MONEY RUSH

Books by Andrew Duncan

MONEY RUSH

THE QUEEN'S YEAR

MONEY RUSH

Andrew Duncan

DOUBLEDAY & COMPANY, INC.
Garden City, New York
1979

ISBN: 0-385-07239-2
Library of Congress Catalog Card Number 73-83628

To Sarah,
who endured the rush without any money

NOTE ON SPELLING

Transliteration from Arabic to English can be a superior form of intellectual snobbery. Experts write Sa'ud and pronounce it *Sow-ood*. Others write Saud, and say *sword* or *sow'd*. Experts say *debay*, others say *d'youbye* (for Dubai). And so on.

There is no definitive authority, so I have kept to spellings most in common use which seem nearest to the Arabic or Persian (Farsi) pronunciation: thus, for example, Shaikh (pronounced *shake*) instead of Sheikh. In the case of names where there are several acceptable alternative spellings, I have given the one used by the person involved even though this leads to inconsistency: *Mohammed* Reza Pahlavi (the Shah), *Muhammad* (the Prophet) and *Mohamed* Mahdi al-Tajir (the ambassador).

ACKNOWLEDGMENTS

A condition of talking to many involved in the money rush is that they are not named lest they be disqualified, or worse, for discussing what is not supposed to be a spectator sport. I am therefore inhibited from thanking many people in the eleven countries I visited.

Amongst those I can thank, but who bear no responsibility for what I have written are: *In Iran:* His Excellency Ardeshir Zahedi, H.E. Parviz Radji, H.E. Amir Abbas Hoveyda, H.E. Amir Khosrow Afshar, Amir Mirfakhrai, Sir Anthony Parsons, Desmond Harney, Roger Cooper, John Owen, Andrew Wright, Senator Khoxeimi Alam, Iraj Sabet, and above all my interpreter and guide, Fereshteh Fallahnejad.

In Saudi Arabia: His Majesty King Khalid, Shaikh Faisal Alhegelan, Shaikh Zaki Yamani, John Wilton, Adnan Khashoggi, Peter Downs, Harb and Anne Zuhair, Izzidin Osman, and my driver, whose glass eye gave him a heroic disregard for traffic.

In Oman: H.H. The Sultan.

In the United Arab Emirates: H.H. Shaikh Rashid, Zaki Nusseibeh, Ibrahin Al Abed, Colonel Sir Hugh Boustead, Humeid Ahmed bin Drai, Neville Brook, Oscar Mandoody, Easa Saleh Algurg.

In Bahrain: H.H. Shaikh Isa, Steve Wyatt, Trevor Goodchild, John Turnbull, Ralph Izzard.

In Qatar: Tayeb Saleh, Issa Kuwari.

In Iraq: Naji Hadithi, Ahmad al Azzawi.

In London: Michael Adams, Jonathan Aitken, Julian Amery, Algernon Asprey, Avril Bloy, Robin Cook, Andrew Faulds, Fred Halliday, Alan Hart, David Housego, Clive Irving, Ken Inglis,

Morison Johnston, Peter Mansfield, Peter Temple-Morris, Ian Skeet, Nicholas Thompson, and, most important, Barbie Canning-Ure who typed endless copies of the manuscript, and Ingrid von Essen, who took it apart and put it together again.

I thank, too, those who offered inducements—$300,000 was the highest—to interpret events in their favor; those who threatened legal retribution when I did not; and my bank manager, John Learmouth, whose nearly always unwavering support made the extensive travel possible.

New York, February 1979

CONTENTS

PROLOGUE

"*My father rode a camel. I drive a Cadillac. My son has a jet. My grandson will have a supersonic plane. My great-grandson? He will have a camel.*"

COMMON PREDICTION AMONG MANY WEALTHY BUSINESSMEN IN ARABIA

FOR YEARS THE Arabs slept. They were defeated in successive wars, manipulated by foreign governments who carved their land into haphazard countries, and were ignored or despised by most people in the West. Then, one day, a change occurred.

Saturday, October 6, 1973, was Yom Kippur, the Day of Atonement, the most holy day in the Jewish calendar. In Israel, the celebrations were a relief from tensions which beset the country. Although security organizations spoke of an imminent Arab attack, the warnings were not taken very seriously. There were more immediate considerations, including an election which was about to take place, and the fact that world sympathy with Israel seemed to be waning. Financial contributions from abroad had begun to decline. But these matters were for another day.

At 1:58 P.M., 500 Syrian MIG-17s began an attack on the Golan Heights. They were followed by a barrage of at least 700 tanks which broke through the United Nations cease fire lines, overwhelmed the defensive forces of 170 Israeli tanks, and advanced toward Kuneitra and Rafid.

Two minutes later, 300 miles to the southwest, 8,000 Egyptian infantrymen crossed the Suez Canal in rubber dinghies and attacked Sinai. The Israeli fortifications along the canal, known as the Bar-Lev Line, were thought to be virtually impregnable. Apart from natural obstacles, there was an ingenious and supposedly secret trap: hidden sprinklers filled with oil which, ignited, would incinerate any invaders.

On this Saturday, the line was protected by 600 middle-aged businessmen, reservists from the Jerusalem Brigade, many of whom had been concentrating on their afternoon prayers. They did not know that Egyptian engineers on a secret mission had filled the oil sprinklers with concrete the previous evening.

The fourth Arab-Israeli war had begun and the consequences were to transform the world in what some said was the most traumatic social upheaval since the Middle Ages.

Within days, the six Gulf members of the Organization of Petroleum Exporting Countries (OPEC)—Iran, Saudi Arabia, Iraq, Kuwait, Qatar, and the United Arab Emirates—announced an unprecedented 70 percent increase in the price of oil: from $3.10 a barrel (42 gallons) to $5.11. A few weeks later, on December 23, the price was again raised: this time by 120 percent to $11.65.

The immediate effect was financial panic, accompanied by political threats and social chaos. Britain's economic decline was accelerated, and the American balance of payments slid into deficit. Japan, more dependent on Middle East imports than any other industrialized country, finally saw its postwar achievements slowing down. Airlines canceled 10 percent of their flights, speed limits were lowered to conserve fuel supplies, and the automotive industry ordered layoffs. Long lines formed at garages as the last drops of gasoline were squeezed from pumps—and one or two people who tried to push in front were shot dead by irate customers. Unfortunately, Europe was suffering its coldest weather in fifty years, so when Shaikh Ahmed Zaki Yamani, the Saudi Arabian oil minister, visited the capitals to explain his country's position, apologize for the inconvenience caused, and suggest blandly that he was "just a simple Bedouin," no one was very impressed. The French, pragmatic as ever, tried to wheedle concessions; the Italians, broke as ever, found they had to go to

110 different banks to borrow $1.2 billion; the British, by now familiar with humiliation, punned "Yamani—or—ya—life." The Americans refused to believe what had happened.

Dramatic predictions were made about the new Arab wealth, with figures so large they became incomprehensible and largely meaningless.

Before 1973, OPEC countries had a mere $6 billion reserves. By 1977 they had $145 billion, and the World Bank estimated they would have $1.2 trillion by 1985. The countries were saving $115,000 a second—enough, according to the *Economist*, to buy all the companies on the world's major stock exchanges in fifteen years and eight months (the London Stock Exchange would take less than ten months. New York needed longer: nine years and three months), and all the United States overseas investments in one year and ten months. The Rockefeller family wealth represented only six days' oil production.

Surely it could not be true that a handful of autocratic Arabs living in faraway deserts who had been bankrupt ten years previously, could, through a quirk of geological luck, disrupt the fabric of Western life and acquire luxuries for themselves which are rewards associated with the Protestant work ethic? It was. Years of cheap, plentiful energy discovered and exploited by the West as a basis for its own progress, were over.

The Middle East, an indefinite term invented by an American admiral in 1902 to describe the area where Europe, Russia, Asia, and Africa meet, now has power of its own and is possibly the only place in the world which the West will defend—or attack—with nuclear weapons.

But how do people from these undeveloped countries react when, overnight, they have the wealth and power to be their own masters? How do others react to them? Do sudden riches help build a vigorous society and provide opportunities, or merely encourage the worst excesses of Western consumerism? What is the result when two autocracies—Iran and Saudi Arabia—jealous of each other's power, become so influential that the United States has to prop up their pride with weapons and give enthusiastic support to outdated political attitudes? Who, and what, is trampled in the money rush?

I traveled to seven countries which have become the last

places on earth where ordinary people can hope to make a fortune without too many restrictions: Saudi Arabia, Iran, Kuwait, Bahrain, the United Arab Emirates, Qatar and Oman—and an eighth, Iraq, which is regarded as Russia's client as well as a terrorist haven for those who wish to upset the pro-Western capitalist sympathies of the others.

It was not easy. Paranoia is a disease of the nouveau riche everywhere, and in the Middle East it has reached epidemic proportions. This is partly because of a passion for secrecy and manipulated information, partly because of the burden of historical prejudice, partly because greed, waste, and preposterous self-deception invite ridicule from any but the most partisan observer.

I began with some pessimism, which was rewarded when not one of my initial letters to the ambassadors in London of the Arab countries was answered. Saudi Arabia was the worst. It took nearly a year of unanswered letters, Telexes from many parts of the world, and telephone calls before I was given permission to visit the country for the first time. I mention this not with a sense of injured pride—anyone with such fragile sensitivity would soon be overcome by the inept bureaucratic muddle which passes for administration in so many of the countries—but because it illustrates the first and most important qualification for money-rush contestants: patience.

It is futile, as well as presumptuous, to apply Western standards of efficiency, or middle-class attitudes about "morality" to countries where such concepts are alien, and to a people whose sense of tranquillity—*kayf*—is based on a belief that God's will—*insha'allah*—is carried out regardless of man's efforts. This fatalism is difficult for a Westerner to accept during interminable stifling hours waiting for promises to be fulfilled or hastily canceled meetings to be rearranged. ("I am sorry, Mr. Andrew, the Shaikh went hunting in Pakistan this morning. He will be away a few days, a week, a month . . . who knows?")

At first, like most newcomers, I was frustrated and angry but after a few visits—I made eight altogether ranging in time from one to eight weeks—I accepted *insha'allah,* expected nothing, prayed for the best, and hoped the translation was accurate. When I told an Iraqi News Agency reporter that some governments in the West felt there was too much blackmail from oil producers, he looked puzzled. I was later quoted as saying there are too many black men in Britain.

I spoke also to sponsors of the money rush: diplomats, bankers, businessmen, confidence tricksters, university presidents, salesmen, and planners who scramble over each other to flatter, bribe, and cajole the half-dozen men who, it seems, control the world's monetary system. No hope is too high, no swindle too elaborate, no suggestion too outrageous, and no fantasy too grotesque to remain unfulfilled. It provides today's pile of money. Is it beginning to produce tomorrow's ghost towns?

Part One

The Rush Begins

1/THE LAST BASTION

"The pot is boiling and no one knows what's being cooked—a frog or some wonderful new thing."
EUGENIO MONTALE, ITALIAN NOBEL PRIZE-WINNING POET

"The Middle East is 'the last bastion where great men can come out of the desert and do unbelievable things.'"
FORMER U.S. SECRETARY OF STATE HENRY KISSINGER

"We've gotten very close to Saudi Arabia."
PRESIDENT JIMMY CARTER

IN NEW YORK, Tokyo, London, Frankfurt, Toronto, Paris, Zurich, even in the smallest town where manufacturing provides employment, maps were scrutinized and visits planned. It all seemed very simple. A quick stopover in Tehran to relieve the Shah of a few millions, then on to Saudi Arabia—not far on the map—to advise the King (one of America's largest banks suggested grandly that they should "handle" all the Saudi oil revenue, bringing their "experts" from New York to plan the country's future), perhaps a quick jaunt to the United Arab Emirates to see those Bedouin who distribute money and watches to everyone. Then to Oman, and back via Kuwait and Bahrain. Possibly Concorde to London, strikes permitting. Leave home on Monday morning, and back in time for a celebration dinner party on Friday. If the mountain was going to Muhammad, there was no need for it to stay very long.

It was forgotten, if it was ever known, that the Muslim "week-end" is on Thursday and Friday, that hotel rooms had to be booked in advance, that Iran is not an Arab country,[1] that communication is haphazard at best, that thrusting business-school skill, so admired back home, is unlikely to be successful in an area where religious taboos, social restrictions, and tradition combine to create an atmosphere that makes Sleepy Hollow look dynamic.

Slow payments and overoptimism bankrupted many firms, but in the beginning the gusher of money was so prolific that there was something for almost everyone. The United Arab Emirates, which only a few years before had been regarded as "economically poor" by the Royal Institute of International Affairs gave away £75 million in 1977 and had enough money to spend on a massive but vain attempt to subdue the scorching climate by planting thousands of trees in the desert with individual remote-controlled sprinklers. It also provided money for eight international airports in operation, or planned. This may seem excessive for an area of 30,000 square miles inhabited by only 600,000 people, but logic is a casualty in the money rush. "I don't think there has been such waste in the history of the world," says Lucien Dahdah, former foreign minister of Lebanon. The objectives of a "radical" welfare state—free medical care, schooling, and housing—were soon accomplished by repressive right-wing rulers who were then left to gratify their majestic whims with monuments by which the West judges success.

Everyone needs airports, seaports, bridges (even if there is nothing for the bridge to cross, a river can always be produced later—and often is), factories, petrochemical plants, and steel works. Prestige projects prosper, particularly those involving education, even if there are not enough students, teachers, or proper facilities. The new university at Al Ain, pride of the United Arab Emirates, has six administrators to every student. Meals are provided at the nearby Hilton Hotel, the world's most luxurious refectory, at a cost which would pay tuition and maintenance fees at a Western university. The money rush is developing a concept of prefabrication, in which it is believed that anything can be bought—even a social system complete with do-it-yourself cultural kits. To some extent, it is made to work.

ed States imported more oil than

omes from Saudi Arabia, which
$15 billion a year on American
uipment, and has investments of

stics and the assumption that the
on in the West is based to a large
the King of Saudi Arabia and
Although the United States pays
eli (a total of $2.5 billion), there
t which real estate becomes more
ealism less persuasive than GNP.
served, so as not to arouse accusa-
tain "truths" are reexamined in a
crisy of politicians as much as the

sident Roosevelt pledged to the
would make no change in Pales-
ulting the Arabs. When his succes-
this promise, he explained to his
ntlemen, but I have to answer to
ple who are anxious for the success
dreds of thousands of Arabs among

ter, nor will his successors. But now
upon Saudi Arabia, than vice versa,
f people anxious for the success of
d against the millions of Americans
olific energy users.
d to present realities. The American
nct. "We have a curious mixture in
eroism. In the First World War we
fe for democracy. In the Second, we
d guys. In Vietnam, Johnson sat in
ering what the hell he had got himself
ur bit. Why the hell should we feel
f the Jews? Someone has to sit on
y's own good."

In 1974 an average of two American university presidents a week traveled to Iran, and many were rewarded with the endowments they sought—thus providing intellectual respectability for a country whose international image bordered on the barbaric, and a useful financial boost for impoverished academics. This cozy arrangement was popular until Japanese commercial firms, with characteristic lack of grace, abused the system by sending salesmen disguised as "professors." That was considered an underhand way of trying to sell audiovisual equipment and other devices so essential to the burgeoning scholastic environment.

Attending conferences is clearly a satisfactory way of becoming identified as part of the international intellectual elite, and bureaucrats of the new "governments" hastened to add to their knowledge. In Abu Dhabi, the Ministry of Information was passed an invitation from the Foreign Ministry to attend a week-long seminar on "Informatics" in Tunis. Three officials went, including the "envelope man" whose job is to deliver spending money, in envelopes, to delegates when they arrive at their hotel. The delegates found the first day's talk confusing but they persevered, realizing only later that informatics is an aspect of computer business. They stayed for the week anyway and wrote a report which was filed, unread.

But no amount of conferences are necessary to give an understanding of the most lucrative trade: arms sales. United States military exports doubled in 1974; the Shah of Iran alone bought as much as the total exports of the previous year.

Arms sellers of the world, who once thought their disreputable trade was destroyed by the First World War, and then again by the Second World War, not to mention Vietnam, jumped with delight into the money rush, shouting familiar excuses as they sped from one country to another with their glossy brochures detailing the latest computer-controlled, 100 percent accurate, artful way of death.

Not that they mention killing—such talk is too sentimental. They are into "the quickest way of bringing Iran into the twentieth century," or "providing awareness and education all down the social scale." Their litany of self-justification is well rehearsed. "I have no moral scruples about selling arms to any country with which the government says I can deal. I lose no sleep whatever on the moral issue. The morality lies with the user," says Ronald Ellis, head of British Defence Sales, who adds, "Ready cash is what we like—that is why we sell so much to the Middle East."

In 1970 peace in the Gulf was kept for $40 million a year. By 1977, the defense budget of Kuwait, one of the smallest countries, was $310 million. In a visit to London, Kuwait's Defense Minister managed to spend enough to guarantee 25,000 British jobs for two years. His Saudi Arabian counterpart, the portly Prince Sultan, was greeted with honor guards and protocol normally reserved for a head of state, when he shopped in England for enough explosive toys to keep an old-fashioned war rumbling for several years. "One of the reasons for the existing cooperation between us, Britain, and France is their total willingness to respond to our requests and provide us with any arms we choose. We do not accept any conditions," he says.

No wonder. He spends $11 billion a year—one-third of Saudi Arabia's revenue—for armed forces of 50,000 men who are helped by a semisecret American force of about 3,000. Iran, with six times the population, spent $10 billion. "If you Americans are going to be so moral, you must apply a single standard to the whole world," said the Shah. "From lack of American comment, Saudi Arabia would appear to be a paradise of human rights."

Perhaps the transformation in Saudi Arabia's economic power has been too rapid for its significance to be fully understood. In thirteen years before the money rush began, it spent only $600 million on military equipment. By 1977 it was buying so much that 500,000 Americans owed their jobs directly to Saudi Arabia —and three times as many indirectly. The United States now has a more substantial financial commitment to the country than in Vietnam at the height of the war.

Robert Haack, chairman of Lockheed, who claims his company now sells to the Middle East "as a result of a lot of hard work and with no cumshaw whatsoever" was asked his views on the United States becoming the arms merchant to the world. "I don't want to be facetious," he replied, "but that is a little bit like asking a plaintiff lawyer what he thinks of no-fault insurance. I think there is a period of unrest in the world. People are

when, for the first time, the Unit it produced.

Nearly one-fifth of the oil c spends in return as much as goods, services, and military eq $60 billion in the United States

Israel suffers from these stati standard of living of every pers extent upon the goodwill of whoever manages to rule Iran. $600 annually to aid every Isra is a point in the money rush a important than people, and id The diplomatic niceties are ob tions of anti-Semitism, but ce way which illustrates the hyp ironies of history.

In 1945, for instance, Pre Saudis that the United States tinian policy without first cons sor, President Truman, broke ambassadors, "I am sorry, ge hundreds of thousands of peo of Zionism. I do not have hu my constituents."

Neither does President Car America is more dependent the "hundreds of thousands Zionism" have to be balance who are the world's most p

Past guilt has to be modifi diplomat in Jidda was succ our character of guilt and h wanted to make the world s wanted to get rid of the b front of the boob tube wond into. Well, we have done saddled with the burning Israel's head for the count

This happened for the first time on May 15, 1978, when the U.S. Senate voted to sell sixty of the most sophisticated fighter aircraft, F-15 Eagles to Saudi Arabia in spite of furious Israeli protests. It was a success for the National Association of Arab Americans (NAAA) over the powerful American Israel Public Affairs Committee, which represents over thirty Jewish organizations and whose executive director, Morris Amitay, had boasted, "We've never lost on a major issue."

John Richardson, director of public affairs for the NAAA was triumphant when he told me in Washington, "The big lie has worked for long enough. Even Arab countries have not advanced their own interests here because they look upon our society as being under Zionist control and money spent here as down the rat hole."

But isn't it naïve, I suggested, to think that influencing arms sales to Saudi Arabia is more than a hollow victory?

"Hollow victory? That term means nothing."

"It means," I added, "that it is no triumph to sell even a cata- pult to such a dangerous area, let alone airplanes the Saudis are not competent to use."

Richardson, who has not been to Saudi Arabia for ten years, replied, "We are not carrying a torch for the Arabs. Our concern is what we perceive as a redefinition of American interests in the Arab world."

If American interests are best served by selling potential de- struction, so be it. But it is exactly this attitude which makes many Arabs succumb to one of the conspiracy theories endemic to the area. They insist that the Middle East has been kept in a state of tension not only by quarrels amongst themselves, nor even by Arab-Israeli confrontations, but by Western politicians and businessmen whose interest in peace is merely cliché-deep. "It is obvious," says Saudi entrepreneur Adnan Khashoggi. "Oil is power. Cash is power. I say God help America and Europe when we unite with the Jews. Then we can really run the show. You could wake up one morning and find yourself occupied by an Arab-Israeli nation.

"The oil crisis was—and is—no crisis. It was created by oil companies to build an atmosphere in which high prices could be justified. You don't think that unsophisticated Arab governments would dare challenge the United States without some encouragement? They wouldn't have the guts. What happened was that oil-company people needed money for expansion and they told some local politicians to go ahead, be heroes, put up the price, and nothing serious will happen. So they did it. At present the Middle East is still just part of the cycle of economic growth of the Western world."

Progress is measured by the number of building sites completed to take advantage of rents which at one time increased by 400 percent a year. "Everyone is so paralyzed with money that they don't bother to think," a banker told me. "Rebels and potential leaders are bought off by stuffing them full of dollars. The old way was safer: we shot them."

But, now that the last bastion is crumbling under the assault of the invaders in pinstriped suits, there is little that can be done to halt the money rush, however harmful its consequences, however dangerous its future.

2/THE SILKEN CURTAIN

"Ideologies of the West must be resisted. They are the forward arm of corruption, the silken curtain behind which hides the greed of the graspers and the dreams of the dominators."

HASSAN AL BANA, FOUNDER OF THE MUSLIM BROTHERHOOD

"The lesson to be learnt is that they have to be brought along slowly. They do not like buying in front of one another and are not really ready for some things."

MR. ROBERT EVANS, BUYER OF ANTIQUE FURNITURE FOR
ASPREY'S, AFTER A TEN-DAY EXHIBITION IN SAUDI ARABIA, JUNE
1978

THERE IS A WAY to postpone the inevitable: censorship. Books, magazines, newspapers, even supplements commissioned by a particular country and carrying government advertising, are censored for the most trivial reasons, often on the orders of semiliterate officials who understandably fear that intellectual freedom is incompatible with their own power.

In Oman a straightforward historical book was banned because its title, *Muscat and Oman,* is the pre-*coup* name of the country. In Kuwait and Saudi Arabia the *Financial Times* was banned for suggesting that the rulers were elderly and not in good health. (The Kuwait ruler died a few months later.) In Iraq even typewriters are considered subversive instruments and are liable to be confiscated at the airport. In Iran the translator of a Molière play was asked to bring the author to the censor's office so that registration procedures could take place.

"Is it not a pity to allow an official who has no idea of the life and death of a certain author to deal with the registration of his work?" asked Empress Farah who was once herself a victim of the censor's clammy embrace. An interview was banned in which she expressed admiration for the writings of a poet who had criticized the Shah. "The people in charge are not bright enough, nor intelligent enough, to see what they should censor," she told me. "Sometimes His Majesty and I have been so angry that he had to see a film that was censored and say there was nothing wrong with it. It is not possible for us to see all the films or read all the books. I believe our people should read all sorts of material to be able to judge; otherwise they cannot tell if our system is better or worse than others. It is sensible to give them all the material, so when people say they believe in you, they really do believe."

But when they stop believing, as Iranians did in the fall of 1978, previous assertions seem ironically inept. "Our own people would not accept a direct insult to the King because he represents the unity of the nation," the Empress had told me earlier. "In the West, you do not believe it is democracy unless someone goes in the streets and shouts against the King."

Nevertheless, thousands of books were said to be banned in Iran, from soft-core pornography to a critique of the Shah's regime, *The Political Élite of Iran*, by Marvin Zonis. I bought a copy at the Hilton Hotel bookshop (owned by the Shah's Pahlavi Foundation), where there was also a great deal less cerebral material ready for those tired businessmen unsuccessful in flirting with pulchritudinous German air hostesses by the pool: *Young and Hot* ("They were two teenagers too hot to wait.") by Ginger Craft, *Lesbian Interludes, Hot Trail* ("two hot women. Sex hungry bandits"), or *Kinky Tramp*. Slightly more inspirational perhaps than the only books censorship allows to remain in the window display of the main bookshop in Riyadh, world capital of puritanism and hypochondria: *Atlas of Surgical Operations, Clinical Concepts of Cancer Management, Clinical Nursing, Eighth Revised Edition of Diseases of Livestock, Jane's World Aircraft 1973/74, The Story of the Bomber 1914–1945*, and *Tool and Manufacturing Engineers Handbook*.

Not that the Shah lacked sensitivity. He withdrew his ambassadors from all the Gulf states because an "Arabian Gulf News Agency" was set up. Persian Gulf is the only acceptable name in Iran for the most vulnerable stretch of water in the world, and any document which says otherwise is forbidden. When I suggested to the Shah that his attitude might appear trivial to outsiders, he bristled. "Why should it? What name did you learn in school? The Arabs are making a heavy-handed policy trying to change historical names. It is childish on their part. We have our pride."

Pride is a dominant emotion throughout the Middle East, and is evident in every aspect of life from driving, to lack of sex equality, to politics. Tribal tradition, vicious family competition, and jealousy are so powerful that it is still not possible to draw an accurate map of the Arabian peninsula. For all the talk of brotherly love, most boundaries remain disputed; Saudi Arabia refused to recognize the United Arab Emirates for three years because of rival claims to bits of desert.

Truth is usually relative, but in the Middle East it is more relative than elsewhere—particularly in Saudi Arabia, where facts are confused with aspirations. They have to be—there are few accurate statistics. It took the American embassy a year and a half to compile a list of senior government officials. "We look in the newspaper for any changes," explained a counselor. He is not helped in his work by the fact that the commercial capital, Riyadh, is 500 miles from the diplomatic enclave at Jidda on the Red Sea. In the mid-seventies, telephone links between the two cities were so tenuous that in order to make contacts he had to fly to Riyadh, take a taxi to a hotel near the airport, and telephone government ministers from a pay phone.

"You must understand it is a curious experience for us, too," says the poetry-writing Saudi Minister for Industry and Electricity, Dr. Ghazi Algosaibi. "We have suddenly become a world power without any of the attributes, simply because of this thing [oil] which is neither permanent nor really important. We have no illusions about achieving in a short space of time what took centuries in the West."

In Arab countries, unlike Iran, money stifles underlying dissent. Elsewhere, it produces culture shock as "petrodollars" are "recycled" to buy banks, businesses, and property in the United

States, Europe, and Japan. Nothing is sacred. A Saudi Arabian
with historical pretensions tried to buy the Alamo for his son's
birthday; others wanted to purchase the site of the Battle of
Hastings, or Fortnum and Mason; and the Arab League even
discussed how to take over *The Times,* which was not for sale, in
the hope of gaining favorable publicity for their cause.

Sometimes such efforts seem superfluous. "Mistakes" can be
made. *The Times* prints a map of the "Middle East" which does
not show Israel but divides the country between somewhere
called "Syria Lebanon" and Jordan.[1] British Petroleum's desk
diaries give Israel her 1949 borders. Other firms stamp "This is a
map of the Middle East" over sensitive areas. Publishers make
fortunate cartographical errors which omit Israel in books designed for a lucrative Arab sale.[2] Even King Carl Gustav of
Sweden changed the name of his black Labrador from Ali to
Charlie after Muslims complained he was demeaning the name of
the Prophet's adopted son, also Ali. Neither religion, nor money,
should be mocked.

Most of the big money goes to Citibank or Chase Manhattan
in New York, but high-living Arabs find the city too much of a
drab urban Zion and prefer London, known as the twenty-first
Arab nation since Lebanese civil wars made Beirut less enticing.
In a neat reversal of historical roles since the days when Cairo or
Port Said were lurid centers of vice for wandering foreign seamen, Soho has become a vast pornographic conglomerate where
the new rich can be titillated, robbed, conned, or ambushed.
"The government should protect the citizens from exhausting
their sexual and financial prowess in London," wails a Kuwait
newspaper *Al Watan,* without specifying how. "Isn't it their task
to direct our citizens toward proper places and keep them away
from immoral places which steal their money?"

British newspapers are not slow to respond with equally
distressing stories about innocent girls in the clutches of rutting
Arabs. The *Daily Mirror* detailed the "Ordeal of a Sheikh's love
slave"—a nineteen-year-old London salesgirl who was "whisked
off in a Rolls Royce to exclusive restaurants" before her unnamed
"dark eyed sheikh" married her and took her to Saudi Arabia
where he force-fed her because he liked fat women "and made
me kiss his feet like other wives. When he was displeased he hit

me with his shoes." She escaped, she said, by fleeing from a
French hotel during a vacation. The *Daily Mail* warned that
there were "Schoolgirls missing after dating Arabs." The girls
were only fifteen, and "fears were growing that they may have
gone off to the Middle East." The newspaper added that "The
London parks and West End are favourite haunts of wealthy
young Arabs on the lookout for English girls." A few weeks later
there was a much smaller story in the newspaper explaining that
the girls had returned home at last. They had been in London
selling ice cream.

Some Arabs and Iranians did squander their new wealth spectacularly everywhere from London to Los Angeles. A twenty-
three-year-old Saudi Arabian, Shaikh Shamsuddin al-Fassi
lavished $4 million on a ridiculous mint-green *palazzo* on Sunset
Boulevard with a burnished copper roof and plaster skin-colored
nude statues adorned with imposing genitals and lifelike pubic
hair. A couple of Saudi princesses, in need of weekend spending
money, had a special after-hours delivery of $200,000 from the
Bank of America; others buy $30,000 worth of dresses at Giorgio
on Rodeo Drive, a high-priced boulevard in Beverly Hills where
"taste" is expensive. "The only proper customer is the man who
earns $100,000 a month. If somebody needs something, he
doesn't belong here," explains Bihan Pakzad, Iranian owner of a
men's boutique.

Millions are wasted on kitsch interior decoration and other
follies which stretch the frontiers of extravagance. One Arab
paid £530 for a pound of strawberries, another $4,000 for choco-
lates, and yet another spent $54,000 chartering a Boeing to take
$1,200 worth of $.10 bricks from London to Jidda so his new
house could be built a few months quicker. An Iranian stuffed
wads of £20 [$40] notes down a nightclub singer's bodice and
rid himself of $44,000 during a night at the Shehrezade night-
club in Piccadilly. London's twenty-four casinos, with a combined turnover of $1.5 billion, increase their profits by 35 percent
a year and one of them—the Playboy Club—helped Hugh
Hefner's empire of adolescent fantasy recover from premature
financial infertility. "A rather pleasant irony," says Hefner,
whose club thoughtfully provides free Arabic newspapers for its
guests.

Nearly anyone dressed in Arab robes could be assured of a fawning welcome and lavish credit. A twenty-two-year-old student booked a suite at Claridges, saying he was the son of the ruler of Abu Dhabi, and ran up gambling debts of $70,000 in West End casinos before he was arrested. A Paris jeweler lost $500,000 of jewelry he gave on approval to a Saudi "prince." The EMI film company was conned into giving a film script to an unemployed Kenyan living in Wealdstone who claimed to be a nephew of King Hussein of Jordan with $10 million to spend on a new film. United States senators were deceived into giving solemn speeches of welcome to a student who posed as the ruler of a nonexistent Arab oil producing country called Halat al Bhudi.

Numerous stories are told about genuine Arabs and Iranians and most of them are presumably apocryphal, like the woman who asked a window cleaner "How much?" and, receiving the reply, "Two-forty" (i.e., £2.40), peeled 240 crisp pound notes from a large bundle. Or buying $20,000 mink coats to use as bathrobes. Or the Saudi businessman who visited the dentist, was billed for £50.00, misread the decimal, paid £5,000, and, when shown his error, told the dentist to cash the check as it would be too much trouble to write another.

Grasping their opportunity, real-estate salesmen put artificially high valuations on houses as an inducement to buy. It is the only way, some claim, to attract the interest of Arabs and Iranians. Houses costing $150,000 in London are advertised for $600,000 in Middle East newspapers. A shaikh from Kuwait became lord of a Surrey manor, and bits of British heritage went swiftly into foreign ownership: Fort Belvedere, "a half-enchanted castle" according to the Duchess of Windsor, where King Edward VIII signed his abdication; Coppins, former estate of the Duke of Kent; even the British homes of Tom Jones and Rod Stewart were bought by Arabs. "Arabs may buy Knightsbridge" threatened the *Guardian*. In the vicinity of London there are at least 40,000 Arab and 15,000 Iranian households. "For fifty or sixty years, we were almost colonized," explained Iran's former Prime Minister, Amir Abbas Hoveyda. "The British could come to our country and buy anything they liked. Now we are in that position. We like to have a flat in London, a British servant, and to be able to pay for these things. It may be the wrong attitude, but it is life."

South Kensington, once an area reserved for the upper-class British, became known as Saudi Kensington, or bedouin and breakfast land. In a pained letter to *The Times* in August 1977, Lord Greenhill, former head of the Diplomatic Service, observed: "A stroll around the Round Pond, Kensington Gardens, on Friday evening last produced the following tally:

Clearly identifiable Middle Easterners	82
Clearly identifiable foreigners	18
Clearly identifiable British	3
Unidentified	6

"No one asked me the way. I was the one who felt lost."

On the pavement outside the Marble Arch branch of Marks and Spencer, veiled women squat, unpicking the St. Michael brand label from thousands of pairs of panties and racks of dresses so that no one will know they have patronized a Jewish shop at the rate of $2 million a week. One Arab with a sense of humor bought a rack of about forty nightdresses. "But they are all different sizes," said the assistant. "So are my wives," replied the Arab. It was presumably a lack of Arab executives, rather than a sense of humor, which allowed the chain store to sell 12,000 dozen pairs of men's underpants carrying a sacred text from the Koran—"There is no God but Allah"—in thirteenth-century Arabic script. The design came from Paris, and they thought it was merely a nice piece of abstract art.

Independent schools and private hospitals, which few Britishers can afford, also prosper by about $2 million a week from the invasion, although blatant overcharging by some doctors began to spoil the bonanza and in 1978 Germany became a favored medical center. Even so, there were still enough foreigners in London to cause problems. "The Government must now start thinking about quotas, staggering the season and, above all, imposing a special tax," said Sir Malby Crofton, former Leader of London's Royal Borough of Kensington and Chelsea. "At the peak season, certain places such as Westminster Abbey, St. Paul's, the Tower, and, indeed, outside Buckingham

Palace, are soon going to be unable to accommodate everyone.

"The purchase of property also requires a close examination. There is too much foreign money chasing too few properties. We have a right to ensure that they will be genuine residents, and not merely property investors who want to secure a politico/economic hedge or simply an annual holiday home."

That does not seem unreasonable. Arab countries shrewdly prohibit nonnationals from owning land in their patch of desert.

Jealousy, resentment, and the excesses of the money rush reinforce popular prejudice. The Arabs are considered to be either Rudolph Valentino in drag, a gang of unshaven camel drivers with exotic sexual appetites, or the romantic heroes of upper-class British homosexuals who sought simplicity in the Middle East as an escape from the restraints of mid-Victorian morality. These opinions are articulated from time to time in a racist manner that would cause uproar if applied to any other group. According to British Labour Member of Parliament, Ian Mikardo, Foreign Office officials are pro-Arab because they share "a common tendency towards homosexuality, romanticism, and enthusiasm for horses." Film producer Joseph E. Levine broke a twenty-five-year habit of staying at the Dorchester when it was bought by Arabs. "They're a dirty bunch of sonsofbitches," he explained. "We were going to buy a house in London, which is my favorite city away from New York, but the Arabs have now bought 'em all." As if to emphasize the point, someone had scrawled an addition to a "PLEASE DO NOT PARK CARS" sign near the Dorchester. It read: "Or camels."

Apart from causing the biggest outbreak of venereal disease in Earl's Court since the Second World War (a responsibility shared with Australians who stopped in Bangkok en route), Arabs were discovered to have curiously un-British social habits. "As well as screaming children, all-night parties and the lack of Western toilet training, the capital's richest residents are now learning to live with the Arab taste for life on the street," reported the *Daily Telegraph*, which had earlier discovered an unnamed Curzon Street hall porter who observed, "We find that they either tend to stuff cardboard boxes down the lavatory or to wash in it. Regrettably they don't seem to understand its purpose and often use the floor instead."

It seems too much of a bewildering reversal that these same people are using their new wealth to buy the loyalty and expertise of talented Westerners. "You must remember that the Middle East has always been a slave-owning society," says an expatriate businessman in Riyadh. "Now *we* are the slaves. The British are reduced to sweeping the streets here."

Even though Zaki Yamani insists that the world's economy will depend for the next fifteen years on Saudi Arabia, and the hapless Shah lectured about the West's "so-called democracy," it is difficult for us to comprehend the shift in power which has taken place. It is much easier if you are a Muslim. Then, you realize, it is simply God's will—*insha'allah*.

3/TOTAL LIFE

"There is no God but Allah, and Muhammad is his Prophet."
THE ISLAMIC CREED

"Isn't there a gambling firm in England called Mecca? How would you like it if we called a brothel Westminster Abbey?"
MINISTRY OF INFORMATION OFFICIAL IN RIYADH, SAUDI ARABIA

THE ONSLAUGHT OF the money rush is shaking the foundations of religious belief upon which Arab—and to some extent Iranian—society is based. Publicly, Saudi leaders declare their faith in Islam and connive at some of its more barbaric punishments. Privately, many prophesy like Zaki Yamani that "in a few years our religion will be part of show business, like it is everywhere else."

In the meantime, an inability to understand or accept the varous interpretations of Islam causes as many problems for money-rush contestants as it creates divisions among Muslims themselves. Those who feel humiliated, aggrieved, or puzzled by modern Arab attitudes should remember that their ancestors conquered half the civilized world, created an empire larger than that of ancient Rome, and spread a way of total life that lasted for 500 years and has had a more profound effect on European culture than any other foreign influence. Arabs themselves have for centuries felt humiliated, double-crossed, and defeated by "infidels" who now line up to pay homage to a God everyone can acknowledge: ready cash.

Muhammad himself would have understood. Islam has no Christian prudishness about money. Why should it be more difficult for a rich man to enter the kingdom of Heaven than for a camel to go through the eye of a needle?

The Prophet was born into a merchant family, the Hashim, of Mecca, in about A.D. 571. He was orphaned young and cared for by a tribal wet nurse in the desert before being brought up first by a grandfather and then by an uncle, neither of whom were rich. When he was twenty-five, he married a wealthy widow, Khadija, who was fifteen years older than himself. Her money helped him to become an adequately successful businessman and also gave him time to study the mysticism which was such an essential part of his life. Some doctors suggest he was epileptic, like Julius Caesar and Napoleon. Others claim his message was drug-induced—assertions which have also been made about Jesus. Tradition says he was illiterate, thus giving authenticity to his "revelations" because he would have been unable to copy them from books.

Every year, he went to the Jebel Nur (Mount of Light) overlooking Mecca to pray. On one occasion, when he was about forty, he returned home terrified to tell Khadija that he thought he had seen the archangel Gabriel reveal to him the word of God. These visions returned, and by the year 613 Muhammad had begun to preach to his family and friends in short verses which were taken down on bits of leather, palm leaves, or camel bone, and became the basis of the Koran (Arabic for "recitation"). The message was simple: submission ("Islam") to one God ("Allah"). The only rule was that they should pray toward Jerusalem, a city associated with earlier prophets Moses and Jesus.

The Torah, the Psalms, and the Gospels are considered by Islam to be divine revelations which have been misunderstood or mistranslated and are, anyway, only part of the story. The whole truth was revealed in Arabic by Allah to his messenger Muhammad.

Flattered as they were to have at last an Arab God, issuing instructions in Arabic, the merchants were not happy with his alleged exclusivity. Mecca was an important port in the spice routes and held a profitable annual trade fair in conjunction with a pilgrimage to honor multiple gods including trees, heaps of sand, and, most popular of all, the pagan shrine Ka'aba which was supposed to have been sent by the moon god, Hobal. It was a large black meteorite standing 50 feet high, 36 feet long, and 30 feet wide in the center of town. According to subsequent religious legend, it was originally given to Adam, and then rebuilt by Abraham and Ishmael after the flood.

The Meccan mixture of Mammon and God to nearly everyone's satisfaction and profit became threatened by Muhammad's increasingly strident insistence on one God. He was accused of plagiarizing a mishmash of Jewish and Christian ideas, and when he could not be silenced by bribes, hostility became so great that he had to leave.

He first tried to settle in the nearby hill town of Taïf, now Saudi Arabia's summer capital, but was also mocked and despised there. Then a group of rival tribes, including some wealthy and more educated Jewish ones from an agricultural settlement at Yathrib 300 miles away invited him to become their arbitrator. He arrived on July 2, 622, with a few followers, and began to build the world's first mosque. The settlement was renamed Medina al Nabi—City of the Prophet—and is the second most holy city for Muslims. Mecca is first, Jerusalem third. The Islamic calendar starts from the date of this migration (*hijra*).

Muhammad quickly began to organize the tribes into a cohesive society, and adopted a unique way of gaining both converts and revenue. He made everyone who did not convert to Islam pay a 50 percent wealth tax. This ensured hordes of nomadic converts, and also isolated the richer citizens who were predominantly Jewish and Christian.

Rules laid down in the Koran had to overcome a contradiction between the "submission" of his religion, and the aggressive pride of bedou tradition—which is why so much individual interpretation is allowed. One of Islam's more enduring successes is its adaptability, and even Muhammad prophesied that his followers would break up into seventy-three sects (there are more than that) and admitted that some parts of the Koran are "ambiguous."

This has led, over the years, to a number of contradictions, most noticeably concerning women. Muhammad's attitude was enlightened. He stopped the practice of burying unwanted infant daughters alive and gave women legal control over their own property and money—an advance unthought of in the West until the latter half of the twentieth century. He allowed polygamy as a practical means of caring for widows of soldiers killed in battle, and he insisted that every wife would be treated in exactly the same way.

The "word" can be manipulated, of course. The Koran forbids interest, but that does not stop Arab banks charging it, and the new Islamic Development Bank provides "partnerships" for those who lend. Then, under the law, they can accept "profits." No one is surprised if these profits coincide with normal interest rates. Wine and gambling are also forbidden. If they were not, perhaps Western casino operators would be even richer.

At first, many Islamic customs were taken from Jewish tradition. But the Jews did not respond to such blandishments. Muhammad was superfluous to their religious needs, an upstart who was merely tinkering with their own beliefs by adapting them to the peculiar conditions of Arab desert life.

In pique, Muhammad ordered that in future his followers pray toward the Ka'aba in Mecca, and he altered the period of Islamic fasting from Yom Kippur to the month of Ramadan. These two rules, plus the creed, almsgiving, and a pilgrimage to Mecca, remain the five pillars of Islam with which Muslims prepare themselves for the Day of Judgment. (See Appendix.)

When Muhammad died on June 8, 632, his religion had begun to spread across the known world, but not with the missionary zeal of other religions. He had no priests, and there was no particular desire to convert. Islam expanded because it was seeking new treasures to finance its growing status and fresh outlets for bedouin militarism. It was helped by the comparative weakness of other religions and internal bickering in countries it conquered.

Persia provided the first major triumph with successful battles at Qadisiyya in 637 and Nihavand in 641. A 3,000-year-old empire found itself bastardized temporarily (although the legacy is permanent) by hordes of uncouth nomads who did not understand the difference between "yellow" and "white" money and were therefore happy to give away gold. One soldier captured a nobleman's daughter and sold her back for 1,000 dirhams. When told he could have claimed much more he replied that he had never heard of a number higher than ten hundred.

For several years, military successes disguised a power struggle within the religious hierarchy, the results of which exist today and are a major cause of hostility among Arabs themselves as well as between Iran and Saudi Arabia.

Muhammad had no sons and left no properly designated successor, thus ensuring the sort of family squabbles which can blight the most modest inheritance and cause centuries of confusion, bickering, and assassination when religious dogma is involved. After two *Khalifats* (successors or caliphs) had been killed, his son-in-law Ali seemed likely to take the title. But he was opposed by his mother-in-law, who favored the Governor of Syria, Muawiya, and Ali was murdered in 661 by one of his former followers.

Those who today support Ali's claim to the succession are called *Shia* (partisans), and constitute about 20 percent of Islam. Iran has been *Shia* since the sixteenth century. Muawiya's supporters are *Sunni*, followers of the *sunnah* ("way," or, more literally, beaten track) of the Prophet.

While this ideological split was germinating, the word of Islam was forcing its way through Europe. It was stopped only when Charles Martel, grandfather of Charlemagne, won the battle for Tours in 732. By then it had spread to China in the east and Spain (at Andalus) in the north, and was to provide Europe in the Dark Ages with a bridge between ancient Greece and the Renaissance.

Although the Arabs brought comparatively little themselves, their strength was in adapting to and developing their surroundings. They were tolerant of other religions, and their occupation is not characterized by the sort of massacres and autos-da-fé which other faiths find it necessary to justify, nor did they behave with the viciousness which they later were to receive from the Crusaders. "The ink of the scholar is more sacred than the blood of the martyr," said Muhammad. His remark was taken more seriously in the Middle Ages than it is today.

Islamic astrologers plotted the orbits of the planets and accurately measured the circumference of the earth at a time when most Europeans thought it was flat. Their mathematicians developed algebra and logarithms and introduced a numerical system which is the basis of modern mathematics. Scientists translated Greek experiments into Arabic and expanded on the ideas (incidentally bequeathing the word alcohol—*al-kohl* in Arabic—and inventing the still). The Persian Avicenna wrote an encyclopedia that became Europe's standard medical textbook for four centuries. The world's oldest still functioning university, Al-Azhar, was founded in Cairo in 970.

But at the end of the eleventh century the Catholics began their reconquest of Spain, the Crusades started to win back parts of the Middle East, and the Islamic empire crumbled with internal dissent and terrorism. Genghis Khan grasped the opportunity. He united the nomadic Mongol tribes, advanced toward Persia and Afghanistan in 1219, and was followed by his grandson, Prince Hulagu, whose warriors destroyed nearly everything of cultural or physical value.

Next it was the turn of the Ottomans, and by the middle of the sixteenth century, the whole of the Arabic-speaking world was plunged into a dark age of subjugation and religious authoritarianism. At the same time, the rest of the world, encouraged to some extent by Islamic cultural heritage, began to emerge from autocratic feudalism into centuries of rapid progress and enlightenment.

Arabia became impenetrable, a land explored by a few adventurous men and hardy women like Sir Richard Burton, Captain Shakespear, William Palgrave, Charles Doughty, Wilfrid and Lady Blunt, Douglas Carruthers, Harry St. John Philby, Wilfrid Thesiger, Gertrude Bell, and Freya Stark. A legend was built of warlike shaikhs, seductive moonlit nights, shifting white sands, flowing garments, and heroism.

The reality was different. The Turks were not defeated until the First World War, and then the Arabs suffered what many of them saw as a final humiliating double-cross: the division of their land as booty to satisfy rival imperialist ambitions of France and England.

Not until the money rush would they accept that the time had come for their own *nahda*—renaissance—and a revival of their faith throughout the world. Islam is now France's second most

popular religion after Roman Catholicism, and has 700 million
followers throughout the world. A golden age dawns, *insha'allah.*
Or does it? Does money provide the happy ending the rush as-
sumes as its reward?

I went to Iran to see if the collision between money and religion could result in anything but disillusion. And there I met the
first casualty.

Part Two
Iran

4/FIRST CASUALTY: THE SHAH

"No other country in the world offers citizens as many causes for anger and frustration as our country. Any one of them would be enough to drive an average Swede or Englishman or American stark, raving mad."

> A. AMIRANI, EDITOR OF <u>KHANDANIHA</u> (TEHRAN), OCTOBER 1965

"The heart of every Iranian is full of national pride, confidence and hope." THE SHAH, AUGUST 19, 1977

[Iran] is a rotten apple, and all we have to do is wait for it to fall into our hands." NIKITA KHRUSHCHEV

A NUMBER OF THINGS take place when modern Western materialism seduces ancient Eastern philosophy with promises of a more sophisticated tomorrow. Tehran, capital of Iran, is the most extreme example of all the worst aspects. From the airplane circling above Mehrabad Airport (described as an accident waiting to happen, because of its sloping runways and heavy winter blizzards, and awarded a black star by the International Federation of Airline Pilots), urban sprawl can be glimpsed through gaps in the yellow smog which drifts like a ragged tablecloth just below the snow-capped peaks of the Elburz Mountains.

In November 1978, I made my seventh visit to the city in order to meet once more a man who only a few months earlier thought himself a symbol of stability in a reckless world, but was now a casualty of forces unleashed by the money rush: the Shah.

Thousands had been killed in demonstrations against his rule, and now, unable to form a civilian government, he had imposed military control over the country. Two of his most trusted former aides, Prime Minister Amir Abbas Hoveyda and General Nematollah Nassiri, head of the secret police, SAVAK (Sazman-i-Amniyat va Kishvar, State Security and Intelligence Organization), were under arrest on charges of corruption and torture, others had committed suicide, his family were said to have fled the country, and, as I arrived, there were reports he had been assassinated.

It was after the 9 P.M. curfew deadline. The car taking me to my hotel was stopped four times by heavily armed soldiers, fixed bayonets on their rifles and determined looks on their faces. At one intersection, a soldier crouched into a firing position and aimed at my driver's head. The driver turned off his engine and lights, and held a special pass to the window. Still the soldier remained crouched, aiming. Another, also holding a rifle, approached cautiously, examined the pass, and then motioned us into the eerie, trafficless night.

So different from my first visit two years previously . . .

Then, everywhere I looked there were grotesquely enlarged photographs of the Shah standing like a Greek statue in the ruins of Persepolis and waving to something vague on the horizon, or brooding over the scene with his beautiful, sad-looking wife, Farah, and the Crown Prince. No one could be immune to the presence of a personality cult so immediate and stretched to such an excessive degree that it would be laughable further down the Gulf (and is, in Oman, where it is vigorously emulated).

Whenever the Shah was interviewed, or made a speech, the whole text was read on television and radio, several times. There was always a picture of a member of the royal family in the daily newspaper, and sometimes the forced patriotism was so intense that it appeared there was no other news. One typical morning the front page of the English language *Kayhan International* had seven stories and a picture. The picture showed "a patient at Pahlavi Hospital in Rezaieh overwhelmed by the presence of the Shahanshah." The stories were: MONARCH KILLS U.S.

ARMS RUMORS; MONARCH STRESSES NEED FOR HOUSING COOPERATIVES; MONARCH CONFIRMS HUGE COAL DISCOVERY; AUDIENCE FOR EX-PRISONERS; SHAHANSHAH, BHUTTO HOLD TALKS; PRINCE DEPARTS. There was, in addition, one announcement: "His Imperial Majesty paid a visit to the Youth Training School attached to the Imperial ground forces this week."

Such excesses, in the best tradition of despotism, contributed to a quiet resentment that was then expressed in ways too poetical to seem offensive. When confronted by television interviewers asking about the Shah's latest triumph, his detractors avoided "No comment." They had a tactical, all-purpose remark: "My heart is too full to express what I have to say." Nevertheless, when a local newspaper asked readers to contribute to a column, "What's Wrong with Iran?" there were 42,000 replies in two weeks. Revolution was simmering.

But there are few places in the world where lies are told with such conviction and apparent good faith, or where a desire to satisfy is so misleading. A Persian saying, "Better the lie that pleases than the truth that hurts," is echoed by a joke in the Iranian humorous magazine *Caricature*. A harassed businessman asks a hotel clerk the time. "What time would you like it to be, sir?"

Fresh from London, I sensed a resentful, sullen atmosphere, but all I saw as I left the airport was an unending traffic jam, and all I heard was the ceaseless hooting of bad-tempered drivers. I shared a taxi with a Dutch businessman, resident in Tehran. "I always advise friends to hire a car at the airport and drive straight into town," he said as we sweated and swayed through the inadequate streets which 1,000,000 cars had made a battleground for the world's most reckless and stubborn drivers—five killed and thirty-five injured daily. "A baptism of fire is the only way," added the Dutchman. "If you look at what happens here, you would never drive."

Nor would you walk. The pavements were lethal with motorcyclists too impatient to use the roads. In a two-day purge, police arrested 2,000 of them. They were less successful with illegally parked cars. The main result of importing hundreds of American wheel clamps was to benefit locksmiths. No true Iranian motorist would deign to pay a fine.

The planeloads of expatriates who arrived in Tehran, inspired by rumors of $200,000 a year salaries and convinced they could make a quick fortune, were not hell-raisers in the gold-rush tradition—pioneers and individualists hoping for a lucky break who, whatever their faults, had some commitment to the country. There were mostly bleak accountants and "consultants" peddling westernization, whatever it means, regardless of its suitability if it could rebuild profits lost in the panic of the oil price rise.

"At first, it was Klondike in a coat and tie," said Dr. Franklin Burroughs, executive director of the American Chamber of Commerce in Tehran. "Americans came here for forty-eight hours before going to Saudi Arabia and expected to be seen by everyone from the Shah downward. They came in like bulldozers and left a bad impression which created potential difficulties in international relations. Their attitude was, 'These people have money. We'll get it.'"

A few had unique ideas. One man tried unsuccessfully to interest the government in a new type of brick made from oil and mud—he sat in his hotel room for a month awaiting appointments. A more astute entrepreneur, perhaps anticipating the dainty habits of the money rush, drove his old motorbike to beauty salons, hotels, and restaurants offering crisp new banknotes in exchange for old ones—less 10 percent of their value. Within months he was driving a Mercedes. Most, though, were more predictable. When the government declared its intention to construct 1,500,000 houses in a few years, the Tehran city planning office was besieged by twenty architects a day, each with a new prefabrication idea. Nearly all left—poorer but wiser. "The Iranians are much cannier and older hands at the game than people imagine," said Desmond Harney, Tehran representative of the British merchant bank, Morgan Grenfell. "They have become masters, over the centuries, of keeping their options open and choosing with discernment between the many suitors for their favors."

A first shock for suitors was the discovery that a confirmed hotel reservation was usually meaningless. Many had to share with others or spend the night on a bench, so great were the pressures for available rooms.

Firms soon realized it was cheaper to find houses for their

employees—with the inevitable result that rents in Tehran accelerated to become the sixth highest in the world. An ordinary two-bedroom flat cost $1,000 a month, and a larger house was at least $4,000. Houses which had cost $8,000 to buy in 1967 were now $160,000. In the center of Tehran office space was $3,000 a square meter in 1976 and had doubled by the following year. It was so difficult to obtain a telephone that installation could cost a $5,000 bribe.

Many new houses were unfinished because of a cement shortage—in spite of large imports and the use of oil supplies as a bargaining counter which caused hardship in other parts of the world. Several small building firms went bankrupt, and hundreds of construction workers were laid off in Port Elizabeth, South Africa's fifth largest city, because the local cement factory had to give priority to an Iranian order for 1,500,000 tons, an amount which did comparatively little to ease the situation or inhibit the black market. The Iranian ministry of education ordered 4,000 tons for urgent school building. They refused to pay the premium price. They received 200 tons.

Meanwhile ordinary Tehranis, who hoped for luxury from the oil boom and had been promised a glittering future, waited helplessly as inflation rose by over 30 percent a year. Food was scarce, or imported—eggs from West Germany, lamb from Australia, butter from Holland, and cheese from Bulgaria. Even though average incomes rose to $2,000 a year (compared with $300 in Egypt, which has almost the same area and population), there was little to spare. Rents took 50 percent, and Iranians who wanted to leave the country had to pay a $400 tax.

The Shah abandoned plans for the 1984 Olympics to be held in Tehran and concentrated on building the new town center, Shahestan Pahlavi, twice the size of the City of London with a military square—Shah and Nation Square—larger than Moscow's. One day, his glittering capital would be a showpiece to the world, but until then, unfortunately, the whole country was designated a hardship post requiring foreign companies to pay expatriate workers financial compensation—sometimes equivalent to three times their home-based salaries.

Problems were inevitable, particularly among military advisers who resented what they felt was their second-class status in a backward country. "What you have here are ex-military professionals, guys who liked Saigon, the mid-level fellows who don't know any other way of making a living. The money is good, so they came," said an official of Bell Helicopters, which had 2,000 employees (with 6,500 dependents) at a 45-acre base in Isfahan. Bored and disgruntled for much of the time, they were arrested frequently for drunkenness, and drove motorcycles through the Shah mosque, one of Iran's most sacred shrines. The American Defense Department, obsessed with hygiene but deficient in tact, forbade its employees to consume local dairy products, considering them inferior. Butter, eggs, and milk were flown in on C-130 transport planes.

Tehran's growth is so rapid that today's exaggeration is tomorrow's truth, and every opinion, however contradictory, can be justified. There are those who describe the narrow canals which stretch along the side of the street as "open sewers." Others claim they are "scenic waterways." Memories of the city can be colored either by the sight of some of the world's most beautiful girls walking to work with arrogant self-confidence—or of beggarwomen with children at the breast trying to cadge a rial from passing drivers,

In the turmoil of the bazaar area the unidentifiable fragrance of a hundred different spices was lost in the overpowering stench of uncleaned streets. Here it was possible to buy anything from boiled beetroot to heroin, from *Qualitative Chemical Semimicroanalysis* to Lenin's *Organizational Principles of the Proletarian Party*. Who read such books? In spite of grand aims, more than half the country is illiterate, and clerks waited outside the Ministry of Justice, their typewriters balanced on the wall, to copy out petitions for those who cannot read or write. The smug assertion by Iranians that they were jumping into the twentieth century, while their rivals, the Saudis, struggled to reach the sixteenth, seemed hollow in a city that is the seething suspicious center of 5,000,000 people on the make but does not even have a telephone directory.

"It's just like Calcutta," said an American banker in disgust.

The more fashionable area was high up in the northern suburb of Shemiran, on the slopes of the mountains, past chic boutiques, discothèques, a Mary Quant shop, Colonel Sanders' fried chicken and Wimpy hamburger restaurants (culinary exports whose ubiquity throughout the Middle East makes them flag-bearers as well as indigestion purveyors to the business invaders).

Spacious and elegant homes, hidden from view by high stone walls like all houses in Tehran, were furnished with French paintings, genuine antiques, Persian rugs, and a luxury more formidable than anything available in the West. Their owners' loyalty to the Shah was unrestrained in public. Privately they were skeptical, despising him for being nouveau riche and distrusting him because he made them sell their land, decreed profit-sharing laws, took strong measures against corruption, and had an ambivalent attitude toward big business—one day he applauded its loyalty, the next condemned its avarice. Consequently, they took about $3 billion of their private money out of the country each year, even before their panic in the autumn of 1978.

"They have homes in Paris, and see a lot of taxi drivers there who were princes in Russia but lost everything during the revolution," said a leading businessman. "They know the same could happen here. Meanwhile, we enjoy ourselves." He shrugged. Comfort anesthetized dissent temporarily, and political freedom could be dispensed with temporarily when every other luxury was available. Or so it was thought.

Tehran high society, the most snobbish and incestuous in the world, will always be devious enough to flatter whoever is in power, and it performed its rituals around the Shah with a precision lost to the rest of the world. The degrees of intimacy with which a newcomer was greeted (handshake, embrace, or kiss) were observed with interest and jealousy because they indicated social undercurrents that have existed for 2,500 years.

I spoke to an ambassador with long experience of the Middle East who saw modern Iran in terms of the Roman Empire. "There is no question of an aristocracy of descent—as in Europe —so purple invests the man. The Shah had to be supported by an enormous cast of bowing and scraping and protocol. When he was present at a party, you had to stand facing him all the time, and no one could sit until he did. To us it seemed a bit grotesque at times, but towards the end ambassadors didn't have to wear morning coats for an audience anymore."

The Shah's courtiers wore several different types of uniform, depending upon the occasion and their status. There were twenty-five heads of protocol—but only one supreme head. Orders were carried out with rigorous attention to detail and an enthusiasm which caused embarrassment. Once, when the Shah visited the University of Tehran, he asked casually whether a student with long hair was a boy or girl. Next day, all male students were ordered to have their hair cut short. A courtier told me a story, presumably apocryphal, which illustrates the Iranian desire to please. "The Shah asked for someone's hat. A few days later one of his ministers came in with it. But the hat was still on the man's head, which had been cut off."

His Imperial Majesty Mohammed Reza Pahlavi, Aryamehr, Shahanshah, still believes he is Light of the Aryans and King of Kings, as well as Shadow of God, and for thirty-eight years his autocratic rule over 35,000,000 cynical, backward, corrupt, and charming people was a performance of unrivaled cunning or, as his enemies said, brutality. He seemed to have precise knowledge of the fickle nature of his countrymen and the duplicity of "friends" abroad. "Because rumors fly so freely, it is my policy to cultivate a wide variety of viewpoints and sources of information," he said. He was so powerful and feared in his own country, and so courted by nations who realized his whims could affect the lives of millions outside Iran, that diplomats and businessmen in Tehran rarely mentioned him by name in case they were overheard. To Americans, he was "Ralph" or "Pepe" (he and the Empress Farah were "Ken and Barbie" or "George and Martha"). The French called him "Smi," an acronym for Son Majesté Impérial. The British referred to him as "the man on the hill" or, more conversationally, "Fred." Abroad, to his detractors, he was the Shit of Persia.

He was likened to a combination of Croesus, Dr. No, and Goldfinger. A State Department profile in 1950 said, "His indecision is monumental and his moral courage debatable." Twenty-five years later, the CIA described him as "a brilliant but dangerous megalomaniac," and an American official in Tehran added that he "has a reality problem." In fact, he was a leader trying to keep an equilibrium between what he wanted to do, what was acceptable, and what was possible, in a country where paradox is the only consistency.

He initiated some of the most advanced social programs in the world, yet he prohibited criticism of himself or his decisions. He claimed to draw support from ordinary people, yet surrounded himself and his sixty-strong family with a servile court of 1,500 costing at least $15 million a year, whose comic mannerisms would be the envy of any amateur dramatic society and whose protocol requirements made the British royal family seem like mere understudies in the diminishing cast of world monarchies. He has a Zurich bank account, extensive investments in England (including a million-dollar house near Windsor for the Crown Prince), France, and the United States, which make him the world's richest ruler. He said his wealth had been made over to the Pahlavi Foundation, a charitable trust. Charities have certain tax advantages, of course, and when the Shah claimed he had little control over the foundation, he was unconvincing. He had food flown from Paris to his villa on Kish Island in the Gulf—yet many of his villagers were starving on five grams of protein a week, and, it was alleged, adults searched for undigested oats in horse droppings[1] and children were sent to graze for their lunch.[2] He reads all the latest military magazines, yet relaxes by talking to chickens and cows and playing with an electric train set he bought in Switzerland. He claims to be deeply religious, yet he curtailed the power of the *mullahs* (clergy) to such an extent that they became a focus for all forms of dissent as well as his most implacable enemies. He believes religion can be "the root of backwardness," and, asked once what happens when the conflict between him and *mullahs* became intense, he replied with only the trace of a smile, "I send them away. I send some of them a very long way away." He talked about the emancipation of women, yet he is a male chauvinist par excellence.

He held power longer than any other modern monarch with the exception of the Emperor of Japan, in spite of a brief exile and several assassination attempts. Like his people, he is easy to misunderstand, deceptive and ambiguous. Like his country, he has a turbulent past, a confused present, and an uncertain future, although initially the money rush provided enough high-level flattery to convince him the days of humiliation were over. In 1973 there were twenty-three official visits to Iran by leading foreign politicians and heads of state—and seven came after the

October war. The following year there were fifty-five such visits, and by 1975 there were ninety.

But had he become an enlightened ruler, or a totem to tyranny? An independent, tough-minded statesman, or America's hired gun in the Middle East who, according to one diplomat, "makes Hitler look like a cream puff," but who nevertheless received twenty-one-gun salutes when he visited Washington because, as President Carter asserted, "Iran is one of the important bases on which our entire foreign policy depends"? A man with a mission for his country, or a self-deluding paranoiac with a barroom philosophy? A despot, a clown, a world leader, or a nut to beware of?

On my first meeting with him, he stood to greet me in the middle of his huge office on the second floor of the Niavaran Palace. He looked a smaller, shyer man than his pictures or public image indicated. To the left was his desk; to the right, a settee, a high-backed armchair, and a coffee table. He sat himself on the chair, bolt upright, even when he made a joke or smiled, which was rare.

His voice was surprisingly soft, and he sighed sometimes as he repeated the message he had given so many times. He had the bored, querulous air of a superior schoolteacher reciting for the umpteenth time to a class of dim-witted fifth-graders, "If things continue on their present track, the disintegration of Western societies will occur sooner than you think under the hammer blows of fascism and communism."

My attention was distracted. Two footmen, immaculate in gilded official court morning dress, entered soundlessly, bearing huge gold trays. On one was a small cylindrical cup for the Shah, an *es takan*, which he took and balanced on the arm of his chair. On the other: a Sèvres cup for me, which had a large bowl and tiny handle through which it was impossible to insert an average-sized finger, thus making it difficult to raise elegantly to the lips, and without appearing to tremble, when it was full of hot tea. Should I grip the cup as if it were a soup bowl, thus ensuring I would not drop it but at the same time adding ammunition to the Shah's belief in the decline of Western standards? Or should I remain a slave to impossible demands of etiquette, and risk appearing terrified or spilling tea over the floor with the added possibility of smashing the cup? Struggling with these complex issues, it was difficult to concentrate fully on what the Shah was saying, and then, out of the corner of my eye, I became mesmerized by the sight of the footmen backing at a steady pace across the yards of floor to the door, their eyes staring unwaveringly at the Shah, their bodies missing the inlaid tables by inches as if guided by remote control, their feet gliding over the loose carpets with cautious aplomb, one white-gloved hand behind each bowing back, the other stretched beneath the large tray. It seemed that acute gymnastic ability, or at least professional accomplishment in ballroom dancing, was essential for the maneuver. I waited breathlessly, with cup in trembling hand, for the whole edifice of ceremony to collapse into a clattering heap of golden accouterments. Naturally it did not, and I turned to the Shah, who continued in a monotone.

"The picture of Iran is distorted abroad, for several reasons. One is jealousy. How can the old, established Western societies be criticized by these newcomers? Actually, we are not newcomers, of course, with three thousand years of history. But for the last three hundred years we lost almost everything. So, in a sense, we are newcomers. Criticism of Iran does not upset me if it is informed, but so much has been unjust. It is the masochist approach of the decaying Western world trying to commit suicide. We have a saying in Iran, 'The dogs bark, but the caravan continues.' People can bark, and it will not bother us. Why should it?"

He had his answer in the autumn of 1978. An eighty-year-old religious leader, Ayatollah Ruhollah Khomeini, who settled in the Paris suburb of Neauphle-le-Château after fifteen years' exile in Iraq, had a clear message which was becoming increasingly influential. "The people will not rest until Pahlavi rule has been swept away and all traces of tyranny have disappeared. As long as the Shah's satanic power prevails, not a single true representative of the people can possibly be elected."

Although considered a "pantomime clown" by many Western diplomats in Tehran and in spite of the fact that he had vague and meandering ideas for an "Islamic republic," Khomeini symbolized a Church versus State conflict which, historically, usually ends in bloody civil war. The Saudis looked on with acute anxiety. They feared they would be next.

The Shah tried to avoid a conflict, although, privately, he suspected it was inevitable. For two years, he had allowed a semblance of "freedom" to dribble into Iranian society. He relaxed press censorship, released political prisoners, and allowed opposition parties to form. But his timing was wrong—too little too late—and he miscalculated the speed of the money rush and the inherent power of religious promises over political reality. "The Iranian people consider me a symbol. I talk their language. I listen to their needs. I cry for them," boasted Khomeini in ironic, but unperceived, mockery of what the Shah had said for years.

But the Shah was caught. Resisting would prove yet again that he was a "butcher," as one of his defecting aides called him. Giving in would be considered weak. Once he chose the latter course, his days as an autocratic ruler were over, and there were elements of panic in the measures he felt obliged to take. He closed the casinos (at least three of which were owned by his Pahlavi Foundation), curtailed such Western manifestations as "adult" movies, liquor stores, women's emancipation, and dismissed the government he had appointed only a year before.

The new prime minister, Jaafar Sherif Emami, announced there would be greater political freedom. "Democratic" elections were promised for June 1979. Speeches, many critical of the regime, were broadcast live on television and radio from the previously docile Parliament. And some indication of the repressed political turmoil was given when, within a few days, more than thirty new groups announced their existence, including the Society of the Sentinels of the Constitution, the Iranian Toilers Party, and the Party of Islamic Freedom Seekers.

When the new government failed to solve problems, the Shah declared martial law and appointed his chief of staff, General Gholam Reza Azhari, as prime minister. He promised to commit himself to "make up for past mistakes, to fight corruption and injustices," but sitting in his palace, surrounded by tanks, he knew he could trust fewer people than ever before. He turned first toward his family and, in particular, Ardeshir Zahedi, a former son-in-law who had been ambassador in Washington for five years. "I believe the only thing I can do is tell him the truth," Zahedi explained to me. "If you lie you are a traitor."

"Iranians have a facility for not exactly lying, but for making the truth appear palatable," I replied.

"There are reasons for that," he said. "It is part of our education never to say no. You must remember we have been invaded many times. If we weren't tolerant we would not be where we are today. If we had been too stubborn, we would not exist.

"But now we are in a very important and dangerous time. The job of the Shah is not easy but he knows he cannot bring his country into the twentieth century with sixteenth-century attitudes. People expect miracles. They forget what Iran was like only twenty years ago.

"He does not have to stay there. He could take the money, go anywhere in the world, have a wonderful time, and say 'To hell with you.' Yet he spends eighteen or nineteen hours a day working for his people. He is really their prisoner."

Until November 1978, that might have seemed a reversal of roles, but now as I drove to see the Shah on a Thursday afternoon (equivalent to a Saturday in the West) it appeared almost true. He had not left his palace, refused to see any but his closest aides, declined newspaper interviews (once his favorite source of public announcement), and was guarded night and day by the most formidable security of any world leader. Nevertheless, his real power had disintegrated far quicker than anyone expected. "We never thought it would happen," said an American diplomat, "but the days when he *was* Iran are over." And a member of the Cabinet warned, "You will find him a different man than before. He feels bitter, very let down, but he is now doing exactly what our constitution demands. He is a constitutional monarch."

I was still not prepared for what I saw.

Once more I went to Niavaran Palace, this time to the Shah's smaller, private office. There was less formality—no tea. The Shah, dressed in a double-breasted black suit, looked tired, gaunt, thinner than I remembered, and he spoke hesitantly with little of the authority I noticed previously. He sighed a lot, sucked on his cheeks in a nervous gesture, and there were long pauses while he struggled to find the right words.

Was this the ogre whose downfall was demanded? Or was he a man whose own admitted follies had now smashed his dream to squash centuries of progress into a few decades without a revolution, thus reversing the trend of history? Could he, indeed, survive? Did he actually want to leave the country and enjoy the wealth he had accumulated?

"Anything might occur in the mind of a human being," he replied.

"But has it occurred to you lately?"

He sighed, paused for a long while, and then said quietly, "I can't say. But I told you this might occur in the mind of a human being."

Clearly it had occurred to him, so I asked if he was surprised by the strength of the animosity toward him. There was no hesitation: "To be honest, yes."

"The caravan," I said, "seems to have slowed down."

He laughed. It was curious that, in spite of his palpable depression, he seemed more relaxed than before, as if no longer burdened by decision-making. He was chastened, and did not find it necessary to make his usual grandiose, self-congratulatory pronouncements.

"The caravan seems to be stopped," he replied with a smile.

"Will it restart?"

"God knows."

"That sounds pessimistic."

"When you are not sure about something, that's what you say. How could I be sure? It's not the first time. It was bad in 1953, too."

Then, he had been forced into exile. Now, it was said, he was no longer in control of the country and was in fact a "prisoner" of his own generals. "Not yet," he said, and laughed again. "Until now, the military obey me."

For how long?

"That remains to be seen. You must remember how many people would like to see the end of this country. We have a strange history. For the last I don't know how many years, the only two people who have really reigned over a pacified territory are my father and myself, so I don't see a few military people ruling peacefully and easily. Or a president." He repeated the words quietly, as if to exorcise the thought. "Or a president. It's a little hard to imagine."

There were those who thought he should abdicate in favor of his son, eighteen-year-old Crown Prince Reza.

"My son is too young. Will the army obey him, as they obey me? How could the structure of the state remain? But this is the day to hear these things. I heard it this morning, and again and again. People just simply think that by my retiring everything will be all right. Will it? That would mean that I am the only target the people want removed. They will accept military rule, but not me?" He shrugged. Clearly it was an impossibility.

Iran had to have a Shah, then?

"Well, so far. [If not], it will be fragmented and finally unified under the red banner. You would be dead, in Europe, within three months. I think the oil of other countries would not pass through the Straits of Hormuz."

But how could he remain Shah when he appeared to be the most detested man in the country? Surely the people were against him personally?

"I hope not. Some people tell me the opposite about the majority."

"They were burning your portraits in the streets."

"Sure, but that could be a minority."

"Do you think it is?"

"That's what they tell me, the people who collect the news. They say that truly the majority does not think this way."

It was a wan, and not very convincing, answer. After all, these same people had flattered him for years into a situation where he was totally unprepared for any opposition. He could command only a sullen obedience with the aid of bullets. Surely "they" did not tell him what was really happening?

He paused for a long while, and when he spoke the sadness in his voice echoed around the room. "It is quite possible."

It seemed, at that moment, that he had lost the will to fight, and would accept more or less anything that was suggested. When I asked if he could guarantee to be on the throne in two months' time, he said no. After another long pause, he added, "Some people say 'Ask the British and Americans' because they are making all the trouble. That's what they say. That you are behind the scenes. I'm repeating to you what people say. I'm not expressing my own opinion."

"Surely you don't agree?"

"Do you listen to the Persian version of the BBC? It's very provocative."

"The BBC isn't the government."

"Nevertheless, it's British and it's financed by the government."

Was he embarrassed, then, to be supported publicly by President Carter or the British Foreign Secretary, Dr. David Owen, who had said, "It would not be in the interest of this country or the West for the Shah to be toppled. Can you just take their money, sell them tanks for strategic interests, sell them cars, persuade them to hold down oil prices in the interest of the world, generally exert influence with them and then, when they come under attack, just back off?"

Those words incited an attack on the British embassy in Tehran. Perhaps it would have been better if Dr. Owen kept quiet?

The Shah nodded. "It's how you say it, what words you use. Some people attacked here because they were criticizing those words."

"So it was an embarrassment to you?"

There was yet another long pause. "I'd better keep quiet," he said finally.

An even longer pause followed when I asked if his relatives had left the country.

Then, softly, he said, "Yes."

"Why?"

He appeared to be fighting with his emotions, before he replied, "With right or false rumors, why should they stay?"

"To support you."

"Hmmm. I don't know how helpful they could have been now."

"Perhaps they should return?"

"I wouldn't advise it."

In a television broadcast to Iranians, he had seemed to beg almost for a last chance, and promised to make up for past mistakes. What mistakes? He agreed, after some hesitation, that he might have underestimated the power of religious forces in Iran.

"Looking at what is happening, you will have to accept *anything* as a criticism. But we are taking many steps—the family, the Pahlavi Foundation—although in the foundation maybe they will find absolutely no mistake."

It is stretching credulity too far to believe that the Shah was unaware of the corruption swirling round his throne, but he still maintained a hurt response when it was suggested.

"How could I have had knowledge? Really. When I had knowledge of it in the armed forces, it was . . . *pfffttt* . . . stopped, eradicated."

But one of his close friends, Sir Shapoor Reporter, had received a secret £1-million commission from the British Defence Ministry for the sale of Chieftain tanks.

"That's nothing. What's £1 million? We bought close to $20 billion of weapons."

Some people might think it was a bribe.

"Well, the British Government paid the money. You did it."

"And you didn't know about it?"

He paused again, sucked in his breath, shook his head, and said nothing.

Corruption charges had already been brought against Mr. Hoveyda, General Nassiri, and several former Cabinet ministers. It appeared everyone was being sacrificed so he could remain on the throne.

"What can I say? The government asked . . . with persistence . . . that these people should be arrested. They really insisted."

"Against your better judgment?"

"Well, I took the position that you do whatever you think is best. But they insisted."

"It could not have been a happy time?"

"Well, you can look at this thing from . . . *pfffttt* . . . many angles." He sighed again.

Maybe the arrest of General Nassiri implied that the Shah was mistaken when he insisted repeatedly that there was no torture in Iran.

"Well, surely. But not at least for the last two years. That's for sure."

Maybe he did not realize what was going on because he was too remote.

"I don't think so. Everywhere I went, I tried to talk to the simplest people. But you can't do without security these days, after the assassination of all those people. They won't let you go."

I asked if he thought his dreams were now shattered.

"Let's see what the future is. It's very early to judge now."

"It doesn't look good."

"Not at this minute."

"Do you think you have been misunderstood?"

There was the longest pause of our discussion, as he controlled his emotions. Finally his words came slowly and almost inaudibly, as he tried to comprehend the reasons for his massive disappointment.

"Yes," he said at last. "And I don't know . . . why."

"By the Persian people as well?"

"If what we hear is really what they think, I would say even more."

"Do you feel lonely at this moment?"

He laughed again, the tension disappeared. "How do you want to console me? We should have had Mr. Homer or Mr. Dante here to ask their opinion."

It is fashionable to condemn the Shah, particularly when he seems at last to be defeated, and to disbelieve most of what he says. It is true that he has an ability to act in a way he feels is appropriate for his audience. But as he sat alone, bewildered and upset, deserted by his family (except his wife and children) and those for whom he had tried to control the money rush, it was impossible not to feel sympathy.

Two months later, on January 16, 1979, he was forced to leave the country, weeping, for an extended "holiday." On February 1, Ayatollah Khomeini returned, and he and civilian leaders began the virtually impossible task of reconciling their ideals in order to create a "new" Iran. As the Shah watched their efforts from abroad, he nurtured the forlorn hope that one day he might return in triumph—as he had once before. At least, he reflected, nothing is predictable—as his own life story illustrates. It is entwined with the modern history of Iran and could keep a convention of psychiatrists arguing for weeks.

5/THIS KING BUSINESS

"The Shah couldn't prove he was Shah if it wasn't written down."
BERTOLT BRECHT, THE CAUCASIAN CHALK CIRCLE

"No hard feelings. You can be what you are, but don't force us to be what you are. We want to keep our identity."
THE SHAH, NEWSWEEK, OCTOBER 14, 1974

BORN ON OCTOBER 26, 1919, minutes after his twin sister Ashraf, in a small house in what became the red-light district of South Tehran, Mohammed Reza was the first son of Colonel Reza Khan and his second wife, Tadj-ol-Molouk (see Appendix). The colonel, who had joined the Persian Cossack Regiment when he was fourteen, illiterate, and a donkey driver, "had risen from the ranks and was renowned for his strong personality, iron will, and extraordinary capacity for leadership, and was clever and ambitious,"[1] useful qualities at a time when Iran was bankrupt, demoralized, and increasingly under the control of Russia.

Colonel Reza Khan first led a military coup against the government and then, in 1925, deposed the last of the Qajar dynasty kings, Ahmad Shah, who had decided prudently not to return from an extended vacation in Switzerland and the South of France.

At first Reza Khan wanted to declare a republic, emulating his hero Kemel Ataturk two years previously in neighboring Turkey, but managed to convince himself that "the tide of public opinion shifted back towards the idea of continuing a monarchical system."

He adopted the name Pahlavi after an ancient Persian language, and crowned himself, just like Napoleon who snatched the crown from the Pope's hands at the last minute because he believed that no one else on earth was qualified to perform such a ritual. The donkey driver had become Shahanshah, Shadow of the Almighty, Viceregent of God, and Center of the Universe.

Standing in the Great Hall of the Gulistan Palace, Tehran, his impressionable son marveled at the magnificence of it all. "You can imagine the awe it inspired in a six-year-old like me," he said.

Despite the extravagance of the coronation, Reza Khan, now called Reza Shah, continued to live an ascetic life, sleeping on a mattress on the floor, dressing in simple army uniforms, homemade socks, and worn shoes. He wanted his son to have a "manly" education, so he created a special elementary school for him and took him away from his mother's control. "My father influenced me more by far than anyone else," he says. "He could be one of the pleasantest men in the world, yet he could be one of the most frightening. Strong men often trembled just to look at him."

Former Empress Soraya recalls the Shah adding, "We were all frightened of him. He needed only to fix his piercing eyes upon us, and we went rigid with fear and respect. At the family table, we never dared express our own views. Indeed, we were allowed to speak only when asked a question."[2]

Clearly much was expected from the son—possibly too much. He was sickly and timid, daunted by the forceful personality of his 6'4" father. Soon after the coronation, he suffered from typhoid fever, nearly died, and began to develop a faith which he claims is his most persistent motivating force. He dreamed that Ali, the son-in-law of the Prophet Muhammad, ordered him to drink from a bowl. "I did. The next day the crisis of my fever was over, and I was on the road to rapid recovery." This "vision" was followed by two others which convinced him that "there is a supreme being who is guiding me." When I asked about his mystical nature, he replied, "It is the whole history of my life, and probably will be to the end. I don't have visions anymore. They stopped when I was seven—and so did the apparitions, and this and that. Sometimes I dream now, but very seldom. It is always mystical and religious. At one time, I dreamed about things that later happened. I was afraid that something really bad would come true, and my actions might be influenced by my dreams. Fortunately, they stopped."

His father scoffed at such mysticism and worried that his son might become a religious fanatic. "It is a pity Ashraf was not born a boy," he remarked to a friend. "She's the one with the balls."

Reza Shah began the practical task of modernizing the country, once more following examples set by Kemel Ataturk. He developed a railway whose punctuality made him inordinately proud, began health and educational systems, and resisted the efforts of Lord Curzon to turn Iran into a protectorate. "Father did not trust foreigners in general, and Westerners in particular," says the Shah today. Nevertheless, modernization meant "Westernization," and as Ataturk banned the veil for women and insisted men should cut their beards and dress in European style, Reza Shah followed the example in the most dramatic way he could devise. One day he ordered his wife and eldest daughter, Shams, to accompany him to the opening of a new teachers' college without wearing the traditional *chador*. "For my personal feelings, I wish I had died today, but for the country I take you there like this," he explained in the car on the way to the ceremony.[3] A few days later, a priest in the religious city of Qum denounced the Empress for her action. Reza Shah went straight to the mosque and beat the priest so hard that his metal stick bent. He had a notoriously violent temper. It is claimed he kicked one minister to death, and threw another out of the window.

"I find that by nature I am calm," says the present Shah, who at the age of twelve was sent from his father's overpowering influence to Le Rosey boarding school in Switzerland, where he saw the advantages of a democratic education—to a limited degree. He did not take his final exams, but returned after four years to the Military Academy in Tehran, copied on the French academy at St. Cyr, where there was no difficulty in ensuring that he became one of the most successful students. After two years, "Reza Shah decided to provide for me a suitable bride. With his characteristic forthrightness, perhaps better adapted to engineering projects than to affairs of the heart—he started an investigation. First, he had the girl's pedigree checked. Negotiations rapidly progressed, and the first thing I knew I was betrothed. That was in 1938. Up to that point I had never laid eyes on the girl."

She was Princess Fawzia, sister of King Farouk, and the next day Mohammed was dispatched to Cairo to meet her. There was only one problem. A future Crown Prince had to be Persian. It was overcome with ease. Reza Shah ordered Parliament to pass a law making Fawzia an instant Persian. A daughter, Shahnaz, was born in 1940, but it was not a happy marriage and the couple divorced in 1948. The Shah's second marriage, to Princess Soraya in 1950, marred because they had no children, ended in divorce eight years later. Empress Farah, whom the Shah married in 1959, and by whom he has two sons and two daughters, has had an important influence on him and on the development of Iran—although, as she was to tell me later, he does not confide in her some of the most fundamental details about the life of Crown Prince Reza. From an early age, the Crown Prince has had his own house in the palace grounds. He attended a special school with the sons of a few carefully selected families, where military training was emphasized and then went to Texas for advanced pilot training. The present Shah tried to cultivate in his son the tough, self-reliant qualities he feels are essential in a ruler. Before his exile in 1979, he planned to abdicate in about 1988. But he realized there was an ever-present threat of assassination or exile. It had happened to his father before him.

Reza Shah was made to abdicate when he refused to let the Allies use Iran as a supply route to Russia during the Second World War. He said he wanted to be independent, but it was felt he had become too sympathetic toward the Nazis. Germany was Iran's principal trading partner and provided much military and educational equipment. There was a Nazi propaganda center in Tehran, which capitalized on the Aryan nature of both countries (Iran is a variation of "Aryan." "Persia" is the English name of one of the southern provinces, Fars. Reza Shah insisted that the country should be called Iran, but today both names are interchangeable and equally correct.)

"If the Allies had not sent huge quantities of war materiel through Persia in aid of the Russians, probably the spring offensive of 1942 would never have succeeded," wrote the present Shah, "and just as probably the Germans would have invaded my country. Some Persians might have welcomed a German victory, believing that it would finally end Russian and British influence in Iran. But my father had authoritarian tendencies which would never have allowed a dictator to dominate him."

This theory was not tested. On August 25, 1941 the British invaded Iran from the south, the Russians from the north, and two weeks later, the Shah was given an ultimatum: abdicate by noon on September 16, or troops would enter Tehran the next day.

"I cannot be the nominal head of an occupied land, to be dictated to by a minor British or Russian officer," he told his son, minutes before he signed the abdication papers. According to one account, he added, "You must devote all your energies just to staying on the throne. They will try to push you off it. So you must be patient, and bend with the wind. Eventually the war will end. You must still be king when it does. Then it will be time to raise your head."[4] As he left on the British steamer *Bandra* for exile, first in Mauritius, then in South Africa, Reza Shah sent his son one more instruction, which he was to repeat several times in letters before he died three years later: "Your Majesty, never be afraid of anything in the world."

Many years later the money rush allowed the Shah to exorcise his fears by buying weapons to protect his country from humiliations which disgusted him in his youth. "I think the British were terribly mistaken," he told me. "But I have no resentment. They have behaved absolutely correctly for the last twenty years, and I do not mix sentiment with politics. Never." His uncompromising militarism began at this time. "I came to the conclusion that besides the Nazis and fascists, there were obviously other moral outcasts in the world. I realized also that unfortunately in this world of ours it is always the one who is stronger who is right. Might is right, and to be strong you need a people who are united, a sound economy, and, of course, adequate weapons. This is a lesson I learned at a very early age."

Until that time, the new Shah had given little public indication of being interested in anything other than fast cars, nightclubs, and women. There was talk of a more active occupation of Iran and the installation of a puppet government, so it was considered something of a compliment to him when Tehran was chosen as the location for a conference between the Big Three—Britain, Russia, and the United States—which began on November 28, 1943 to plan a final assault on Germany.

In snubs that still rankle, Churchill and Roosevelt sent for the Shah to call on them. Only Stalin followed the protocol of a country where lèse majesté was taken with utmost seriousness. He treated the Shah as a world leader, visited him without a bodyguard, brought lavish presents, and offered a regiment of T-34 tanks and fighter bombers. "Don't worry," he explained. "Communism will not come to your country for sixty years."

The Shah declined the military gifts, and, at the end of the war, Russian designs on his country were made explicit when the Soviets refused to leave until President Truman exerted strong pressure. On the other hand, British troops departed by an agreed-upon date, but considered that their part ownership of the country was taken for granted.

When the Shah visited England in 1943, he spoke to Ernest Bevin about the possibilities of developing Iran. He recalls, "I said we had minerals in Kerman. He exclaimed, 'Oh, in our zone?' I had to tell him that the whole of Iran was the zone of a free country. He was very embarrassed and tried to explain, 'No, no, that's not what I meant.' But he did."

It was an easy mistake to make. For years, Iran had been a useful source of revenue for the British Treasury, thanks initially to a high-living adventurer, William Knox D'Arcy, who made a fortune from the Morgan gold strike in Queensland, Australia, and then retired to live opulently in Grosvenor Square, London. In 1901 the then Shah gave him a sixty-year oil concession covering five-sixths of the country.

But no oil was found. At the beginning of 1908, with five dry wells completed, George Reynolds, the geologist chosen by D'Arcy to take charge of the exploration, is said to have received a cable telling him to return home because funds were exhausted.[5] There is no copy of the telegram in official records, but

in view of what happened five months later, it is not impossible
that it was removed. Reynolds refused to accept the order, and,
on May 26, 1908, oil gushed fifty feet above the top of the der-
rick at Masjid-i-Sulaiman (the Mosque of Solomon) 150 miles
northeast of Abadan. It was the beginning of the oil industry in
the Middle East and the first flickering indication of the money
rush that was to come.

The local Bakhtiari tribe, which had demanded protection
money during the drilling, was given 3 percent of the profits in
return for maintaining law and order, and the Anglo-Persian Oil
Company (later Anglo-Iranian, then British Petroleum) was
formed. By 1950 it was paying the Iranian Government $32 mil-
lion in royalties—and $101 million in tax to the British Govern-
ment.

Such enforced largess, combined with Iran's status as an honorary colony (*"Dogs and Persians Prohibited"* is one sign that
former Prime Minister Amir Abbas Hoveyda recalls seeing
painted on the side of a railroad car), the squalor in which most
people lived, the corruption of the government, and the lavish
wealth of a few landowners, inspired an increasingly strong na-
tionalist movement. It found its apotheosis in a shrewd politician,
Dr. Mohammed Mossadeq, who was represented to the British
as the caricature wog of their imagination, dressed in pajamas,
crying a lot of the time, an ever-running nose, fainting at convenient moments. He was about seventy years old when he became Prime Minister on April 29, 1951—and immediately nationalized the oil fields, declaring that he was opening "a hidden
treasure upon which lies a dragon."

Gunboat diplomacy was considered inappropriate on this occasion, unlike at Suez five years later, and on October 4, 1951,
the last of 2,000 British employees of Anglo-Iranian gathered
forlornly at the Gymkhana Club, "the centre of so many of the
lighter moments of their life in Persia, to embark for Basra on
the British cruiser *Mauritius*. Some had their dogs, though most
had had to be destroyed; others carried tennis rackets and golf
clubs; the hospital nurses and the indomitable Mrs. Flavell who
ran the guesthouse and three days previously had intimidated a
Persian tank commander with her parasol for driving over her
lawn, were among the party, and the Rev. Tyrie had come

sadly from locking up in the little church the records of those who had been born, baptised, or had died in Abadan. The ship's band, 'correct' to the end, struck up the Persian national anthem and the launches began their slow shuttle service. The cruiser *Mauritius* steamed slowly away up the river with the band playing, the assembled company lining the rails and roaring in unison the less printable version of Colonel Bogey."[6]

(It should not be assumed that such brave colonialism is now extinct. The British Empire is still alive and thriving, but has shifted itself to some of the hottest and most inhospitable parts of the world, as I was to discover. The American Empire, a more recent development, the boastful French Empire, the cunning Japanese Empire, and the ruthless German Empire are all resurrected for the money rush. The difference is that few administrators claim altruism as a motive. Most take the money and run. Many had to run very fast when the Shah left in 1979.)

Unfortunately for Dr. Mossadeq, he had chosen the wrong time to fight—there was no world shortage of oil. Anglo-Iranian organized a boycott of Iran by other major companies which were happy to comply because they realized that if one Middle East country succeeded in nationalization, the others would follow. Even when Mossadeq offered oil at one quarter of the market price, there were no buyers. Finally, in June 1953, he was forced to ask President Eisenhower for an American loan, adding the Red Threat as an inducement. The Russians, he said, were willing—even eager—to provide economic and military aid. For a month Eisenhower did not reply, giving America's answer to the Red Threat—the CIA—time to plan. Allen Dulles, head of the CIA, flew to Switzerland where he met Princess Ashraf. Meanwhile, a colleague of Dulles arrived in Tehran "to see some old friends."

General Norman Schwarzkopf who, as head of the New Jersey State Police, had been in charge of the hunt for the Lindbergh baby kidnapper, had also been in Tehran from 1942 to 1948 reorganizing the police, a task he performed with such dramatic efficiency that he was known as the "gang basher." He professed surprise that he was referred to as "this notorious agent of American intelligence," and left Tehran after forty-eight hours, having met the Shah and other leaders of the anti-Mossadeq faction.

On July 6, 1953, thirty-seven-year-old Kermit Roosevelt,

grandson of former United States President Theodore Roosevelt, arrived at Qaar-e-Shirin on the Iran-Iraq border, and entered the country recorded as "Scar on the Left Cheek"—the Iranian immigration official having copied the passport entry for "distinguishing marks" as his name. Roosevelt's job was to mastermind Mossadeq's overthrow, but he found the Shah depressed and unenthusiastic. Mossadeq's public boast that "I have muzzled the Shah" was justified. The Shah was made to sell estates inherited from his father, had to sign a receipt if he wanted to borrow the crown jewels, was confined to his palace and spied upon by guards loyal to Mossadeq. The resulting frustration and boredom encouraged his enthusiasm for childish practical jokes. He threw lifelike toy spiders and frogs at women guests and did uncannily realistic imitations of dogs barking during film shows. He was disillusioned and ready to leave the country. He was not, it appeared, the sort of man for whom revolutions are planned.

Roosevelt sent for Princess Ashraf, who returned to Tehran incognito on July 25 "to encourage us to act," according to Soraya. This "encouragement" alternating between shouts, threats, and curses inspired the Shah to nominate a new Prime Minister, General Fazollah Zahedi (the father of Ardeshir), in place of Mossadeq. Unhappily, as so often happens in Iran, the plan was disclosed prematurely, and Mossadeq was able to denounce it as an attempted coup d'etat.

The Shah left Tehran hurriedly for his summer palace at Ramsar on the Caspian Sea. From there he and Soraya were forced to flee to exile in Rome. Meanwhile an uprising was organized in Tehran, financed with CIA money variously estimated as anything between $70,000 by the Shah himself to $19 million by others[7] which was distributed in 10-rial notes to those who shouted *"Javid Shah"* (Long live the Shah). Three days later, Mossadeq was overthrown.

It was clear now, even to Anglo-Iranian and the British Government, that American influence in Iran was paramount and that some reward would be expected for organizing the coup. But what? There was a world oil glut, and the Iranian boycott had actually been a blessing in disguise both to the companies and to the Arab countries—particularly to debt-ridden Saudi Arabia, which had been able to sell more oil. Moreover, production costs in Iran were considered high in an industry with extraordinary profit margins: 14 cents a barrel, compared to 8 cents in Saudi Arabia and 6 cents in Kuwait. Today each barrel costs about 30 cents to produce.

Eventually it was agreed that the National Iranian Oil Company formed by Dr. Mossadeq would remain owner of the oil fields and refineries, and sell to a consortium. The arrangement gave Iran a considerably increased income—from almost nothing to $490 million over the next three years—but it was soon insufficient to pay for the Shah's plans.

By 1961 overspending and widespread corruption resulted in a budget deficit of $500 million. "Let me tell you bluntly," said the Shah, with psychic disillusion, "that this King business has given me nothing but a headache."[8]

He needed money to implement what later became the Shah-People Revolution, a nineteen-point program whose basic socialist principles appeared a contradiction in a country where communism was outlawed. They were milestones on the way to what the Shah saw optimistically as his Great Civilization (see Appendix) but were ambitious beyond the capabilities of a country whose income was controlled by foreigners with their shareholders in mind.

The consortium agreed to a bookkeeping maneuver in order to help overcome the Shah's immediate financial difficulties. Accounting procedures were changed from the Gregorian to the Persian calendar, which began in March, thus providing an additional three months' money in one year. "The Shah frittered away Iran's oil through the sixties, then ruined the world by upping the price in the seventies," says one of the consortium's senior members whose opinions, although necessarily biased, are echoed by others outside the industry. "He made the world believe there was an ever-increasing supply of cheap oil. He pushed us all the time to produce more, and the world has still not learned to withstand the shock of the sudden price rise. He has made more mistakes than anyone when it comes to volume and price." Certainly the Shah's later talk about oil as a basis for 70,000 different products, and "too noble to be used just for making electricity and heating houses," seemed a conversion initiated more by expedience than long-cherished scientific idealism.

But flamboyant declarations are an essential requisite to rebuilding a nation, and the Shah had returned from his few days' exile with reawakened faith both in himself and his country. He began to demand respect and, perhaps to disguise the parvenu nature of his "royal" line, he put increasing emphasis on the distant past, back to 559 B.C., when the Persian Empire under Cyrus the Great stretched from Greece to India. "Ours is the world's oldest continuous civilization except that of China," he said. "Our empire was flourishing centuries before that of Rome, and it was in fact we who showed that it was possible to govern and administer on such an extended scale." He claims several pastoral inventions for Iran: the windmill, tulips, peaches, alfalfa, roses, narcissus, lilacs, jasmine, sherry, sherbet, backgammon, and polo. As a final proclamation of his authority, he decided to crown himself—just as his father did—on October 28, 1967. "Now, at last, I feel I have something to show. There is no pride, no job, in being king of a poor, divided, occupied land," he said, and, regretting his inability to invite many heads of state as witnesses, he added, "We simply have not the means to accommodate them. By 1971, when we celebrate the 2,500th anniversary of the Persian Empire, we might be in a position to ask everyone."

He was, and he did, but not everyone accepted. President Nixon sent Spiro Agnew, later to become a frequent business visitor to the Middle East. Prince Philip and Princess Anne represented Queen Elizabeth. Jacques Chaban-Delmas stood in for Georges Pompidou. There were, though, nine kings, including Haile Selassie, who brought his black chihuahua wearing a diamond collar, five queens, thirteen princes, eight princesses, sixteen presidents, three prime ministers, two governors-general, two foreign ministers, nine shaikhs, and two sultans mingling with the 600 guests who came from 69 countries. "We want people to see what Iran is," explained Empress Farah. "Other countries pay so much money for public relations, and we are getting it free."

Not quite. The meal of quail eggs stuffed with caviar (the Shah ate artichokes—he is allergic to Iran's most famous food), crayfish mousse, saddle of lamb, peacock, and fresh figs, was cooked by 180 chefs flown from Maxim's of Paris, the Hôtel de Paris in Monte Carlo, and the Palace Hotel in St. Moritz. The total cost of the celebrations was between $14 million and $100 million, depending upon which items are taken into account.

The Shah denied extravagance. "The cost was less than for the twenty-minute inauguration of a United States president," he told me.

Nevertheless, criticism was unrestrained. "It would be easy to hail this as the greatest non-event of our time," wrote the London *Observer.* "A creation of royal despotism taking advantage of the bedazzled mass media. It was the Field of the Cloth of Gold without a purpose, the Congress of Vienna without any business, a picture of unparalleled vulgarity."

International prestige and respectability are not nurtured by extravagance. They need another essential ingredient for which the Shah had to wait two more years: power. Many of those who scorned or privately ridiculed his grandiose ambitions and posturing were first in the money rush, giving him a quickly accepted opportunity to adopt their patronizing attitudes for himself. "We think the West is passing through a very, very difficult time, and you don't have much to offer us. No doubt we can still learn tremendously from you. But not in the mode of governing or ruling. That you can keep for yourselves."

When it was suggested that the oil price rise would create chaos in the industrialized nations and be a burden on poor countries, he replied, "That is true, but as to the industrialized world, I think that they will have to realize that the era of their terrific progress and even more terrific income and wealth based on cheap oil, is finished. Eventually all those children of well-to-do families who have plenty to eat at every meal, who have their cars, and who act almost as terrorists, and throw bombs here and there, will have to rethink about all these aspects of their advanced industrial world."

A ruler who saw his country's income rise in one year from $4.8 billion to $18.5 billion could perhaps be excused the orgy of indiscriminate spending which took place, but it laid the foundations for future problems. "It was like a chap who did not know he had an uncle being sent a telegram to say that not only did he have an uncle, but that the uncle had left him $20 million," says one of the Shah's few close confidants. "What would you expect him to do?"

Apart from massive spending on weapons, loans were promised throughout the world: $1.2 billion to the British Water Authority, $1 billion to France in advance payment for nuclear reactors, $1 billion to the World Bank, $3 billion to Italy for joint ventures, $7 billion to developing nations in Africa and Asia, a $3 billion trade agreement with Russia. The Shah tried without success to buy into Pan American for $300 million, offered $75 million credit to the Grumman Corporation which produces F-14 fighters for Iran and the United States Navy (his offer was declined because foreigners cannot buy into U.S. defense contractors), bought nine jumbo jets from TWA for $16.6 million each (and sold one back to the company for $22 million in 1977, before it had even left the TWA hangars in Kansas), spent $100 million on 25 percent of Krupp. "Americans buy minority interests in European companies, and this astonishes nobody," he said in reply to criticism, "but when we buy this little twenty-five percent, so-called liberals profess to be shocked."

Nothing seemed able to stop his determination to make Iran within a generation the world's fifth most powerful nation, after the United States, Russia, Japan, and China. One day in August 1974, he met his Cabinet in the conference room of the Ramsar Palace, from where twenty years previously he had flown into humiliating exile, and said in a flat, undramatic way that he had decided to double the money spent on the Fifth Development Plan, which ran from 1973 to 1978. Suddenly Iran had $68.8 billion to spend, instead of only $35.5 billion. It did not seem to matter that there were not enough qualified people to administer such a massive increase—after all, he had ordered twenty atomic reactors even though Iran had only four resident technicians.

Money could overcome every problem, it was thought, and the most important first step was, naturally, education. He decreed that it was to be free and compulsory for all children, regardless of the fact that such an order required an additional 30,000 teachers. His then Prime Minister Hoveyda explained that college students could fill the gap, and that within two years televised lessons would be broadcast to schools via Iran's own satellite. But most of the 65,000 villages did not have electricity. No problem. "We will use batteries," he said. Next there was an order that school-children should have a glass of milk and a piece of cake every day—a feat totally beyond the capability of the dairy industry, and impossible even with the importation of dried milk.

Politically, too, the Shah became unpredictable. In March 1975 he announced that Iran would have only one political party: a decision which made very little practical difference because the two existing authorized groupings were known as the "Yes" and "Of Course" parties. But it caused embarrassment to Hoveyda who was campaigning for a summer election at the time, and involved the Shah in tortuous explanations as he had always declared himself opposed to a single-party system.

The following year, by a decree effective on March 21, the Iranian New Year, he altered the calendar. It had been based on the date of Muhammad's flight from Mecca to Medina (the *hijra*). Now it had to coincide with the reign of Cyrus the Great (see Appendix), a reversion which many Iranians were surprised to note "re-affirmed their basic faith in their glorious Monarchy," according to an advertisement in *The Times*. It served no tangible purpose, and, if anything, put Iran even farther away from the Western civilization whose advantages the Shah was trying selectively to emulate. When, in the fall of 1978, religious pressure forced him to revert to the Islamic calendar, there were no brave advertisements.

But perhaps the most symbolic act, a plan conceived out of pique, or with a sense of humor, was an attempt to buy 17 percent of British Petroleum when the British Government sold part of its shareholding in the company during the summer of 1977. The day before the issue closed, the National Iranian Oil Company, under direct orders from the Shah, sent an application for the whole lot and a check for $400 million. "It was sheer bloody stupidity," said a former director of BP. "Not even a lunatic would do that sort of thing when the British Government had made it quite clear that the shares would be spread around among as many people as possible. It was arrogant, high-handed, and inept. But he is so vain, isn't he? He is shut up in his palaces all the time and has to rely on visitors for a view of what's going on in the world. Most people don't dare tell him what is happening."

It was difficult for the Shah to avoid noticing for himself. As his spending became legendary, more and more people tried to become beneficiaries. Imports quintupled, bringing $93 billion worth of goods in five years. Ships waited 250 days to unload, and the government had to pay $1 billion demurrage fees a year. Fruit went moldy, and was thrown into the Gulf. Cargoes of rice cooked themselves gently into pilaf in the steamy holds of freighters. Even when goods were cleared, there were not enough trucks to take them to their destination. So the Shah bought 4,000 from an American firm for $6,000 each. He did not realize that they were too large for the roads and lacked adequate spare parts. More important, Iran did not have enough trained drivers. The trucks were still unused in 1978, rusting in sand up to their axles.

A modern railway system was planned by the Shah to carry passengers at 150 miles an hour along thousands of miles of the most modern track and signaling devices in the world. For political expediency, the main projects were awarded to four countries: Britain, France, West Germany, and Japan. In addition, the Russians, Danes, Swiss, Italians, and Indians were working on smaller contracts.

It soon became impossible to coordinate the various schemes, and, while Iranian State Railway officials were fired every few months, competing nations began to design railways with no regard to each other. The Germans had trains running on the right, while others went on the left—leaving speculation about what would happen when the lines eventually met in Tehran.

"There is no doubt the country was taken for a colossal ride in a number of ways," says a European ambassador in Tehran. Exploitation was hardly one-sided. Suspicion and misunderstanding were so widespread that soon many firms, including some of the largest, like IBM, suspended activities in Iran. Others lost millions in aborted contracts. Some respected businessmen did not dare enter Iran for fear of arrest followed by an unfair trial. The Iranian Government, meanwhile, thought it was a target for the biggest rip-off in history. "It's okay for people to try," the Shah told me, "but it is up to us not to be duped."

His wife, Empress Farah, looked on and nodded. But was she duped? Have the women who tag along behind the money rush been duped? Sometimes it seems as if they have.

6/EMPRESS FARAH AND THE BLACK PANTHER

"Oriental countries keep women in subjection less by the rigors of laws than by the severity of the custom."
SIMONE DE BEAUVOIR, THE SECOND SEX

"Women are important in a man's life only if they're beautiful and charming and keep their femininity." THE SHAH

AT TEN O'CLOCK one evening in the small Caspian Sea resort of Rasht, there was a knock on the prison door. Her Imperial Majesty, Empress Farah Pahlavi, Shahbanou of Iran, had arrived for an unexpected visit. It was so unexpected that the guards did not believe it was her, and they refused to open the gates for fifteen minutes.

I did not believe it either. I had spent the day with the Empress as she toured the town in an open Mercedes 600 visiting a library, a school, a factory, and listened to the flowery welcome speeches which are an integral part of royal duties anywhere in the world but seemed even more fawning in a country where the autocrat's wife had co-star billing. That morning she had been met at the tiny airport by 200 obsequious officials who stood in a trembling row, the women in their finest long-sleeved frocks, the men in morning dress, perspiring as the temperature reached toward the hundreds.

She is exquisitely beautiful. Her face is hardly lined, and her dark brown eyes have melted the most icy bureaucrat. She dresses well, and the thick hair streaked with auburn which curls gently round her face makes her look several years younger. She was born in Romania on October 15, 1938, the daughter of a diplomat who died of cancer when she was ten. She went to school in Tehran, and, later, to the École Spéciale d'Architecture in Paris. It was there, among a group of students, that she first met the Shah, who was on a private visit. She shocked court officials by asking him why student grants were being cut. A year later, she again met him at the home of his daughter, Princess Shahnaz, and her then husband Ardeshir Zahedi, former ambassador to the United States (see Appendix). The marriage took place in December 1959 and the new Empress found herself the most influential woman in a Muslim country where female emancipation was not notably progressive.

I was told about the prison visit by one of the rather fey officials who surrounded her, and he obliged with further details. "When she went into the prison, a former policeman dashed up to her. He said he wanted justice. It was very moving. The Empress asked the prison governor, 'What has this man done?' The governor said he had shot someone. 'Is he guilty?' asked the Empress. 'Yes,' said the governor. 'Has he been tried?' the Empress wanted to know. 'No.' Her Majesty looked shocked. 'Well, how do you know he is guilty?' She was amazing. You should have been there."

To expect people to believe a prison visit in the middle of the night seemed overambitious, so when I met the Empress again six months later in her study at Saadabad Palace on the northern outskirts of Tehran, I asked about civil rights, and if she had ever been inside a prison.

"No," she replied, to my satisfaction, but then she continued. "Except once, in Rasht, a few months ago. I was not supposed to go, but I wanted to see the conditions. Quite often people are in prison for small reasons—they owe money or something. Perhaps we could help them. Unfortunately, I went too late at night, and the man with the list of their crimes was not there. The guard was very upset that he took so long to let us in because he did not believe it was me, but I complimented him. He was right. Anyone could come and say it was some person or other."

"Do you believe that prisoners are tortured in your prisons?" I asked.

"I could not know for sure. I know that in every country when they want to get information for the security of the country they are hard on people. Two or three years ago I heard there was torture. In my opinion that is not human, but how could I find out about it? I could not go to see for myself. What is the use? They know I am against it, and if they perform things like that, they are not going to show it to me.

"It happens in other countries as well. A policeman is not told to push or to be rude to people, but sometimes he is. It's people themselves—not the system—who sometimes overdo things."

There was resistance to her influence, particularly from religious leaders, although she claimed not to have noticed it. "My power shows exactly what is happening in this country. The possibilities I have been given show there are equal rights for women. I have never had any difficulty. Of course, I act with delicacy in some fields because we have to think of the mentality of our people. They expect me to take care of the needy, to be involved in education and social welfare. Some officials might be upset when they have told His Majesty that a particular project is all right— and then I see it, and tell him it is not all right."

But does the Shah really take any notice of her? He once said, "What do these feminists want? You say equality. Oh, I don't want to seem rude, but . . . You are equal in the eyes of the law, but not, excuse my saying so, in ability."[1] He added to me later, "The interviewer wanted to provoke me. I told her that women are cruel, and can be more cruel than men. I asked the interviewer if there were any women who are great musicians, composers, painters, even cooks."

"So," I said to the Shah, "you are not influenced by your wife? Are you influenced by anyone?"

"No, fortunately not."

The Empress sighed, lit a cigarette, and thought for a while before she explained how her husband could sound like such a male chauvinist. "I think I will have to answer that question for the rest of my life. I say that acts are far more important than words, and look what His Majesty has done for this country. That shows what he believes."

"Women are still not allowed to leave the country without permission from their husbands."

"We have a few points we are working on—but diplomatically. Some people believe it will ruin the status of the family if women can go wherever they want. I don't personally believe it, but you must remember that something which is good in the West may not be accepted by the majority here. We absolutely do not want to be like the West.

"Our values are not tangible or material. People do not understand. They think of cars, roads, houses, food, and things like that. Our challenge is to develop without losing our own culture, which is very difficult because material progress goes so fast. We do not want to repeat the mistakes of the industrialized nations. Whether we succeed or not, only the future will tell."

She did not know then that those, in Iran and abroad, who felt progress had been neither just nor equitable would soon overwhelm her and her family, although she had her warnings. Every time she visited the United States, she attracted demonstrations from masked protesters, abuse, and insults.

"There are demonstrations, but usually the numbers are exaggerated, and the students who protest are not always Iranian. Some are professionals who do not care what the subject is. But, putting that aside, many of our students come from simple families in small towns or villages and are not yet mature enough to understand what Iran has been through.

"Our students go to industrial nations and they see big differences from their own country. They don't realize that industrialized countries have been working for centuries to arrive where they are today. So the students get frustrated. It is very normal. They complain that the government is not working well. Also, they are homesick, away from their own environment, traditions, and habits. They are vulnerable to any group which wants to use them. It might be Communists or people who are not pleased by our oil policy. Iran has been retarded all these years and is now finding its place in the world. We are a very juicy fruit, and there are countries who would like still to have political and economic control over us. Today, though, we act Iranian, think Iranian, and are independent. That does not please everybody."

Every year the Empress made several visits to various regions of Iran. Often she was accompanied by the Prime Minister, and there was always at least one other minister present. "People ask me to visit because it helps get things done. The moment they know I am coming, everybody does a little more.

"I receive about 80,000 letters a year, often about private, personal problems, and I try to answer as many as I can. Sometimes a private problem gives you an idea about difficulties throughout the country. I try to help my husband in some of the fields he has not time to see in detail—social, cultural, education. These cannot be separated from politics, of course.

"It is important to see people in their own environment because when you are in Tehran you are involved with so many national and international matters that it becomes too much. If you see people in their small villages, you can understand their needs."

The traveling and her duties in Tehran left less time than she would have liked to spend with her four children: Crown Prince Reza, Princess Farahnaz, Prince Ali Reza, and Princess Leila (see Appendix). "I try to balance the two, but there is not much time for private life. During vacations I see them a lot, and I try to spend some afternoons with them during term time. At first, I worried about the responsibilities that would be put upon the Crown Prince because one never knows the personality of a child. Now I see him more and more involved in the interests of the country."

I asked why Crown Prince Reza needed his own house in the grounds of the Niavaran Palace. "The reason for that," said the Empress, "is because when my fourth child was born, there was not enough rooms for them all in the palace. My son was growing up, and he likes to be alone by himself."

"You also bought him a house in England?" It is near Windsor.

"I am not aware of these things," she replied with some uncertainty.

"You don't know if he has a house there or not?"

"I have heard. I know he has bought a house. But I don't know the details. I don't ask."

"That seems to contradict some of the things you have said about women's rights."

The Empress lit another cigarette. She began to blush. "No, it's not that," she said. "It's not the Iranian side of a woman—not asking her husband what he does."

There was silence for a while. Then she continued, "We have a very good relationship within the family, and I want to keep it like that because it is important for a king that it is quiet at home and there are no little problems which annoy him. They can be more upsetting than those he faces in his work.

"Obviously there is intrigue and gossip around us. It happens to any group which is in an important position in any system of government. It is normal. People have their eyes on you, and the gossips crawl around. They say the Shah has a fourth wife. That sort of nonsense does not hurt. I have been used to it since I married. But there are things which are really unjust, and one wonders why they are said. Political things, for instance.

"People think that no one can talk to my husband, that they must always say yes. But if you talk intelligently, he will accept your ideas. We talk a lot. Sometimes he acts on my suggestions, sometimes not. It is a very normal relationship."

But over it all hung the fear that stalks any world leader. Assassination. There have been several attempts on the Shah's life.

The Shah said he was not worried. "For fifteen years, death has meant nothing to me," he told me. "It did at one time. Now it is totally irrelevant."

The Empress was more cautious.

"Sometimes I have fears and anxieties, but I do not really want to think about it. If you start worrying about these things, it becomes impossible to live. You have to be fatalistic in a way because accidents can happen to everyone—whether a king or a simple person. Sometimes one is pessimistic to see what is happening around the world, and I wonder if I am too naïve or idealistic. Progress brings pollution, corruption, and the disappearance of human contact. People are just working to make more and more money. But we all have to remain hopeful and do our best for a future we have dreamed of throughout history—a world of peace, social justice, cooperation, and friendship. If we realize we need each other, and cannot live apart from each other, there is hope."

It must be hell for the Empress to have a sister-in-law like Princess Ashraf, whose energy is as prodigious as her ambition and whose influence on her twin the Shah could never be equaled by a mere wife. The two women are wary of each other, and sometimes their hostility erupted into cautious bitchiness at social gatherings, much to the delight of the chattering tongues of exclusive Shemiran which relay with gusto and some exaggeration the latest conflict between two determined women.

The Empress was more concerned with pastoral, domestic matters whereas Ashraf has spread her considerable talents internationally since 1948 when she first met Stalin who she found "so kind and very gentle." She spent half the year in Europe, mostly at her apartment in the Avenue Montaigne off the Champs-Élysées or at a villa in Juan-les-Pins. Her third husband, Dr. Mehdi Bousheri is managing director of Maison d'Iran in Paris. For many years she led the Iranian delegation to the United Nations. She later visited China as the Shah's special envoy to initiate diplomatic relations between the two countries. She was also President of the Iranian Human Rights Committee, which some think is a cynical contradiction in terms, particularly when she appears to make flippant remarks. Asked about one of SAVAK's alleged new inventions, a red-hot table to which prisoners are strapped, she replied, "I'm not sure what you call it." An aide intervened. "Toasted, Your Highness?" They all laughed. "That's it. Toasted. No, I can assure you these stories are one hundred percent lies. Anyway, there are now more sophisticated ways of getting the truth." What sort of ways? "Injections."[2]

Princess Ashraf's private life is also unconventional. She was engaged at fourteen to a man she had never seen, has three sons, and is now married for the third time (see Appendix). In her late fifties, when she should present a grandmotherly image of lace and docility, she finds herself ambushed returning in the early morning from a gambling casino. She has the reputation of being a luxuriating pussycat rather than the "black panther," as she is called.

I met her at her opulent home in Tehran. She bounced skittishly down the circular staircase into the overdecorated drawing room, where a portrait of a suitably somber Shah hung at one end, sat on a settee, folded her elegant long fingers onto the skirt of her couture dress, pouted in the attractive manner of a woman twenty years younger, smiled, and said, "Yes?"

"Do you have a powerful personality?"

"I hope so," she replied.

"And a temper?"

"I lose my temper—and how. But not for long. I lose it very, very quickly, and after five minutes, it's finished. His Majesty is different. His strongest quality is his sangfroid. When we had a bad time in the past, he never lost his temper—not once. He is quiet and calm and you would think that nothing had happened. He has a stern image which is the opposite of his real character. He has the most gentle heart, but if you want to govern a country like mine, which has been up and down, up and down, you have to be strong. For thirty-six years he has been King. People change.

"I try to help because he can't do everything himself. I don't interfere in political affairs although it is not right that he has to approve everything in this country—simply everything. Iranians won't make decisions. I remember it was the same in my father's reign. He said he only wanted one thing: people who are conscientious and who will take responsibility. The trouble is that Iranians think that so long as the King is there, everything is done, and everything will be okay."

The Shah allowed women to progress cautiously. He made a gallant concession for International Women's Year 1977 by easing the law whereby women must have a father's or husband's written permission before every journey abroad. He decreed one permission valid for seven years.

"It is still an insult to some of the world's most beautiful and self-willed women," I suggested.

"Yes, women are very furious about it," replied the Princess. "I am not furious because I know it will be resolved. The biggest problem for women here is that they are not men."

"That sounds sexist."

"It is true. Do you think it is a paradise for women here? Do you think that men are giving up their place easily? No. For two hundred years women have been like slaves. Universities were opened to them only forty years ago, and they have had the right to vote only since 1963. You cannot comment on the situation today until you understand what it was like before.

"We have jumped so fast. In the villages you can see how backward women still are. They do not want to integrate or become part of society. They want to stay in their home and have children, and not go out. In some villages there is ninety percent illiteracy. We cannot reach them. If we do, it is difficult to make them know their rights and tell them they have to change their way of life. We have to fight with them."

Men in Iran are no longer allowed to take more than one wife without court permission, granted infrequently. Nevertheless, women are still treated as possessions to be sold to the highest bidder and even, on occasion, subject of an antiprofiteering court case. A story in the Tehran newspaper *Kayhan* in January 1977 told about a farmer, Mehdi Asakoreh from Khorramshahr, who sold his wife for £1,000, but decided a year later he wanted her back—only to find the new husband charging £10,000. Mehdi was told that the cost of living had increased tenfold, and the new husband had been obliged to spend a lot of money on the wife who was a hypochondriac. "Officials explained to Mehdi that the law has no price tag on 'women' because it is not a marketable commodity and sent him to the local branch of the Women's Organization," reported the local newspaper.

"It cannot stay like that," says Princess Ashraf. "The world is becoming so small that there is no frontier, no limitation, and sooner or later countries will have to follow each other. I have been to Mecca and was very well received by the Saudis but I find their attitude to women very strange. They have to change, too. And they will."

A few weeks after I met the Princess, I was in the South of France when she was attacked by gunmen on her way back from the Cannes casino to her villa at Juan-les-Pins. Her lady-in-waiting was killed. Was it a political demonstration? I recalled what she had said.

"It's not foreigners who behave badly to me, it's Iranians. They find out where I am going and make trouble."

"Does it worry you?" I asked.

"*Noblesse oblige.*"

For Mahnaz Afkhami, who was Minister of State in Charge of Women's Affairs, *noblesse* did not *oblige*. "If you really want to change things, you have to understand national and local politics," she told me. "Look at New York. The Equal Rights Amendment has not been passed, and only eight percent of women are in politics compared to four percent two hundred years ago. What sort of achievement is that?

"Here in Iran we cannot wander off into the world chanting slogans and getting a lot of personal publicity. We have thousands of illiterate women who would not understand anyway. There would be an upheaval if we had the sort of talent that is available in America."

Mrs. Afkhami studied literature and languages at the University of Colorado and returned to Iran to join the government as Minister of State in Charge of Women's Affairs in 1976 when she was thirty-seven. She does not suffer from the slick posturing of American feminists, nor the vacuous daydreams of their frail Arabian counterparts, nor the smugness of many European women.

"In England, of course, women are very conservative. Margaret Thatcher appalled me when I met her. She said she did not expect too much success for women's rights. That way, she explained, she would not be disappointed. She has a very bright daughter who did not seem to be doing much. 'That's all right, though,' Mrs. Thatcher told me during a conversation, 'because she's a woman.'"

Mrs. Afkhami, whose husband was also in the government, spread out her arms helplessly. I was about to ask a question, but she continued.

"You have this tremendous separation in the West. Women either want to sit at home and be mothers or they say, 'Why shouldn't we all be lesbians?' And neither side likes each other.

"You get so upset by small details as well. You are not even allowed to advertise for a man or woman in a particular job. Absurd! We agree jobs should not be limited to either sex, but why shouldn't you advertise for what you need?

"Here, we wanted women in the army to help with the literacy corps. We advertised so everyone knew about it, and that made people interested in the job. The very concept of getting women to put on a uniform, go into a remote village, and teach the inhabitants to write was horrifying at first. But they went, and some stayed to become village leaders.

"Of course there is resistance to change. Unconsciously, because of our history, women feel inferior, but we should be judged by the realities of our past and not by what goes on in California. We are trying to make the most of this period of adjustment—the money rush—to make sure that women have a place in society when it is finished. We don't want what happened in the United States during the Second World War to happen here. Women helped all through the crisis and afterwards went back to being wives and mothers, and were treated as inferior. We want healthy integration of our women into society."

In September 1978 Mrs. Afkhami was fired, a sacrifice to fundamentalist religious fervor that was to alter the country dramatically. So the question remains: Can Iranians escape their past and develop a free society or are they, as the Shah believes, similar to Turgenev's description of the Russians: "formed for despotism, its paternal thrashings, and its Byzantine chicaneries."

The secret police were the people to ask.

7/THE WATCHDOGS

*"If people are against the régime what do you want us to do—
put them on a throne?"*   PRINCESS ASHRAF

*"The suppression of political opposition is carried out by SAVAK
with extreme ruthlessness, using a system of informers which
permeates all levels of Iranian society, and which has created an
atmosphere of fear."*

AMNESTY INTERNATIONAL, BRIEFING ON IRAN, NOVEMBER 1976

SAVAK, run along Israeli lines, advised by Americans, and operating clandestinely in the West, caused frissons of apprehension
whenever it was mentioned. Some critics claimed it employed
300,000 people part-time, that wives could not trust husbands,
nor sons their fathers. One of Ayatollah Khomeini's first acts was
to disband it.

During seven visits to Iran, I spoke to dissidents, people from
aristocratic, middle, and working-class families; I had Iranians
visit at my home in London. Many were openly critical of the
Shah, and few exhibited the fear of SAVAK ascribed to them by
foreigners. On the other hand, I met many expatriates in Iran
who muttered deep warnings and always knew someone "who
knows someone" who had been tortured. In London I spoke to a
British university lecturer, considered an authority on Iran, who
said he had received the most barbarous treatment at the hands
of the secret police. He asked not to be named, declined to give
specific details, and, despite an alleged beating which would

have prevented most normal people from returning, still traveled merrily back and forth to Iran.

It would be naïve to assume that SAVAK was totally without fault, for as an ambassador commented, "No one seriously denies there has been torture—not even the Shah. But if it exists now or did exist as much as is alleged, you would meet people, as I have done in other countries, with their fingernails plucked out, and so on."

The Shah himself said there were 3,000 SAVAK officers and tacitly defended the occasional act of brutality when he made the distinction between what should happen to those who endangered his security and those who plotted against the State. "In case of betrayal of one's country, I should say anything goes. There is not a single man, though, who has been shot who has planned against myself. I have never pardoned anyone who has plotted against the country in order to put it in the hands of a foreign power."

He admitted his secret police operated abroad and was flattered that their reputation was more substantial than their results, thanks to a universal desire to believe in the superefficiency of bogeymen. "ARE SHAH'S SECRET POLICE WATCHING ME? DEMANDS M.P." was the headline of a story in the *Sunday Times* on August 1, 1976 about Labour Member of Parliament Stan Newens. The Confederation of Iranian Students had occupied the Iranian consulates in Bonn and Geneva and "found" documents instructing SAVAK agents to investigate the relationship between dissidents and the M.P. "There is no evidence to prove the documents are genuine," Newens was reported as saying, "but I have known these people for a very long time, and I have never found them so far to mislead me."

Newens campaigned vigorously against the Shah's government to "mitigate the harshness with which it treats its opponents. It was an uphill struggle." It is especially uphill because Newens had never been to Iran. "I don't accept that as a handicap," he told me. "For me to go to Iran for a fortnight and pretend I'm an expert would be nonsense."

I asked if he really believed that the Iranian Government would watch him. "I do not believe for an instant that the Iranian Government would interfere with a British Member of Parliament. It would be madness. I have never said that I have been watched. I have no evidence. I have a letter, and a translation handed to me by a member of a group. It could be a forgery. That sounds like James Bond—not that I have ever seen a James Bond film or have any interest in such things."

Newens talked about the "reign of terror" in Iran and said, "The regime has never relented." I asked what he meant.

"I would have thought the evidence for torture is not all that difficult to prove. There is a very considerable amount of evidence to support it." When I asked for details of one recent case, he replied, "I believe there has been a change. For all practical purposes, it has stopped."

That was as doubtful a proposition as some of the allegations of torture suggested by Amnesty International, which noted the "atmosphere of fear" in its *Briefing on Iran,* published in November 1976, an eleven-page pamphlet written by a well-meaning woman from Hampstead, London, Anne Burleigh, who has never been to Iran and admitted, "We know very little about the country and have great difficulty in getting information."

The man allegedly in charge of torture was at school with the Shah— "My special friend was a boy named Hossein Fardoust."

I went to see him.

At the corner of a suburban street in Tehran, three policemen stood casually watching as cars passed. There was nothing to indicate that the detached house they were guarding was the office of one of the most feared yet least known people in Iran.

Two tall men, immaculate in lightweight gray suits, greeted me in the driveway and asked me to accompany them upstairs. One walked in front, the other behind, as in spy movies. They chatted amiably about the difficulty of finding the place, the weather, the appalling traffic conditions in Tehran. They had American accents tinged with the merest hint of their Iranian mother tongue.

We walked along a corridor into a small waiting room. In one corner was an old-fashioned hatstand, its curved wooden arms unpolished and scratched. On a wall there was a fading black-and-white poster of the Shah. The carpet was threadbare, and the few pieces of furniture were of a dingy, open-market variety. One of the men sat opposite me and lit a cigarette. His colleague stood nervously by the door.

There was a view from the window of higgledy-piggledy houses and apartments. A few children were playing in the street. Not a car was in sight; they were all jammed together on the main thoroughfares. From the corridor came discreet grunts of recognition as people passed each other.

"Lovely day," repeated the man who was sitting. "What are you writing about?"

"God knows." Sometimes in the hurly-burly of the money rush it is difficult to know what you are doing or even where you are. No wonder so many retire bewildered and return to more sensible pastimes at home.

"This is a difficult country to understand," continued the man. "I've spent a lot of time in America. Well, it's very different here."

Silence again. The man by the door began to fidget. It was like waiting for the dentist, except there were no magazines to read.

Suddenly the door opened and a short, stocky man shuffled in. He had the hangdog look of the Iranian working class, melancholic and dispirited. I thought he was bringing tea, then saw his hands were empty. He wore an old double-breasted fifties-style brown suit with cuffs and a shiny seat. His black lace-up shoes were scuffed and small, the sort you would expect to see on the feet of a ten-year-old boy.

The two men jumped to attention, and the one who had been smoking stubbed out his cigarette into a glass ashtray. "Your Excellency," they said almost in unison. "Good morning."

One rushed to shut the door while the other motioned General Fardoust to a chair. He waddled across the room, eased himself down, and sat hunched, as if trying to curl into a ball. For the first hour of our conversation, filtered through an interpreter, he muttered slowly into his chest. Occasionally he glanced up. His face was pudgy and lined. He looked ill. His pallor was accentuated by bushy black eyebrows, immobile as two satiated caterpillars sleeping on his forehead. Now and again he managed a smile which invariably spread to a huge grin so that two rows of off-white teeth separated his jolly chin and lower lip from the squat nose and somber brown eyes which retained an impassive, unflickering glare.

This, then, was one of the Shah's most trusted friends, a companion at school in Switzerland, a bridge partner ever since, and head of the Imperial Inspectorate Bureau which, amongst other duties, comprises the Special Intelligence Bureau and oversees SAVAK. The former head of SAVAK, General Nassiri (executed in February 1979), was another school friend, but the Shah's Machiavellian impulse to have ambitious enemies competing for positions of power was not compromised by appointing schoolmates to the most sensitive security posts. There was also J2, the military intelligence, which had become increasingly important as Iran's wealth and military ties with the United States made the country a natural playground for Russian spies to test the ingenious toys now used by agents and their Iranian collaborators. Former Major-General Ahmed Mogharebi, a logistics expert in the Iranian Army had a superfast transmitter in his home which was capable of broadcasting twenty minutes of data in twenty seconds to a Soviet diplomat operating it by remote control from his car nearby. Another Iranian KGB informer had instructions sent from Russia by satellite to a receiver that looked like a pocket calculator. When the calculator was turned upside-down, the digits, activated by satellite, formed letters which were the basis of a coded message.

General Fardoust, chief covert watchdog of Imperial Iran, did not give the appearance of a man who operated successfully, as he did, in a world of such sophisticated electronic gadgets. He seemed miserable, like a grocer trying to sell a few rotting cabbages, and it is perhaps not surprising that he had never before been put on public view.

"I personally do not believe in publicity or propaganda," he said. "We do publicize ourselves through public facilities such as newspapers, but I am not deeply in favor of that, even. When you indulge in propaganda, people believe you have things to hide. We have nothing to hide. What people actually see is the true propaganda, and what they see in this country creates enthusiasm."

"Not abroad," I said. "Iran's image could not be worse."

"As a one hundred percent loyal Iranian, I am surprised by that. We have to consider the ideologies of those who write about us. What is their attitude to world politics? Their ideology is my main concern. I stress it is individuals who criticize us—and not their governments. The laws of these countries give people freedom to write what they want without having to justify it to any responsible people. If they did, the government would take steps to negate what they say and show that they had been telling lies."

"Are you suggesting that other countries should become as repressive as Iran?"

"In the last fifteen years," he said blandly, "England and the United States have been more repressive than we have been here."

He surely could not believe that. "What about torture?" I asked. The answer was predictable.

"Torture is not needed with modern methods of interrogation. Science has taken over, and nowadays we can discover what we are after in a humane and civil manner. We have translated a book from America called *Interrogation*, which is used by the FBI, CIA, and Israel. Besides, torture cannot be correct because if someone tells you something under torture, he won't be telling the truth. If we used such a system, we would not be able to combat terrorism. There has been no torture here since we had contact with countries who had a good knowledge of scientific methods."

"How long is that?"

"In the past. Ten or fifteen years ago. But I don't mean to be specific."

"Why not?"

He gave a smile composed equally of menace and amusement, as if undecided about his reaction. "In the past," he repeated. "In an age that I cannot remember—perhaps because I was not born. There is undeniably evidence that torture existed then, and of course there have been more recent incidents because people did not have the full knowledge of proper interrogation." He paused, then continued, "I have the impression you want to see me just to find out about torture. I cannot help you. There is no such thing here."

"Have you seen anyone tortured?" I asked.

"I have not personally witnessed any torture. Look, there may have been wrongdoing twenty years or so ago, but it was because of lack of knowledge."

So I went to see the Minister of Justice, Gholam Reza Kianpour, official watchdog of a nation's virtue, a man who read poetry (he said) on the way to his luxurious office where fresh carnations stood in a vase on his bookcase, as if in obeisance to the scales of justice nearby. "My job is not easy," he said. "The Shah is impatient. He wants everything. We have been sleeping for two hundred years and have to catch up. We used to be like Katmandu or Nepal. Whoever heard of those places now? But everyone knows about us."

"Most people know about Iran because of its military aspirations and its apparent lack of human rights. Does justice exist here?" I asked.

"Let us have a definition of justice." The normal Iranian prevarication. "Justice in society is a way of carrying out the measures which Members of Parliament, on the basis of the will of the majority, say are right. In that case, yes, justice is done here.

"But do not measure us by any other society. For example, in your country a man and woman can kiss each other in the street. Here it is a crime. The penalty is two months in prison. If I go to Disneyland or Hyde Park and I see a man kissing his sweetheart, I don't criticize them. That is your custom. Okay, don't criticize me because of my laws. Iranians are safe if they keep out of trouble."

Are they? A few months later, Kianpour lost his job in the purges which accompanied martial law. There were calls for his arrest, and he had time to reflect on various "customs."

By Western standards, the Middle East is repressive, brutal, and backward. By Middle East standards, the West is patronizing, greedy, and hypocritical. "Who do you think runs America?" asked one of Iran's leading businessmen. "The Mafia, of course. And when they talk about democracy, what they mean is people with money buying those without it. It's not so very different from here."

The vital difference is that in the West change takes place without revolution. How many years will it be, I asked the Shah, before that sort of democracy exists in Iran? "When everyone is literate and has the right to vote, we will have secret ballots. It will come. But what is democracy?"

"Political parties, free people, free speech, free press . . ."

"We are trying to lead the people to that stage, when they participate in every aspect of the life of our country. We are starting with economic democracy. The main wealth—oil, gas, copper, forests, grazing land, water—cannot belong to individuals. So it is nationalized and belongs to everyone. Factories are being sold to the people, and soon every individual will be a shareholder in his place of work.

"Liberty of the press, yes. But within the law. Freedom does not mean that you disrespect laws. If you do, you will have a permissive society. Your freedom cannot take freedom from someone else. Why should we have a press which is full of libels, lies, accusations, and disgusting things?"

Is that like the Western press?

"I have examples to show you, if you like, so many. But I won't because I don't want to enter into that. It might hurt other people in power. But newspapers bully governments and push them into dangerous policies. If they publish a lie and you want to rectify it, they will not publish what you say."

He had no such trouble, being a dictator.

"I consider myself much more like a father, like the head of a family. I don't want to brag about it, but maybe sometimes a teacher. Today's children will be adults, and they are going to do what they want for sure. I can't see our society being helped, though, by any change in the form of government. If I did, I would advocate such a change. We are used to our system."

But the "children" grew up quicker than expected and, like other children before them, they decided their "father" had been wrong all along.

8/TRUNDLING OUT THE DUKE OF KENT

"All this modernity is a façade, a pretence. The calculating machines have not made us less calculating."
ESMA'IL POURVALI, <u>WHAT IS CIVILISATION?</u> BAMSHAD (TEHRAN), SEPTEMBER 1964

"No doubt we can still learn from you. But not in the mode of governing or ruling. That you can keep for yourselves."
THE SHAH, <u>NEWSWEEK,</u> MARCH 1, 1976

MANY OF THOSE sent to Iran to recycle the petrodollars returned home bewildered and broke, frustrated that they had not been treated like the saviors of the Third World they imagined themselves to be. On one of the holiest Fridays of the Muslim year, equivalent to the Christian Christmas Day, a chemical firm representative from Manchester arrived unannounced at the home of Ken Lewis, then Chairman of the Anglo-Iranian Chamber of Commerce.

"Thank Christ for you, mate," said the salesman. "I came here to try to help these buggers, and they've all gone off on holiday. You're the only person working."

It was not an isolated case. Although international competition was intense, the inexperience of the participants was often so overwhelming that Tehran began to evoke distrust simply because few people understood each other—yet they were convinced that they did. "I met many who have been here three days and say, 'I've got the big one now,'" recalls Ken Lewis.

"They are still here three months later, wondering what happened."

A contract which looked straightforward in London or New York became a nightmare of maybes and tangled dealing in Tehran. "The Iranian public sector is the most procrastinating and difficult in the world," said a British trade official. "In any other country, you have a deal and that is that. Not here. There is no coherent corporate structure, and no one wants to make a final decision." There were enough bureaucrats to allow the game to continue for a long time. The Ministry of Economic Affairs had 10,000 employees, whose personnel files alone were one kilometer thick. Payment for work on government contracts sometimes required sixty signatures on numerous documents. Sending a car from the General Motors assembly plant in Tehran to a dealer required thirteen forms.

"If you want to work here," explained the trade official, "you send a contract bid to the Plan and Budget Organization. They make one or two changes and pass it to the relevant ministry where a Harvard graduate alters a few clauses and returns it to Plan and Budget for ratification. This time it lands on the desk of a young man who has done two years at MIT. He tinkers with it a bit and gives it to his boss, who has done four years at MIT, and has to emphasize his superior experience by modifying the bid slightly. It is returned to the ministry, where the Harvard graduate transforms it to his original conception and passes it again to Plan and Budget. It can go on forever. You must realize they enjoy the game and have an innate passion for bazaar bargaining, which *they*—not the Arabs—invented.

"There may be fifteen clauses, and you think you have agreed to each one. The following day, when they bring up an objection, you must not become annoyed. If they say, 'Everything we agreed last night is fine. But there is the matter of the cabbages,' do not lose your temper and say, 'I thought this was a contract for a school. What have cabbages got to do with it?' Remain calm, agree with them, and say, 'Yes, not only cabbages, but I was thinking we need cauliflowers, too.' It usually works. If it does not, you have to relax. They will last longer than you. Naturally they have a proverb for it: Patience is from God. Haste is from the devil. But I prefer Iranians to be arrogant and proud, which they are now—rather than arrogant and servile, which they were a few years ago."

Iranians enjoyed the ironies of their new power and knowing that their actions—even their rumors—affected the rest of the world. When it was thought that the British firm Richard Costain might have a £600 million contract with Iran, the price of the company's shares increased by 40 percent in a few weeks. When John Laing and George Wimpey appeared to be having trouble with payments for a $1 billion military base, the price of the shares fell 50 percent in a year.

It was also instructive, at first, to watch civilized Westerners outbribing each other, so eager were they to please their new customers. In lobbies of hotels throughout the Middle East, it is possible to meet middlemen who claim the right connections to fix a contract—for a nonreturnable advance of a few thousand dollars. Alas, in Iran there are only a few genuine entrepreneurs, and their influence fluctuates. Some have been in prison, others stay abroad—just in case. But foreigners who take part in the money rush need guidance about the rules, and one of the first and best guides was fifty-six-year-old Sir Shapoor Reporter.

He has British nationality from his father, a Parsee who left Bombay aged twenty-seven, in 1893, to look after Zoroastrian interests in Iran. Sir Shapoor talks softly, confidentially, and has developed a devastating combination of the opaque Persian attitude toward truth and the outward qualities of unassuming, upright Britishness. Not only did he manage to be paid several million pounds by the British Government in undisclosed commissions on arms sales, but he also received money from individual firms who supplied the weapons. And he was given an unrivaled start in the money rush by being knighted in 1973 "for services to British interests." He has all the credentials one would expect in a man of charm able to understand the somewhat eccentric ethics of Iranian business: a former correspondent for *The Times,* British intelligence agent, and "political adviser" at the United States Embassy in Tehran until the overthrow of Mossadeq, when he became one of the Shah's closest confidants, traveling with him abroad, advising at home, ever discreet, ever courteous, ever worldly.

The British Defence Ministry found Sir Shapoor indispensable (it has 400 civilian and military employees in Iran doing "backup work"—that is, helping the armed forces in the same way as the Americans, although on a smaller scale), and he allowed them to think he was instrumental in the sale of many weapons, including $200 million of Chieftain tanks for which he was paid $2 million commission not mentioned in the contract. "One does not boast about this sort of payment, not because you are ashamed of it, but because the fewer people who know, the better," admitted Sir Lester Suffield, former head of defense sales.

It was probably unnecessary, and certainly did not help Sir Shapoor, who was already very rich, regain his declining influence with the Shah. The original Chieftain was not a great success either for the Defence Ministry, which may have just broken even on the deal, or for the Shah. "It is underpowered and cannot go more than 220 kilometers before it has a snag," he told me.

Not much good for a war. Not even adequate for street control.

"Habib Sabet owns ten percent of practically everything in Iran," a New York banker told *Fortune* magazine in October 1974. A few months later, Sabet was arrested for profiteering and thereafter spent most of his time abroad, based in Paris, delegating the business to his son Iraj. When I met Iraj at his $15 million home in Tehran, a replica of Le Petit Trianon, with all modern conveniences, he had just been charged with distributing Pepsi-Cola containing oil and cockroaches (sabotage, he claimed), and had received a tax demand of $2.5 million (incompetent public officials, for sure). He was remarkably philosophical as he sat in his living room—twenty meters by twelve—and told me, "They want to make an example of someone important, to show they are doing something. You have to join what my father called the p. and p. club—patience and perseverance."

His father, Habib, son of a textile retailer, began work in a bicycle shop, saved $70 to buy himself a taxi, then started a furniture factory and bought a Dodge distributorship. At the beginning of the war, he sold everything and emigrated to the United States, returning in 1949 at the invitation of the Shah to help construct the Great Civilization. He set up three independent television stations, eventually compulsorily purchased by the government which now controls all broadcasting, and he developed interests in forty-one major enterprises, making him the richest man in Iran next to the Shah. He could afford to spend $441,000 on an antique desk in 1971, the most expensive in the world. "That has given me more pleasure than anything," he says. "I started out building things like a kitchen door for my family, and now I can afford the most expensive furniture in the world."

Iraj graduated from the Wharton School of Finance at the University of Pennsylvania, and returned to Iran in July 1957, when he was twenty-five, to develop the Pepsi-Cola concession—particularly valuable in a largely teetotal country with very hot summers. "I arrived in Abadan and worked night and day to beat the opening of the Coca-Cola plant. I did—by three weeks."

Ruthless competition has not ceased since then, with the Sabets claiming prejudice against them because they are Bahi, a religion not officially recognized in Iran. Some *mullahs* maintain that Pepsi is *haram*—forbidden—because profits support the Bahis, who are dangerous and unclean. The *mullahs'* indignation rises in proportion to their *baksheesh* from rival firms.

There are worldly obstacles, too. Shopkeepers leave empty Pepsi cases outside their shops at night to be restocked with the same number of full cases. Fifty thousand disappeared and were not replaced, causing a significant drop in Pepsi sales. Mr. Sabet knew what to do.

"I went to SAVAK and said, 'I have five hundred workers who are becoming very upset. Any day now they could start a fight with the people who are stealing our cases.' So they went to the company which was organizing the thefts, and everything was settled quietly. You cannot rely on the police or the army, so you need other people. In my opinion, none are more patriotic or efficient than SAVAK.

"When I have an industrial problem at one of the factories, I telephone SAVAK to send a representative. A person comes along—not a thug or a gangster, and he does not hit anyone on the head. He just says to the ringleader, 'Don't try to be a big shot. Don't try to be a hero. The government has enough problems without your troublemaking.' In England that type of man would be a respected trade union leader, wouldn't he?"

After a while, he showed me around the house, about which one foreign diplomat had warned, "The first thing you need is a large whisky to cope with the vulgarity. Being strict Bahis, they don't drink. You will have lots of Pepsi, though."

Iraj admitted, "It is not *all* an exact replica of Le Petit Trianon. It has the spirit, the ideas, and some of the details. It took us quite a time to find a proper architect, and eventually we got a Frenchman who had worked on restoring buildings and castles. He stayed with us for eight to ten days to see our social habits, our friends, our children—to understand what we wanted. The interior was designed by the man who did the 2,500 anniversary celebrations at Persepolis."

There is tapestry from Belgium, doors from a French château, and marble from Iran. "The door handles come from France, and some of them had not been made for a hundred years. The workmen had to go back to their original catalogs and casts. There is no design in the world so perfect as that of Louis XVI. You have everything—the gardens, the buildings, the interior, the lights, the floors, the furniture. . . ."

For rural simplicity, Sabet has a hideout twenty minutes' drive away—isolated, moated, and overlooking the plains. It is a circular one-story building on a stem—a design he copied from a picture postcard of the Philippine pavilion at the 1964 New York World's Fair. We sped there in his black Cadillac de Ville with his attractive wife, Nikka. While the two servants prepared lunch, he expanded on his hopes: "Iran is not in as desperate or impossible a position as many people think. It has a major role in the future, once we get rid of the petty jealousies and prejudices which are eating our heart out. The government cannot continue to upset business people. In the United States it does not matter, because there are thousands of entrepreneurs. Here, we can be counted on the fingers of two hands."

In the garden, we picked apricots and pomegranates, before visiting one of Sabet's bottling factories. Only half the work force had turned up. "There was a time when people would beg me for a job. Now I have to chase them here. They don't take it seriously enough. They must be given the right ideas.

"The trouble is that everyone is waiting to see how they can milk each other. We have tasted money and it has gone to our heads. Materialism is ruining the country. People have to realize there is a limit to what they can buy. You don't need twenty cars, forty suits, and a forty-bedroom house. You find that four suits are problem enough."

Some people might be churlish enough to suggest that one $15 million home is enough. "I accumulated all that I have in the last twenty-two years here. I sweated it out, and it has been worth it, but I have taken a lot of knocks. Many people ask why I don't sell up and leave. There may come a time when I say, 'Okay, uncle, I've had enough.' But if everyone abandons ship, there will be no crew."

Many foreigners abandoned ship, beaten because they mistook ambiguity for malice, and a love of bargaining for bloody-mindedness. Prevarication is essential to the Iranian way of life. It is business by seduction rather than rape, and, as some nationalities are better at it than others, indignation accompanied each new twist in the sales game, and contempt was feigned at every trick of one-upmanship. "President Giscard came here and started kissing the Shah. It was disgusting to watch," says a British merchant banker. "All we do is trundle out the dear old Duke of Kent now and again." Finally, though, after much lobbying from businessmen, the British Government decided to use its most devastating commercial weapon: they arranged for the Queen to make the money-rush circuit—with the exception of Iran —during February and March 1979.

Not that the French are so successful as they like others to believe. Many trade protocols, signed with such a flourish by political leaders, remain more hopeful than real. They did win a contract to build the Tehran subway, and it was not until initial excavation began that their rivals were able to laugh. Tehran has no sewage system. Two thousand five hundred years of Persian history may be a cause for celebration; two thousand five hundred years of consolidated Persian feces seeping into cesspools through which tunnels have to be dug is not such a salubrious undertaking.

Bribery influences every action and is an integral part of the money rush. Each competitor denies that he is involved; each one knows it will continue to exist. An Iranian businessman who has been paid millions by governments and international companies explained the refinements. "It is very simple. A company gives a fee of $300,000 for the 'client' to study wildlife in Timbuktu. No report has to be produced, and it keeps the accountants happy.

"If governments ask for an affidavit that bribes have not been paid, there is no problem. Two people have an understanding that a new company will be set up *after* the contract is signed, into which money is channeled for one nonexistent project or another. The law is not broken. There is no proof the money is a bribe. And everything is fine. The going rate in Iran is about ten percent. In Saudi Arabia it is thirty to fifty percent. No government will ever stop it, however hard they try!"

A director of one of Britain's largest defense contractors added, "Business, from time immemorial, has required the advice of experts with local know-how. The Americans are the most uncultured people when it comes to these activities. The Lockheed method was 'To hell with the competition—we'll just buy it out,' and so the whole defense business was distorted. They behaved in an outrageous way. We British did not compete. You cannot win a pissing match with a skunk."

In the early years, such squeamishness did not matter. There was more than enough business for everyone. Then, in the summer of 1975, things began to go wrong. The money was running out. It was discovered that unauthorized clerks had signed contracts for millions of dollars, that proper control was negligible, and that corruption permeated the highest level. Princess Ashraf's eldest son, Shahram, accepted $705,000 from the Northrop Corporation for such arduous tasks as finding a good Iranian architect—at a time when Northrop was part of a consortium that received a $200 million telecommunications contract. Although there was nothing legally improper in the payment, the Shah was furious with his nephew for making so much money so publicly and so easily. Another leading personality, Admiral Ramzi Abbas Ata'i, head of the Navy, was sentenced to five years' imprisonment for embezzlement. It is claimed the Shah noticed the admiral's wife wearing a $500,000 necklace he had wanted to buy for Empress Farah.

Corruption seemed to be the national sport. Seven hundred civil servants were jailed for taking bribes; and, in one month, 12,000 shopkeepers caught charging more than government-controlled prices were either fined, imprisoned, or exiled to remote villages. In some cases, Persian ingenuity was triumphant. The controlled price of beer was $1. Pistachios to go with it, previously free and therefore unregulated, now cost $2.

By 1976 Iran had a deficit of $1.7 billion. "We overspent with our eyes open," claimed Prime Minister Hoveyda. "I don't shed any tears about a couple of miserable billions of dollars deficit."

Others did. They said they were not being paid and that contracts were dishonored. Recriminations began. "By and large it pays—even in Iran—to tell the truth," said a man close to the Shah. "When you feed a nation on exaggeration, there is bound to be reaction. My God, they talk about a subway, but they can't provide enough food for the people, and I can't read at night because of power cuts. At the rate the Shah is going, trying to do too much, I don't think he can pull through. One of the worst aspects is the way others are always blamed. Nothing can ever be the fault of the Persians."

That was not quite true. The Shah announced, "It is time to stop dreaming and get down to work." He dismissed Hoveyda in the summer of 1977. The new American-educated Prime Minister, Djamshid Amouzegar (known as Jim at Washington University, where he received a degree in engineering) warned of a "spirit of indolence and sloth. We are ill advised to forget that our fathers did not have oil, and neither will our children."

Amouzegar was ill advised, too, to believe that anything in Iran is permanent. He was fired a year later for failing to quell riots throughout the country.

And then, in January 1979, it was the Shah's turn to be humbled. He was simply the most dramatic example of many for whom the Iranian experience is not a dream. It is a nightmare of tragedy, legal problems, damaging accusations, and financial loss.

9/THE $24 MILLION NIGHTMARE

"To become outstanding in any field of endeavour in Iran requires an appetite for corruption and a taste for personal decay."

THE POLITICAL ÉLITE OF IRAN

"A power failure early in the party left everybody in romantic candlelight for quite a long time."

TEHRAN JOURNAL, JUNE 14, 1977

The power failures "have incited our disgust and caused us unease."
THE SHAH, AUGUST 19, 1977

THROUGHOUT THURSDAY, December 5, 1974, there were heavy snowfalls in Tehran. Traffic was more than usually chaotic, and many people canceled plans to leave town for the Muslim weekend. Flights from Mehrabad Airport were delayed or canceled so the main hall was comparatively empty.

At 2:50 P.M., the roof collapsed, bringing down 250 tons of debris. The damage was so extensive that it was not until thirty hours later that the last body was removed. Officially, it was claimed that 17 people had died, but some reports put the toll at 250.

In London, Patrick Brown, an executive of the international consulting engineers, Brian Colquhoun and Partners, was planning to leave for Tehran to set up his firm's new office. Now he had a different mission. He was part of a four-man British team sent to investigate the cause of the collapse. Colquhoun had ad-

vised on the interior of the airport, and, although its work had
been completed ten years previously, the company was concerned about the tragedy—with reason. The Iranian Government
was to blame the company for it, and to suggest that it were liable for $24 million compensation, a claim which seems extraor-
dinary on the available evidence and one which impelled Brian
Colquhoun to disregard Foreign Office advice and issue a public
warning a few months before he died in October 1977.

"We won't go back to Iran if we can help it," he said. "If we
did, we would be put in jail and then if there were any court
proceedings, we would—we would never get out again." He
added that the Iranians were "trying to run before they can walk.
They're in financial difficulties, and many firms, especially the
smaller ones that I know of, are not getting paid and have come
out of Iran bankrupt.

"My firm has had a continuous involvement in the Middle
East since 1948, and on most projects, technical, political and
personality problems are solved as progress is made. Such problems have never been so difficult as they are in Iran. I advise
that on all appointments the conditions are translated by a translator well versed in legal work, both from the original into English and, if necessary, vice versa.

"Engineers who accept appointments there should be aware
of the risks involved to them as individuals. Concepts of justice
can depend upon factors which have long been changed in the
more developed parts of the world. Until modernization of the
legal system and commercial code takes place, I advise that
every scrap of paper connected with the project is microfilmed
and the film stored in a safe place indefinitely."

The external structure of Mehrabad Airport was completed in
1951 by Sentab, a Swedish firm, but further progress was curtailed during the Mossadeq era. In 1954 a World Bank loan allowed building to continue, and Brian Colquhoun and Partners
were appointed as supervisors by the Plan and Budget Organization. The Shah opened the airport in 1959, and responsibility
for the maintenance was handed to the Iranian Department of
Civil Aviation.

Nine years later, the roof began to leak. Instead of removing
the existing three-quarters of an inch asphalt protection, a new

layer was placed on top, doubling the thickness and increasing the weight. In addition, two and a half inches of plaster was added to the ceiling. Further modifications took place in 1974, when it was realized that existing office space was insufficient. A new building was erected adjacent to the terminal, and concrete pillars were cut in order to provide added strength. In fact, this action considerably weakened the pillars.

"The building would have been completely safe if it had not been for the disastrous and almost criminal works which were carried out on it between 1968 and 1974," said Colquhoun. "A structure of this nature does not stand up for over twenty years and then suddenly collapse without interference with its stability from outside sources." He pointed out that it had withstood a severe earthquake in 1962.

Nonetheless, an Iranian committee of inquiry—consisting of members of the Plan and Budget Organization and the Department of Civil Aviation, who were themselves vulnerable to blame—reported in May 1975 that Sentab and Brian Colquhoun were jointly responsible. "The establishment closed ranks," claims Patrick Brown, with some predictability. However, the firm was not represented at the inquiry, was not asked for any opinion, has not been shown a copy of the report and has had no direct contact with the Iranian Government since the day of the disaster. Their information came from "rumor and innuendo," which Colquhoun claimed was harming his business.

The former head of Sentab in Iran, seventy-nine-year-old Jacob Milligard, had retired to live in the country. One day in March 1977, he was tipped off that he was about to be arrested, and he left for Sweden, where he suffered a heart attack. In his absence, he was sentenced to two years in prison. Sentab was not indicted, but was banned from further business in Iran. Brian Colquhoun and Partners learned that the case against the company was being left open. In the United States relatives of the victims began civil proceedings against Iran Air, the Department of Civil Aviation, and the Empire of Iran.

Ironically, a few days after Milligard was sentenced, ten members of the Department of Civil Aviation were convicted of corruption, including the engineer who had been in charge of maintenance at Mehrabad from 1964 until the disaster, and the

head of the department, Abdulhassen Mushang-Arbabi. He was
sentenced to five years and fined $2 million.

"Statistics are like a bikini, my dear," Hoveyda told me in the
safety of his prime-ministerial office. "They usually show everything but the essentials." In Tehran the essentials are hidden beneath so many layers of subterfuge and "misunderstandings"
that no two people have the same recollection of an event in
which they have both been involved. When a cast of worldwide
merchant bankers, businessmen, doctors and governments are
competing for a multimillion-dollar contract, memories become
particularly selective. A typical high hurdle in the money rush
was the Great Hospital Bonanza, and it is impossible to say with
accuracy who tripped whom. The only certainties are that everyone involved fell and blamed the others.

At the beginning of 1974, sixty international groups were lured
to Tehran by the prospect of a nouveau riche Third World country providing itself with one of the main criteria of "modernization": a hospital building program. After much discussion,
three letters of intent were signed, and the successful companies
returned home to prepare detailed plans. From England: Cementation International, part of the large Trafalgar House
Group, in partnership with Taylor Woodrow and advised by the
Orion merchant bank and S. G. Warburg. From the United
States: Medicor. From France: Sedim. The English firm was to
build five hospitals, while the others were commissioned for four
each.

Lionel Edwards, managing director of Cementation, said it
would take two years to prepare designs for the completely new
hospital concept that was required. Initial estimates suggested a
cost of $40,000 per bed. In April 1975 he went to Tehran to see
the Minister of Health, Anushirvan Pooyan, and was asked to
use existing hospital plans as a basis for his design. The rush was
so great that working drawings would be completed as construction progressed. Under those conditions, the Minister asked
if Cementation could have something ready within fifteen weeks.

"Impossible," replied Edwards.

"Are you telling me that you are throwing away the chance of
a lifetime?" asked Pooyan.

"Yes," said Edwards. He left the office and made arrangements to return to London. His business was to make money and to avoid crazy schemes.

However, the next morning the Minister relented, allowed Edwards an extra month, and gave specific instructions. The hospitals, with a combined total of 2,000 beds, were to be completed and staffed within forty-five months. The Shah demanded swift progress, and the deadline had to be met, regardless of cost, which was to be fixed at the beginning of the contract and would contain heavy penalty clauses. Edwards explained that it would be enormously expensive and pointed out that many items were being requested which were not included in the original estimate of $40,000 per bed. It seemed a hazardous project, but Cementation was urged on by the British Government. "It was a large contract and the economy needed a boost," explains one of Cementation's directors.

Taylor Woodrow dropped out, so Cementation continued alone. Draftsmen and architects spent 100,000 hours producing 2,000 drawings and 100 volumes of specifications. "Every hospital had to be completely self-contained," says Edwards. "We needed housing for expatriates and third-country laborers who would have to be flown in. We had five people in Iran looking at the labor problem alone. We planned to work three shifts a day, seven days a week—which meant double the number of supervisors, and extra housing. We needed airplanes to ferry people around, because the hospitals were more than a thousand miles apart. We were going to use steel because it's quicker than reinforced concrete. Our suppliers had to meet the same time scale."

They presented their proposals on September 9, 1975. The cost was $650 million—eight times the original estimate. But, as Edwards points out, that was for a different and far less rapid scheme. "No one realized when we started that the figures would be so astronomical," he says. "But no one in their right mind is going to put a keen figure on a fixed price job lasting four years. There is no way that you can know what inflation is going to be, and you can soon land yourself in the manure business."

Nevertheless, by the end of the month, a new specification had been submitted which reduced the price by increasing the time available and using more local labor. By December a third plan was produced which halved the cost by substituting a less sophisticated design than the Iranians had originally demanded.

But by now the Ministry of Health had been reorganized and had become the Ministry of Health and Welfare under Dr. Shojaeddin Sheikhol-Eslamzadeh, a suave forty-six-year-old who had obtained his doctorate of orthopedic surgery in the United States. In three years' time he was to be arrested for alleged corruption, but now he was one of the Shah's more favored ministers. He looked at the cost of all the hospital plans—the British, American and French figures were more or less compatible, although there were major design differences—and was appalled. "Unfortunately, they thought there was gold in the streets of Tehran and wanted to collect it. They thought we would just approve the price and accept anything they said. Well, they made a very, very big mistake.

"I have a personal interest in hospital construction because I have studied it. I found it very interesting that the plans the British submitted to us were almost the same as those for York Hospital in England. I sent a team to evaluate the costs there."

York Hospital, which was opened by Princess Alexandra in July 1977, has 812 beds and cost $23 million—$28,000 per bed. It is considered to be one of the most modern in Britain.

Dr. Sheikhol-Eslamzadeh continued: "I said to them, 'You are building York Hospital for us, and that is fine. I accept it. But we know how much it cost to build in England. What extras exist here?' They said that our labor and social security is more expensive—which it is not. Then they claimed that costs were increased because we are in an earthquake area. I do not think we have more earthquakes than anywhere else. Anyway, the extra fortifications for earthquake protection add only another five percent to the construction cost.

"So I asked them, 'How much profit do you want? Fifteen percent? Fine.' They had nothing to say. I sat down for hours and hours and talked with them. I told them straight, 'If you are fair and talk about a fair profit, you are welcome here anytime.' But they were not thinking about a fair profit. They wanted a one hundred and fifty to two hundred percent margin. So that was finished."

A director of a bank associated with Cementation admitted that the design was an "adaption" of York Hospital. "Because of the time scale, it had to be more of a carbon copy than was desirable."

Lionel Edwards denies that the profit margin would have been anywhere near Sheikhol-Eslamzadeh's prediction. "We told them that if they did not accept our price, they should put it to international tender," he said. "From our point of view and in terms of reality and common sense, it was a complete waste of time."

There was, too, a fundamental problem which was not to become public for another year, but was already resulting in a reappraisal of the budget. The Shah had begun to realize that lavish, uncoordinated expenditure had placed his country in debt once more. "The time-honored way of cutting back is either not to pay, or to delay payments. They wanted the hospitals, and if their policy had remained the same, it would have been all right. But they can't admit they changed their plans, or that any Persian can ever be wrong," said a banker in Tehran, unconnected with the hospital contract.

In an attempt to rescue the project in January 1976, the British Secretary of State for Social Services, Barbara Castle, arrived in Tehran at the end of a Middle East trip which had taken her to Saudi Arabia and Kuwait. She had a "sharp discussion" with the Minister of Health, and went from there to see Prime Minister Hoveyda, who reminded her, "We are not from the other side of the Gulf, you know." Mrs. Castle, not one to be intimidated, replied, "Maybe you behave like it sometimes."

The following month, the Iranians not only refused to pay Cementation's design fee of $2 million, but they also claimed damages from the firm. Prime Minister Hoveyda had taken a close interest in the situation. We met in Tehran a few weeks before the Shah "elevated" him to Court Minister in August 1977, after twelve and a half years as Prime Minister, and more than a year before his arrest for alleged corruption. I said his government's suggestion that hospital prices were "exorbitantly high" was treated with skepticism by those involved. Hoveyda banged his fist on the table and exhibited the gamut of his considerable indignation. It was more impressive than convincing—he is a be-

nign and sophisticated man whose aestheticism is indicated by
the fresh orchid he wears daily in his buttonhole, and his histrionics are no match for his more natural pipe-sucking urbanity.
"Let them make a libel against us," he exclaimed. "Let them."
And he called for an aide to dispatch a curt, warning letter to the
companies involved. "The Spanish are building the same hospitals—at one-fifth the price.

"It is true that it is very difficult to do business in Iran because
we look after our own interests. We have been occupied by you
people—the British and the Russians. We know there is no love
for us. I am talking about governments, not individuals. There
are Britishers who love Iran more than the Iranians. But we have
been cheated a lot and we know you are not in love with our
blue eyes. We don't have blue eyes, anyway.

"People say we have a lot of money, and they want to get it.
There are three prices: the international price, the OPEC price,
and the Saudi Arabian price. But if it is *so* difficult to do business
here why are so many more coming here all the time? They have
all sorts of plans. One person told me he wanted to make the
Caspian just like California. I said, 'Why California?' Look, when
I want to go to California, I go to California, and I enjoy it. It's a
beautiful place. But in Iran we don't want California.

"What do people want us to be like? America? England? Do
we want to be like that? After all, we have our culture. Why
should we be like other people? One day we were considered
just carpet exporters, but then, when we had more capacity for
imports, people had to be more agreeable to us. And, little by little, they realize we don't say stupid things. We have our short-
comings—yes. Either you have no development and no problems,
or you have development—and problems. I will tell you very
frankly that Iranians are no angels. But the majority of foreign
companies are not ethical. They do deals which are absolutely
incorrect. I will show you examples right away."

With a flourish, he produced the annual report of an American
company (which he asked me not to name) in which it was
claimed that $6 million had been spent on representation "at
high level in the Iranian Government." The $6 million had now
been deducted from the company's final fee. "Maybe some of

the money goes to Iranians, but we have proved that most of it goes to directors of those companies.

"Is it all right for companies to come here, tell us it is difficult to do business, and then cheat? Should we accept the principle that cheating from Western people is very good, but for Iran to defend itself is very bad?

"I know personally how much corruption is in all your societies. I know about it because you bring it to us. If this Western philosophy—this beautiful Western philosophy—was really something substantial, all of you could get together and say, 'We don't pay a dime [in bribes] to Iran.' And—*if* we are the corrupt people, what should we do? Not buy anything?

"English companies are overinvoicing all the time when they sell here, and they underinvoice for our exports. I have a list. But the first responsibility for us is to stop this, not to lecture. I don't resent what people have done. I think it is our duty to fight it."

While we spoke, a digital clock on a bookcase behind him ticked off the minutes. A tape recorder lay on the desk, and, behind me, a secretary took shorthand notes. He gave the impression, as do many Iranians, of haughtiness, of overwhelming self-confidence, of certainty that soon the West would realize how dependent they were upon Iran. Alas, he could not know that soon he would travel a road well known to his countrymen, the one that led to prison.

Now, though, he sat back and told me how much he enjoyed being criticized. "I love it because it gives me a way of fighting something. Either it is true, and we should correct ourselves—or it is wrong and we can have a beautiful discussion. I can't say that I do not bother about world opinion, but it is not going to make me sleepless."

He had another appointment and provided one of his official cars for my journey back to the hotel. It was driven by a slim, tough man in a dark suit, whose eyes shone with the challenge of Tehran in the rush hour. A journey which should have lasted an hour took ten minutes as, lights flashing, we sped by on the wrong side of the road, swept over red lights, were beckoned onward by policemen, glared at by motorists, and miraculously missed two beggars and several pedestrians. Few demonstrations of power are so conclusive as an ability to drive at sixty miles an hour, unharmed, through downtown Tehran, and few demonstrations of Iran's bleakness are so evocative as the Park Hotel to which we sped. There, at the usual table in the dining room, were the Irish chargé d'affaires, Donald Hurley, his French wife, and their seventeen-year-old son heroically struggling with the limited menu as they had for the last eight months while he tried in vain to find a house. They had never been out of Europe before he became Ireland's first representative in Iran. He thought of himself as John the Baptist as he attempted to improve his country's £22.5 million trade imbalance.

The lights dimmed. Candles were lit—mainly for atmosphere, but also in anticipation of the inevitable power failure of up to four hours each evening. A British trio began to play, the same tune as every other night.

> "A love like ours is a love that's hard to find
> We've come too far to leave it all behind. . . ."

A solitary middle-aged couple danced self-consciously, watched by scavenging salesmen from all over the world, who drummed their fingers on food-stained tablecloths, drank another vodka with lime, and glared at the waiter who hovered, expecting a tip above the 15 percent already added to an overpriced bill. They cursed their offices for demanding impossible results on inadequate expenses and wondered if they could survive another day in a drab room haunted by the drone of the air conditioning (if it worked) waiting for promised telephone calls which never came.

Night life was uninviting except for those with money to escape to the northern suburb of Shemiran, where Tehran's rich and elegant gathered in discothèques to obliterate the present and imagine they were back in Europe—the men soigné, the girls beautiful and braless. Downtown, there was very little: cinemas showing imitation third-rate American thrillers or Bombay melodramas starring voluptuous seminaked Orientals. Occasionally, before the purges of fall 1978, more exotic entertainment was glimpsed. A newspaper report of a play at the Shiraz Arts Festival:

Finally the soldier grabs a mother and her two-year-old son. This time, however, he generously offers to spare the child and instead rape the mother. The act was better performed than in any film I have seen. It vividly showed how it is performed in an aroused atmosphere.

Later:

Receiving no response, the killer sharpens a knife on a wheel and simply chops off the man's hand still holding the burning cigarette.

And then the finale:

A man committed suicide in a rather unusual way. He went up to a table, pulled down his trousers [another big shock?], thrust a pistol into his anus and shot himself.

It is unwise to assume that such permissiveness swept the country. In the same month, a German engineer was fined $500, dismissed from his job, and deported for kissing his girlfriend in public.

What anticlimax awaited those who thought that here, in Tehran, the road to success and riches would be revealed. The money rush withered their souls, confused their morality, frustrated their ambition, and cost them far more than they anticipated. Could there be anywhere worse?

There could. Not far away is Iran's chief rival for world influence, a country which one of the Shah's senior advisers told me "we could take over in 48 hours without any trouble—and the whole of the Gulf before anyone else knew what was happening"—the land of what Iranians call the *soosmar khor*, lizard eaters—the El Dorado of the money rush where problems are smothered in a cascade of riches and nations tremble to think anything might spoil the boom as it had in Iran: Saudi Arabia.

Part Three
Saudi Arabia

10/HOSTAGES TO MONEY

"The political future of this sparsely populated nation, possessing a resource vital to others, will continue to be of utmost concern. . . ."

> UNITED STATES SENATE REPORT ON SAUDI ARABIA, JANUARY 1977

"Time was when the donkey ruled Jidda. That wasn't very long ago—only 1952." SAUDI GAZETTE, JUNE 20, 1977

"Where else in the world would you have to import bellboys?"

> RAYMOND KHALIFE, MANAGER OF THE RIYADH INTERCONTINENTAL HOTEL

IF THE MONEY rush created a stream of disillusion in Iran, it will become a torrent eventually in Saudi Arabia, where more money is paid to fewer people, making the opportunities for carpetbaggers correspondingly greater. The rise in oil prices gave dramatic momentum to a situation which had been developing for years, but the start was slow.

"It peaked between July 1975 and May 1976," says an American diplomat in Jidda. "Sometimes we had seventy to a hundred businessmen coming to the embassy every day. We couldn't handle so many, so we ran them through briefing in batches of twenty—telling them where to send telegrams, to buy toilet paper, and so on. At times, we had more than thirty sleeping on the consulate floor because they couldn't get into hotels. It looked like a relief camp."

Salesmen arrive in such numbers from all over the world and with so many adventurous misconceptions that any slum masquerading as a hotel is able to charge £60 a night for a room with peeling paint, rock-hard beds, perilous electrical fittings, unworkable telephones, dingy lighting, and spasmodic water supplies.

"Why is there no hot water?" I asked the desk clerk at Riyadh's Zahret Alsharq Hotel one morning. "And why are the elevators still not working? And why has a cable sent to me from the Shah's private office somehow been mislaid?"

His reply left no room for maneuver and scant opportunity for indignation. "Hot water is not important," he said. "It is very hot outside."

As in Tehran, confirmed reservations are no guarantee, and, according to ambassadorial talk, the Danes had to pay $2,000 to ensure a suite for one of their government ministers in Riyadh.

Costs are almost double those of Tehran, and attractions are even more restrained, although every outing is an adventure of sorts. There are innumerable traffic accidents, and 17,000 deaths a year (twenty-four times the ratio of most Western countries) each accompanied by hysteria suitable for the Apocalypse and formidable police inquiries with the victims remaining in jail.

"If you are involved in a crash, just lie on the ground and howl in agony when anyone touches you," advised a veteran of two incidents. "In extreme circumstances, cut yourself, bite your flesh, do anything to ensure you are taken to hospital and not to jail. Once in, it's almost impossible to get out."

The Arabian American Oil Company (Aramco), mindful of its responsibility and the fact that the number of cars is doubling each year, has erected signs along the road from Dammam to their refinery at Ras Tanura. In Arabic and English they advise: "Drive Defensively."

Not that there is anywhere to drive. Riyadh has no entertainment area (movie houses and theaters are forbidden), nor a vast stadium (although the $400 million sports center being built seven kilometers from the city center will have the largest arch in the world—221 meters—with a restaurant at the top reached in four minutes by motorized gondolas, seating for 80,000 spectators, and a mosque), nor a Parliament (although one has been promised for years), nor even a good restaurant (one, serving Japanese food was closed temporarily because waitress service was provided, so determined are Saudis to keep their women behind locked doors), and no bars, of course, as alcohol is officially prohibited.

No, the central attraction of Riyadh, a structure to inspire visitors and remind them where they are, is an elegant blue-and-white mushroom-shaped water tower.

But what is this? "The Desert Swingers," says a newspaper caption underneath a picture of assorted grinning men and women. Ah, nothing more permissive than a group of American square dancers who, with the aid of a battery-operated turntable, perform their ancient rites in the sand dunes every Friday morning.

No one seriously seeks entertainment in the money rush—certainly not in a country where oil revenues of $85 million a day gives the economy a wham-bang-thank-you-ma'am frivolity, with few questions asked and no killjoys to suggest that it is not even fun while it lasts.

Ambition to make money quickly, or even desire to escape the clutches of an alimony-hungry wife, provides sufficient temporary compensation for some. But in order to enjoy the country and remain within the law, it is necessary to be male, chauvinist, teetotal, and ascetic—qualities found in early explorers who provide so many Arabian myths, but not noticeable in those 500,000 skilled foreigners (soon it will be 1,000,000, and, by 1980, two out of three workers will be expatriates) who are transforming the world's most closed and puritanical society into a kaleidoscope of Western fantasies.

Many cannot stand the strain and even though the annual cost in salaries, benefits, and travel of having an executive and his family in Saudi Arabia is between $120,000 (for the British) and $240,000 (for the Americans), unofficial figures suggest that 65 percent leave after a year. Even the largest companies calculate that one third of their employees will return home before scheduled.

On one of my first days in Riyadh, I met the managing director of a multinational firm who had been in the country for six years. At last, he felt, he could allow himself the luxury of honesty. "We are prostituting ourselves here, simply for the money. The Saudis do not know what they are doing and have not really bothered to ask if all this development is necessary. It is not.

"I really don't think there is much future for them. They gave nothing. They are giving nothing. And, eventually, they will go back to nothing. Everything is brought in from outside to give them a cushy life, and all they want to do is sit under a tree all day. Muhammad knew that—the old rogue. That is why he made them get up and pray five times a day—it's the only exercise they take. I don't suppose he realized that he was creating a police state, with religion as the prison.

"Naturally I am grateful that they have bought so many of our weapons, but they couldn't use them and don't understand how they work. Even if they did, who are they trying to frighten? They are lousy pilots. They point and pray. One got into a sandstorm near the airport the other day and crashed into a house because he just gave up. *Insha'allah.*"

There is one memorable occasion when a Saudi pilot and his American instructor flew to Beirut on a "training mission," bought a case of Scotch whisky at the airport, and then returned in the direction of what they thought was Riyadh. Unhappily, their compass was 180° inaccurate, and they found themselves buzzed by Israeli planes when they inadvertently strayed over the border and were forced to land at Tel Aviv.

Realizing that no warlike act was intended, the Israelis repaired the airplane's instruments, fueled it, and sent the erring couple back to Saudi Arabia, where they were given a public red-carpet welcome fit for heroes.

Action behind the scenes was different. The American was sent home, and the Saudi now has a dehumanizing desk job. The whisky remained on the plane. Its fate is unknown.

A central irony of the money rush is that the "enlightened" West, and even once proud Iran, is dependent on the goodwill of a country created less than fifty years ago from a disparate collection of warring nomads. A country which, in spite of the sophistication of a few ministers, is at the same level of development as medieval Europe, where even the census figures are confidential because there are embarrassingly few native Saudis,[1] where press censorship is absolute, where there are few "official" facts and those which do exist are frequently inaccurate, where women are forbidden to drive cars, where some remote villagers still believe that boys menstruate because their urine is bloody—a symptom of bilharzia, where criticism is rewarded with expulsion or jail, where adulterers are tied in a sack and stoned to death, where thieves convicted for the third time have their hand cut off, where rapists and murderers are beheaded in the main square of town after midday prayers on Friday, where public floggings are commonplace.

It is a country ruled by a family clique (there are 3,000 male members of the royal family, and several thousand dependents) who distribute largess to keep potential enemies docile, and whose public attitude to legality is based on rigid observance of the austere, antifeminist *Sharia* (Arabic for "path to God") law devised by Muhammad for poverty-stricken seventh-century desert tribes.

The fact that these rules, however virtuous, are inappropriate for a modern state did not really matter in 1933 when King Ibn Saud granted the first oil concession to Standard Oil of California (SoCal) "because the United States is far away from Arabia and, unlike any European power, has no designs on it"; nor in 1964, when his son Faisal came to power and the country was so broke that he had to borrow from the oil company; nor in 1970, when the oil income was about $1 billion a year; nor even in 1973, when it was considered such a backward country that the West German Trade Ministry was unable to find one technician to go to Saudi Arabia to help expand the telephone system, and President Nixon could announce with credibility that the Arabs risked losing their markets if they tried to act too tough.

But now it does. The oil beneath the sand is so tangible a weapon that if Saudi Arabia burps, the rest of the world has indigestion. When fire broke out at the Abqaiq oil field in May 1977, the Tokyo Stock Exchange closed temporarily because of resulting panic, and the Bank of Japan sold $130 million to stop the yen collapsing. On the other hand, when Saudi Arabia decided to limit oil price increases in December 1976, the London Stock Market had its best day in eighteen months.

American involvement in Saudi Arabia is crucial for both countries, with the United States an increasingly dependent partner. The value of the dollar drops if the Saudis merely suggest they might like to be paid for oil in any other currency.

"We are really hostages here," says a senior diplomat of his 30,000 fellow Americans living in Saudi Arabia. The country has agreed to produce more oil than it needs for its own financial requirements so that America's gluttony for energy can be satisfied without too many traumatic domestic problems. In return, the United States supplies weapons, technology, and diplomatic pressure on people who have now become a bargaining counter: the Israelis.

The Corps of Engineers, headquartered in Riyadh, provides a semisecret army, internal security, and is responsible for at least $20 billion of development. It has been active in Saudi Arabia since building a military airfield at Dhahran on the east coast in 1951, and now has about 750 technicians brought in from the Virginia office. The corps is responsible for military construction, although the Saudis do not advertise the fact. Now that the money rush is played for real stakes—life and death—the Pentagon should not be seen to be pulling the strings of Saudi militarism.

Besides, the Saudi Minister of Defense, Prince Sultan, has a rival for power in his half-brother, Prince Abdullah, head of the National Guard. They buy different weapons, commission separate hospitals, and behave like empire-building competitors for chairmanship of a multinational corporation—much to the discreet glee and lavish profit of Western entrepreneurs and arms dealers who are happy to provide whatever is requested and welcome the opportunities to outwit each other.

The French are said to offer military aircraft on approval. "We certainly would not do that," says the director of a rival firm. "Maybe we are too conservative, but there is far too much commercial risk. There will be very long discussions when the French try to get their money. 'Well,' the Saudis will say, 'we didn't really like them, and I'm afraid we've pranged [crashed] half of them, and of course they are yours—not ours. So we'll buy those that are still flying.'"

Not that money is a problem. When Sultan's soldiers deserted for higher-paid jobs in neighboring Arab countries, there was a simple solution: he doubled their salaries. A private now earns

$700 a month, and a general $4,000 plus $1,400 housing allowance. If Abdullah's traditional tribal support wanes, he merely cuts down on gratuities to the relevant chief.

Companies contracted by the Corps of Engineers have a particular advantage. Instead of an agreement with a Saudi ministry, which could involve kickbacks to princes and is fraught with potential problems, as many have discovered, they deal directly with the American Government. Any dispute is first adjudicated by a senior officer in the corps, and, if this is unsuccessful, it can be decided in the American courts.

Consequently, the United States Government is responsible directly for at least one-sixth of all development in Saudi Arabia, not including arms sales.

In addition, aid has been given indirectly since 1955 by Aramco, using what critics suggest is shrewd manipulation of the tax laws, sanctioned by successive administrations in order to help the oil companies and give Saudi Arabia financial assistance which would not have been forthcoming if Congress had to approve it in the normal way. Most countries have reciprocal laws which ensure that an international company does not pay double tax. But what is tax, and what is a business expense or royalty? In 1955 President Eisenhower and his Secretary of State John Foster Dulles, influenced the American Treasury to agree that money paid by Aramco to Saudi Arabia was tax—not merely a royalty. It was therefore allowed as a credit in the United States. As a result, the American companies involved—Esso (now Exxon), Texaco, Mobil and SoCal—paid scarcely any United States tax on their Saudi income. In 1975 this was nearly $3 billion. U.S. tax paid: nil. The Internal Revenue Service began to close the loophole in June 1978, but until then it had been "foreign aid by another name," as the CIA calls the bribes it pays to various Middle East leaders.

Many other major American companies are active, although without the same tax concessions. The Vinnel Corporation helps train and recruit the National Guard, assisted by imported British officers. Avco Corporation instructs the Coast Guard. Lockheed and Raytheon arrange air defense systems, with competition from British Aerospace, and ever-ambitious French defense contractors.

Civilian enterprises have been overseen since 1968 by a group of eleven "experts" imported from the Stanford Research Institute. The director for the last four years has been a thirty-six-year-old Englishman, Ray Kelly. In keeping with the jittery state of expatriate nerves and the disinclination of most Saudi Arabian Government officials to make anything but the most minor complaints about the curious development of their country, he talks to no outsider without direct permission from his minister.

He has a small office in the Ministry of Planning, first base in the money rush for other "experts" from every part of the world. "Spiro Agnew comes here every month, selling construction companies . . ."

Spiro Agnew stepped on Saudi sensitivity when he was quoted in *Playboy* as saying, "I think the Crown Prince [Fahd] is a dangerously corrupt man," a remark he did not deny specifically, although he rebuked the source of it with his usual elegance: "I have been commercially exploited by a horse's ass in desperate need of a buck."

"Well, it takes a dedicated man to stay here," Kelly continued. "We're going through the nouveau riche stage, and there are those who say Riyadh is beginning to look like Las Vegas or Blackpool. I'd like to think things will straighten out, and there will be more sanity in the air.

"We are trying to understand some of the lunatic suggestions put forward by various governments and companies. The British would love to build new towns here on the lines of their own, but how can you transplant to the outskirts of Riyadh a system that works in Hemel Hempstead?"

You cannot. Nor can you apply traditional business methods, partly because the contracts are so large. The telecommunications system, so spurned in 1973, four years later developed into one of the largest industrial contracts of the century, worth a minimum of $3.5 billion, and the source of vicious rivalry between three international consortia headed by ITT, Western Electric, and Philips.

At first Philips, represented in Saudi Arabia by Prince Mohammed, son of Crown Prince Fahd, was said to have offered $7.5 billion, with Prince Mohammed taking about $300 million commission from the deal. This was denied by the company, and a British banker involved on the periphery of negotiations told me at the time, "In fact, the tender was for $3 billion, and he was going to get $300 million."

But publicity forced the contract back into the market so that prices could be seen to be readjusted. In December 1977 Philips was awarded the job with its partners Ericsson of Sweden and Bell of Canada. The price: $3 billion.

Jonathan Aitken, Conservative Member of Parliament for Thanet East, who is chairman of R. H. Sanbar Consultants, which represents Prince Mohammed's interests in Britain, denies the commission is 10 percent. Although he does not know the exact figure, he suggests it is between 1 and 2 percent on most deals.

The Confederation of British Industry, however, privately advises members that commissions in Saudi Arabia increase in percentage with the size of the contract—the reverse of the situation in Iran—and that it can sometimes be 25 percent. I met few expatriates, diplomats, or lawyers in Saudi Arabia who denied privately that bribery was an integral part of life. "Everyone here is involved in graft," says an American diplomat. "It goes all the way to the top."

In public, Western governments have to deplore bribery. Privately, it is condoned with a nod and a wink. State Department employees, interviewed for senior appointments abroad, are asked to imagine they are commercial attachés in a Middle Eastern country. A businessman comes for advice. He can win a huge contract, but it means paying a bribe. What should he do? The correct answer is not "Well, sir, our government has strict regulations about that sort of thing and we would advise you to have nothing more to do with the contract." It is "That is your decision entirely, sir."

"It's a whole different world out there," says a high-level State Department official. "This commission business is an aspect of their welfare-state system, a way of spreading the money around. It was not important until the figures became so large."

And until the people involved became so important. The Saudi Arabian royal family, encouraged by money-rush flattery to inflate a moderate political aptitude into world statesmanship, is credited with at least one record: the largest attempted bribe in the world. They offered Shaikh Zayed of Abu Dhabi $60 million in August 1965 to side with them in a border dispute against his brother Shakhbut.

"We think some things are commission which Americans might classify as a bribe," says Shaikh Saleh Touimi, director of the Riyadh Chamber of Commerce. "It depends how you look at these things."

Western companies wading through the murky no-man's-land of bribes and commissions sit back, hope for the best, and are sometimes caught. Well-bred young businessmen, educated not to haggle, would be happier in the vapid corridors of senatorial self-righteousness elevating purity to a branch of public relations, rather than sifting the ruthless pleasantries of the money rush, where it is often difficult to clarify if a firm yes means more than a definite maybe until a large amount of money is paid into a numbered Swiss account.

Or perhaps they should work for the new Lockheed, deodorized after accusations of worldwide bribery. "A year ago, I would have said being in Lockheed's public relations was like being a cosmetician in a mortuary. Now I feel more like a prophet preaching the second coming," wrote an executive in the house magazine in April 1977.

Anxious to witness this second coming, I called Dorm Veirs, Lockheed's vice-president in Riyadh, who gave precise instructions about his location. "Go to University Street, through two traffic lights, turn left at the roundabout [traffic circle], and that is Seteen Street. Actually, you won't know that because it is not named. Go to another roundabout, and two blocks along you will see a building with a big concrete grid covering the front. That's us."

One problem with rapid development is that it is not worth putting up street names. They are all changed within a few months.

Veirs was not loquacious about the second coming. "I can give you a statement from our chairman," he volunteered.

I asked about bribes.

"Procedures are less structured here. Sometimes that is an advantage because government contracts in the West can become tedious, bogged down in rules and regulations. I can give you a statement from our chairman," he repeated.

Lockheed, of course, has the same frustrations as any foreign company trying to operate in Saudi Arabia. I saw one of its compounds of 160 houses built specifically for American employees. It was two years behind schedule, the price had risen 300 percent in two years, and a swimming pool had been erected on the surface instead of being excavated. "God knows if it will withstand the water pressure," said a harassed Lockheed director in charge of the project. Telephones had been promised, but the lines extended only to the edge of the compound, and no one was willing to take them further without a large "consideration." The member of the royal family who owned the land, Prince Misha'al, had built himself six houses on the compound, finished within a few months, and now suggested renting them to Lockheed.

"You sit, you talk, and you negotiate," said William Weisbruch, a C-130 program director. "If anyone is here for anything but the money, let me know. In time it gets so you need more from life than looking at your bankbook to see how much you've saved. A pool and a house can wear thin in a hurry—especially for the wives."

Lockheed's rival, British Aerospace, also has difficulty interpreting local customs. When one of its senior workers summoned engineers to fix his telephone, he was told it was in perfect working condition.

"But I can't get a line," he said.

"The problem is quite simple," replied the telephone company engineer. "You haven't paid your bill."

"I haven't *had* a bill."

"Quite right. We don't send bills."

"How do I know when to pay?"

"When you collect the bill from the telephone office."

"How do I know when to collect it?"

"When the telephone is cut off."

They have overcome many similar problems by leasing a hotel for five years from Shaikh Rahi, a former moneychanger who is now one of Saudi's wealthiest entrepreneurs. This limits the cost of food and lodging to about $12,000 per person a year, while not wholly depriving them of pioneering aspects of life in a developing country. The hotel, on the main airport road, overlooks one of Riyadh's most popular open-air toilets.

British Aerospace (formerly the British Aircraft Corporation) has worked in Saudi Arabia since 1963, creating contacts in the traditional way. The company paid a $30,000-a-year retainer to a senior member of the royal family for several years. They also used Khaled Philby, a stepbrother of Kim Philby, as translator. Khaled is the son of a wife from the royal household presented to Harry St. John Philby by King Ibn Saud in November 1945. Her name was Rozy, but Philby called her Firuza because he thought she was Persian.

"We pounded the beat here until 1966 before we sold our Strikemaster and Lightning aircraft," explains managing director Alec Atkin. "I think the activity we are involved in is extremely good. People ask me how the hell I can believe that. Well, the Saudi objective is to establish their independence, and the only way they can do it is by military deterrent. They see abysmal poverty all around them, and it would be lunatic not to have protection."

There are now 2,000 British Aerospace employees in Saudi Arabia, working on a $1 billion contract to expand and maintain the Royal Saudi Air Force. "It's a fascinating business," says the former general manager, Air Commodore Paddy Kearon. "In a perfect world, arms selling would be unethical, but I have no qualms whatsoever about helping to build a defensive force. I would go further, and say that throughout the Middle East we ought to push the sales of arms. It is a highly profitable business, and we must survive economically. If we don't do it, others will. Edmund Dell (the British Trade Minister) said, 'To survive we have to compete.' I'm having that framed in my office, even though I'm not an admirer of socialism.

"The Saudis are important because of their restraining influence on others, and they are a great power for good in the world. They think their enemy is world communism—not Israel, as most people assume. They believe the West grossly underestimates the menace of Russia, and so do I.

"Don't be misled by the fact that you see soldiers here holding hands. There's nothing effeminate about them. They're a fighting race, and damned fine pilots as well."

Air Commodore Kearon's trade has no time for romance, but he has worked in Saudi Arabia for nine years—time to develop an imaginative and sentimental attitude to a way of life that is fast disappearing. "It is not a repressive society. All right, there is no parliamentary democracy, but you have something far more effective. Anyone who is patient enough can get to see the head man, and something will be done.

"There's so much that interests me here. The desert. People say that if you've seen one bit, you've seen the lot. That's arrant nonsense. It changes in different lights, at different times of the day, and so on.

"There is another fascination, too. I met a Swiss multimillionaire at a party the other evening. I said, 'Why on earth are you here?' 'That's easy,' he replied. 'This is the last frontier.'"

11/SEX OBJECTS?

"Forces as uncontrollable as the droughts which so often killed them in the past, have destroyed the economy of their lives. Now it is not death, but degradation, which faces them."
WILFRID THESIGER, ARABIAN SANDS

"We have no illusion of achieving in a short space of time what took centuries in the West."
GHAZI ALGOSAIBI (SAUDI MINISTER OF INDUSTRY AND POWER)

THE LAST FRONTIER it may be; democratic it is not. Romance, idealism, and innocence should be abandoned at the starting post of the money rush. There is one advantage: lawyers should also be forsaken. As *Sharia* law is flexible when applied to Saudis in conflict with foreigners, international attorneys are not much help. "We find they rotate," says the laconic Mr. Weisbruch of Lockheed.

Saudi passion for secrecy, based on the paternalistic belief that "leaders" know best, infects all those with whom they do business. Public discussion of any decision is discouraged until it becomes a fait accompli. The British even designated a "memorandum of Technical and Economic Co-operation" signed between the two governments as a classified document.

But, as befits leaders of the money rush, no secret is so well kept as the destiny of the millions of dollars of spare cash—estimated by Morgan Guaranty to be $100 billion by 1980. It is deposited throughout the world, enshrouded in nominee names, with a privacy that defies accurate analysis[1] because Arab countries threaten to withdraw their funds at the slightest "leak," and their influence has prevented too intense a probe by Senate investigating committees.

Politicians are terrified because they fear Arabs have built a $60 billion "weapon" of short-term deposits in the West which could be withdrawn to precipitate a financial crisis. Banks are also unnerved. In spite of large profits on international operations—$836 million in 1977, double the previous year—they have taken short-term deposits which have then been loaned over a long period to countries with weak economies and cautious attitudes toward repayment. Zaire, for example, refuses to repay loans until new credit arrangements are agreed.

Ironically, the loans are made to counteract rising prices created by the money rush. In 1973 developing countries owed $40 billion. By 1977 it was $180 billion, nearly half of which comes from commercial banks nervous lest Arab cash is withdrawn for political reasons. But where would it go?

The Saudis in particular have an attitude to money which transcends histrionics. Their realism stretches from doing business with Jewish-run firms (one of Prince Mohammed's advisers described with some admiration how ruthless Arnold Weinstock, chairman of one of Britain's largest firms, GEC, had been in keeping the Prince's commission agreement below 1 percent) to understanding that they have little alternative to depositing their money in American banks. The Germans discourage Arab investment, Switzerland charges negative interest rates, and Britain is considered too volatile. As an ambassador in Jidda explained, "The threat of a money 'weapon' is as empty as saying, 'If you don't do as I say, I will come along and slit my throat on your doorstep. It will make a frightful mess, and you will have to clean up afterwards.'"

Dr. Mohammed Jamjoom, director of economic research at the Saudi Arabian Monetary Agency (SAMA), equivalent to the central bank, admits, "The increasing reserves are causing us problems. It is difficult to manage so much money."

Lack of qualified people is a continual hindrance. Only one Saudi in eight can read. It took four months just to print 14,000 copies of the annual report. "Very frustrating, but you can't change human beings," says Dr. Jamjoom. "It is impossible for us to develop as fast as our incomes. We need five years before everything will run smoothly.

"Of course, you can get things done if you know the right person. How do you know the right person? That is why there are bribes. Even then, it doesn't always work."

However confusing the statistics, however debatable their accuracy, however empty the threats, the reality is still uncomfortable. Shaikh Zaki Yamani known by his enemies as an Arabian Uncle Tom, was not mocked when he explained Saudi's refusal to raise oil prices more than 5 percent in December 1976, against the wishes of other OPEC members. "We are extremely worried about the economic situation of the West, about the possibility of a new recession, and the situation in Britain, Italy, even France and some other nations. And we do not want another regime coming to power in France or Italy. The situation in Spain is not so healthy, either, and the same applies to Portugal."[2]

As the decision was the first major acknowledgment of Saudi Arabia's determination to compete with Iran for influence in the Middle East, it was predictable that the Shah would be displeased. Moreover, he now saw an Arab as a personal rival for charismatic fame in the West, so he denounced Yamani as Washington's colonial appointee sent "to pump all the oil of Saudi Arabia and give it to you freely."

When I met Iran's then oil minister Djamshid Amouzegar in Tehran a few weeks later, he added, "We were annoyed because Shaikh Yamani said he would agree to a ten percent rise, then when he came to draw up the contracts, he said his government had decided to freeze the price of oil. This surprised everyone. Why a change of heart within a week? He explained it was a political decision, and they wanted to exchange a price freeze for American support in solving the Israeli-Palestinian problem. The Americans denied that, so he then said he was worried that some Western countries might turn communist. That made us all laugh because it is far too simple a way of analyzing the inherent problems of Italy and Great Britain. It could not have been the real reason. Later he said he was worried about the developing countries—but we had already agreed to give them increasing aid. So we are in the dark and do not know his real reason."

The attacks continued with increasing viciousness, so I later asked the Shah if he really believed Yamani was a "colonial appointee." He replied, "Why not? Who benefited by the cheaper Saudi oil? The consumers did not. Who profited except American companies?"

"The point is that it was a decision taken by the Saudi Government, and not by Yamani himself."

"Well, we have to have a scapegoat. We can't name other people, so we name Yamani."

No one wants to upset people whose development plan of $142 billion—twice that of Iran's—is so lavish that newspapers applaud ministries for spending money. "The success of the Transport Ministry is all the more important when one realises that some other Ministries and Government agencies were as much as fifty per cent short of their targets," said an editorial in the *Arab News* in June 1977. "Of course, spending per se is hardly a criterion, but we assume that all the money is spent wisely."

One airport alone—Jidda—is costing twenty times as much as the whole three-year development program of neighboring North Yemen, which has about the same population as Saudi Arabia.[3] It is typical of the escalating ambitions created by the money rush. When first planned in 1964, it was going to cost $35 million. By 1970 this had been revised to $200 million, but the money was not available. Three years later, it had become a $300 million project: and by 1975 a new master plan was created making it the world's second-largest civil engineering project, after the Washington subway, at a cost of $4.5 billion. A partner in one of the American consulting firms said, "They decided they had built everything too small, and their attitude is, 'If you think it should be big, build it bigger.' That kind of thinking can't last."

But while it does, there is every effort to encourage it, and the flag precedes trade with a regularity which keeps Saudi ministers to-ing and fro-ing for official welcomes at Riyadh Airport and further dislocates an already confused bureaucracy. No figures are available from the Saudi Government, but American sources catalog an impressive array of visitors for 1976: 23 heads of state,

19 Prime Ministers, 30 Foreign Ministers, and 78 other ministers.

An avalanche of consumer goods followed—$2,000 worth for every Saudi—and began to create the most unwieldy pile of airfreight in history as well as clogging docks which soon resembled mammoth, sand-covered, open-air warehouses. Nearly every unused site in Jidda was packed with brand-new cars from Detroit which, bearing in mind local driving conditions, was a more humane solution than insisting that dealers collect them. Eventually, though, something had to be done, and it was announced that goods not collected within a week would be auctioned.

Slapdash buildings appeared almost overnight to house these costly gewgaws and, as in Iran, there was soon inflation of 40 percent a year, rent increases of 600 percent in eighteen months, and the inevitable cement shortage as construction increased from $1 billion to $16 billion in three years. "Most people were intoxicated with financial abundance and thought they could buy anything," said Deputy Minister of Planning Faisal Bashir. "But it took us only six months to realize the problems, and we readjusted beautifully. It took Iran three and a half years to do the same thing. The single biggest cause of waste in Saudi Arabia is administrative inefficiency, but we have done wonders."

Money does ease some problems, and when port congestion made cement so scarce that the black-market price rose to $27 a bag, compared to a normal cost of $3.50, the government hired eight Sikorsky helicopters from Frank Carson of Perkasie, Pennsylvania, and forty Vietnam veteran pilots to work four-hour shifts from dawn to sundown for a year. They unloaded 12 million bags at a cost of $55 a ton, and the price dropped.

Stevedores from Chicago and dockers from Liverpool were also hired to help with decongestion, and the problem was soon overcome. By the middle of 1977, there was little waiting time at any of the 130 ship berths in the Gulf region. Nevertheless, 353 new ones are planned, and 140 are under construction. Eventually Jidda will be able to handle 10 million tons of cargo a year —double the 1977 amount.

But what will all this cargo be? Is it possible that in a few years, Saudi Arabia and Iran will be rivals only as junkyards of the world, vying for the most petrochemical factories, steel plants, drydocks, and crumbling buildings soon to become ghostly monuments to the salesmen's art, faint reminders of rip-offs which were attempted as a matter of routine in the rollicking early days of the money rush?

One man tried to sell a $340,000 computer system for $20 million. It is common for firms to set prices that are more than double a fair rate and three or four times the amount they would charge elsewhere. "We know firms colluded to fix prices," says Planning Minister Hisham Nazer. And another minister added, "The streets are full of bankers and thieves, and we can't tell them apart."

Ghazi Algosaibi, Minister of Industry and Power, canceled contracts worth $1 billion with German and Japanese firms whom he accused of fraud and price rigging. "We know this isn't Paris," he told me. "There are difficulties living here, so we expect to pay more—but not two or three times more.

"Apart from that, people try to give us the biggest and best of everything. We wanted an industrial park costing about $160 million. The consultants came back with specifications for one costing nearly $4 billion. Why? Because they receive fees which are a percentage of the cost—either that, or they want to build monuments to themselves.

"Let me give you an example of how they should behave. I am building myself a small villa, and my architect fights with me all the time. I say I want an extra room. He says I don't need one. He feels it is his job to save me money. If a minister says he wants a hospital with a thousand beds, the consultant should ask him if he really needs that many. Here it happens the other way round. They say you need five thousand.

"Well, a medium-sized shoe factory in Europe, with a $4 million a year turnover, has more qualified staff than one of our ministries dealing in billions. I haven't got twenty accountants in the whole of this ministry, so how could I possibly monitor such massive contracts? You need attorneys, contract officers, engineers doing nothing else all day long.

"I sometimes think we are too harsh on ourselves. We are impatient of our bureaucracy because we forget the enormous tasks they are asked to perform and the little training they have been given. They have to deal with all sorts of nationalities. The

Americans are the best to work with because they set a price, and that is that. Then the Germans, French, Koreans, and English. A lot of English firms have been so anxious to get the business that they have not costed things properly, or worked out whether they can afford to fulfill the contract."

Algosaibi is one of the articulate, non-royal family ministers. He has a master's degree in international relations from the University of Southern California and sees the problems confronting his country more clearly than most. "Unless you take into account the yearning of our people for a human existence after more than three thousand years of inhuman existence, you can't understand why we hurry so much.

"When I was born, in 1940, we did not even have candles. We used kerosene. We had no lights until I was ten, and I don't think I saw soap until then either. My mother died of typhoid because there was no doctor in town. Later, I almost lost my eyesight because there was no oculist. At that time, the highest of the highest lived in conditions that the lowest of the low live in today.

"Now we are exchanging old problems for new ones. Fifteen years ago, there was no electricity. Now we have power cuts. In another fifteen years there may be no power cuts, but the charges will be too high.

"With all the pressures of becoming an important country, I hope our traditions and religion will keep us in order. There will be change, and it is not easy to say what they will be, but they will be less than Westerners suspect. Sometimes at the moment we feel like a pretty girl. No one knows if we are liked for ourselves, or as sex objects."

Sex objects they are not. But as the Saudis' desires increase, their come-hither overtures entice the world. The problems of consummation are another matter.

12/HONEY AND ONIONS

"You get all sorts of figures in this country."
HISHAM NAZER (PLANNING MINISTER)

"The Arabs are said to have invented the zero. It may explain why their aptitude for figures is nil."
SAUDI BUSINESS, MAY 26, 1977

"Yoam asal, wa yoam basal—one day honey, another day onion."
SAUDI PROVERB

"WELCOME," said Saudi Arabian Minister of Information Shaikh Abdo Yamani. "I am sorry it took so long for your visa, but we confused you with someone else."

This is not an unusual occurrence. When the understandable siege mentality of the world's fastest-growing country competes with the labyrinthine formalities of the Egyptian-style bureaucracy which is being grafted onto it, the result is inevitably inertia or confusion.

Even Prince Abdullah, the third most important man in the country, could not arrange an immediate entry visa for a British colonel from Durham imported for his National Guard. Telexes and messages wafted between London and Riyadh and became mislaid, ignored, and increasingly urgent. The colonel traveled back and forth from London to Durham for three months until the visa was eventually granted.

Two Scotland Yard detectives were less fortunate. They

wanted to investigate a murder which had taken place on board a British ship in Jidda Harbor, but received no replies to their visa requests even after soliciting the help of the British ambassador. Their fundamental mistake, later explained to a fellow diplomat by the Saudi Arabian ambassador to London, Shaikh Faisal Alhegelan, was to apply for visas for two *policemen.* They should have made a request for "two sailors" to join the ship, thus preventing the fear that foreign police might meddle in Saudi Arabia's arcane legal processes. "What they don't know in Riyadh won't harm them."

Death—especially—creates opportunities for officialdom to exercise its power. A British yachtsman, resident in Bahrain, was washed overboard, drowned, and his body picked up in Saudi waters. Having "arrived" in the country without authorization, he was unable to "leave" until the most strenuous diplomatic endeavors managed to prove he was not an illegal immigrant, spy, or threat to the kingdom.

Although many of the money-rush countries are difficult to enter, Saudi Arabia is the only one requiring proof of non-Jewishness in the form of a baptismal certificate, a regulation which deters no one sufficiently determined. The visa charade is reciprocated, for protocol reasons, and has one unexpected bonus: the British embassy in Jidda earns $500,000 a year in fees.

"Now you are here," continued Shaikh Abdo Yamani, "you are our guest. We will arrange for you to see anyone you want, *insha'allah.* For us, the best propaganda is the truth." His deputy, Dr. Abdulaziz Khouja, nodded agreement. "We don't mind what anyone says about us because we are confident that what we are doing is correct."

He provided a guide and a car, and sent me to one of his officials, Abdul Kareem. "Unfortunately you have come at the wrong time," explained Kareem. "I will try to make some appointments for tomorrow. The problem is that all the responsible people are at the airport saying good-bye to His Majesty, who is going to the eastern province. Actually, many of them are going with him."

When King Khalid travels within Saudi Arabia, he is accompanied by about 1,800 people—officials, ministers, various contingents of the armed forces. The previous evening, five Army trucks full of soldiers going to Dammam to provide an honor guard had crashed into each other, killing 14 and injuring 100. News of the accident was suppressed, and did not appear in the local newspapers. Truth has its limits.

For the next six days I went to the Ministry of Information at 8:30 every morning and sat drinking black tea until 12:30 when the day's work appeared finished. Every day appointments were made for *bukra* (tomorrow), and every day the offices were half-full of functionaries who sat yawning, reading newspapers, scratching their crotches, picking their bare feet, stroking their moustaches, playing with worry beads, smoking cigarettes endlessly, and cracking their knuckles.

Occasionally the telephone rang and was watched with fascination for a few seconds before someone answered. The others listened to the conversation before such excitement palled and then returned to gazing at newspapers, yawning, and snoozing. There was one five-minute prayer break when offices emptied and corridors became makeshift mosques.

No one could accuse the Saudis of overachieving, but behind the sloth there is obvious danger. Desert Bedouin still comprise one-third of the country. Few of them can read or write, and life expectancy is forty years. Yet it is probably the easiest place in the world to earn a fortune, be a success, and have a position in what passes for society. There is only one qualification: be born a Saudi. Most foreign firms are required by law to have a local partner who may or may not work for the privilege, but who will certainly earn a percentage of any transaction.

For those without opportunities, there is always a government job. Even automatic elevators have operators, and most offices have four or five male receptionists. Women are not in evidence, and there is no provision for them to be so in future: government buildings are constructed without women's toilets.

Expatriate Arabs, prevented from bringing adult relatives into the country, are restless. An Egyptian engineer earns less than a Saudi cleaner. A Syrian or Palestinian who speaks several languages is paid $800 a month. A Saudi office boy earns much the same. When inflation was at its highest, Saudi Government employees had a raise of 50 percent. Non-Saudis received nothing. "It gets worse every day," complained a Syrian. "Apart from everything else, we live more expensively than them. They only eat rice and meat. We like vegetables and all sorts of things. But what can you expect? We are only here for the money. What else is there? Sand? The only advantage is that they can't throw us out. The country would collapse. The undersecretaries can't even write proper letters."

Further delay and confusion is caused by the strictly observed Ramadan fast, and by an annual migration of the whole government from Riyadh to Jidda and thence to the summer capital of Taïf, a beautiful hill city whose facilities would be strained by an annual Rotary Club dinner. Boxes of files, contracts, bids, papers, and documents of every conceivable nature are all transported there and then moved back to Riyadh at the end of the season. Many are mislaid, creating panic in a country where the simplest maneuver needs a multiplicity of forms and signatures—three are required before official government drivers can fill their own cars with gasoline.

Large firms, anticipating the problems, equip each employee with seventy passport photographs so that every request is duplicated and delays kept to a minimum.

Until recently there was a further complication: no one knew the correct time of day. This did not really matter because the Saudi attitude toward time, developed over thousands of years, makes Iran seem like a paradise of punctuality. There are still three separate methods of calculation within the country. Muslim Sun Time establishes midnight at sunset. If you are invited to dinner on Tuesday morning, it means Monday evening—that is, if you are on Greenwich Time (add three hours for local Saudi time), or Aramco Time (add another hour for daylight saving).

As they tussle with these dilemmas, even the most optimistic adopt a philosophy known as the IBM factor—*Insha'allah* (God willing), *Bukra* (tomorrow), *Ma'aleesh* (Never mind, anyway). However well prepared, nearly everyone loses money on the first business deal. Sitting at home, or in an office, it seems the warnings must be exaggerated. There is, everyone knows, a market for anything: live sheep from Australia,[1] prayer mats, sand, pure water from Loch Katrine in Scotland, reinforced plastic domes from Aberdeen, 200,000 lunches a day flown by chartered Boeing

747 from France, sandwiches from Wolverhampton, $2 million of chickens a year slaughtered in a way acceptable to Koranic law, plastic palm trees, electrically operated hubble bubble pipes. . . .

And it is well known that Arabs are prepared to pay over the odds for anything that might buy an entree into the prestigious areas of Western politics or social life—witness London's Dorchester Hotel or the banking shares of Bert Lance, President Carter's much-criticized former Director of the Office of Management and Budget.[2]

But a baptism of indifference awaits eager entrants to the money rush. After long days sitting in outer offices, drinking cups of scented tea, and listening to ever more enthusiastic promises about *bukra,* they are cabling desperately for more money. To be successful, even a medium-sized firm must be prepared to lose $200,000 in the first year.

"You have to know the undercurrents," says an American diplomat. "We find it a bit like working in the Soviet Union. You learn to feel the pulse, develop an instinct for what is really going on both in politics and business. It is impossible to walk in here and leave a week later with a sackful of money."

A booby trap awaits those who try, who misjudge optimism for commitment, and base their future on what seems like a promise. Phoenix Shipbuilders of Beverley, Yorkshire, was put into receivership after a $90 million contract to supply tugs to Jidda went wrong. They claim that their "agent," Prince Faisal bin Turki, a brother-in-law of King Khalid, took 18 instead of 10 percent commission, as well as other unauthorized payments. This caused a cash-flow problem.

Many another firm discovered that Saudi ecstasy quickly turned to precoital tristesse. In August 1977, the *Financial Times* announced: "£54M. SAUDI HOTEL AND HOMES DEAL FOR BRITAIN. The Elliott Group of Peterborough has won orders from Saudi Arabia worth about £54 million. Over a two-year period six hotels and 200 two-bedroomed houses are to be built. The contracts will be self-financing, and the Elliott Group will act as main contractor."

It was nearly double the group's turnover of the previous fifteen months, and the shares went from 15 cents to 90 cents—

good news for company chairman Edmund Smeeth, who was having problems repaying a Barclays Bank overdraft. During the next three weeks, he sold 335,000 of his 524,633 shares for $270,000—at an average price of 80 cents.

Unfortunately, there was no contract. In October deputy chairman Alexander Houston announced a "misunderstanding over the terminology of the word 'order.' At the moment there is no contract, and we are proceeding with negotiations. There are well-known difficulties in dealing with Arab countries."

Ah yes, said Smeeth. "You have to pay to get this sort of valuable experience." His fellow shareholders, who saw the value of their shares drop to 28 cents, feel the money-rush entrance fee is too steep. And damn the experience.

They are not alone in finding the Saudi Arabian facts of life increasingly difficult. America's early lead is being sabotaged by what participants claim is government naïveté about the realities of international trading. An official in Jidda was distraught. "First the Lockheed scandal encouraged a Mr. Clean attitude towards bribes. Then we announce we are cutting back on arms sales. Now Americans abroad are having their tax advantages whittled away.[3] Then there's the problem of the boycott. Next they'll start investigating Saudi Arabia's civil-rights record, and we'll all be sunk."

The British have 1,150 companies on the Arab blacklist, but, relying as usual on dreams of a celestial "special relationship," they decided not to copy the American Export Administration Act of 1977 which makes it illegal for firms to comply with boycott demands. Too much—$6 billion a year in exports—is at stake. Department of Trade official Peter Corley, was dispatched to reside in Riyadh to help overcome the delicate problems involved. At first he worked from a desk in his bedroom and must have wondered frequently whose side his government was on. They had a way of canceling trade visits at the last minute, particularly if there was antiboycott fuss at home, and he had to provide excuses to Saudi ministers with whom he had taken weeks to arrange an appointment.

The French quietly decided to comply with the boycott by revoking a law which banned commercial discrimination against Israel. They did this in August 1977, taking advantage of the fact that no one is really awake during the holiday month. The Italians used charm and infuriated the British by winning a $30 million contract for air conditioning at Riyadh University Medical School. Fixed-price bids had been requested as usual. "The Italians bid low, got the contract, and hey presto!—they had an escalation clause put in," says a British trade official. "It all depends on who you know here."

British ambassador John Wilton is not convinced. "There are various theories, but I'm not so sure anything is better than having a good product at the right price ready for delivery. The Mercedes diesel truck is the most common in this country. Do you suppose Mercedes get into discussions about financing, or that the German ambassador and his commercial secretary spend eighteen hours a day trying to land their contract? No. Mercedes has a good agent and a good product. In those circumstances you do not need to bribe a prince."

BL (formerly British Leyland) also claims it did not have to bribe their prince. It merely paid $1.5 million into the Chase Manhattan account in Geneva of the brother-in-law of Prince Abdullah, Commander of the National Guard. In the same period, between 1975 and 1976, a further $1.2 million was paid into the Geneva bank account of another Saudi to ensure that BL sales went smoothly in the country.

Bribing your prince, indeed.

As Western companies found the glamour of the money rush evaporating in the heat and frustration of Saudi Arabia, others came to take their place.

In 1973, when the South Korean embassy was opened in Jidda, there were only two Koreans in the country. During the next two years, others came to do business worth $750 million, but the real Korean money rush started in 1976 when they trebled the value of their contracts to $2.4 billion. Now there are 25,000 Korean laborers in Saudi Arabia—mostly bachelors well disciplined from rigorous army training at home. "It will keep Westerners on their toes," says Minister of Commerce Sulaiman al Sulim. "They are working for hundreds of millions less than other countries."

How sentimental it would be to suggest that this is because

the Korean workers have no rights, no status, and are paid about half the wage of other workers. How ironic that they are now poaching jobs in Saudi Arabia because of the gap left in their economy by the withdrawal of American troops from South Korea. Truly there is an equilibrium in world trade.

The Koreans' largest project, involving the Hyundai Company, is a $9 billion complex at Jubail with four petrochemical plants, a steel mill, aluminum factory, two refineries, and a port (a few miles from the large port at Dammam). When 4,000 Korean workers demonstrated for better pay and conditions, there was little fuss and no publicity. "If they behave in a difficult way," says Planning Minister Hisham Nazer, "we ship them home."

He sat smiling behind the large desk in his office, a confident man with direct responsibility for spending $142 billion, a key contact in the money rush. As he tries to reconcile the rigidity of Saudi life with the freedom taught him during his Western education, some of his former professors at the University of California at Berkeley might wince.

"Until we can train our own people, we have to live with the agonies and distresses caused by the importation of foreigners. Of course it has adverse effects, and the fact that some of them are unhappy is of concern to us—although we have no alternative.

"They are here for the money, and they are getting it. If they want to stay, they must abide by our laws. As far as we are concerned, we want only their expertise. As long as they want to sell it and we can buy it, that's fine. Let me tell you something. The majority are not Europeans or Americans. They are Asians who do not even try to speak our language, so how can they affect our society? Go and look at the Koreans. They are regimented, very disciplined. They come here, do a job efficiently, are paid, and go home. That's all there is to it.

"At the moment we suffer from this Hollywoodish image. All sorts of stories are told, but I notice the people are not named. There is the old one about the Shaikh being driven to London Airport and his chauffeur asking, 'What shall I do with the Rolls?' The Arab replies, 'Keep it.' Well, nothing like that ever happens to me, and I am very close to people who have those sort of cars.

"Can you imagine the effect when someone in Italy reads that sort of thing? He comes here thinking he can sell anything—even toys. Yes, toys. They suggested, for instance, that we should place television cameras in the main squares so we can watch from our offices and see what is going on outside. A try is a try, but I often wonder how many of these things have been invented.

"I read in the *Herald Tribune* the other day about a scheme to tow icebergs from the Antarctic. Great big headlines. I was intrigued. Water is a gift in many countries. Here we pay $1 a cubic meter for desalinization. But I know the story was not true."

In fact, the story illustrates one of the dilemmas of a feudal society. Members of the royal family can produce schemes of their own without any reference to overall planning, logic, or the minister concerned. In June 1977, a week after I spoke to Hisham Nazer one of his colleagues, Prince Mohammed Faisal, a nephew of King Khalid, was underwriting a conference in Paris at which he launched International Transport of Icebergs Ltd., a company backed with $1 million of private money. In partnership with a French firm, Cicero Company, he proposed that six tugboats could haul an iceberg wrapped in eighteen-inch-thick plastic from the Antarctic to the Red Sea. The iceberg would be a mile long, 1,000 feet wide, and contain 20 billion gallons of water. It would take six months for the 7,500-mile journey, and Cicero promised first delivery within months for a fee of $90 million. Prince Mohammed reckoned the ice would sell for about 20.6 cents a cubic meter.

Alas for brave ideas. A few months later, as Prince Mohammed was sponsoring an International Conference on Iceberg Utilization at Iowa State University, Cicero went into liquidation, just like icebergs in the desert sun.

"Well," continued Hisham Nazer. "Well. We do receive all sorts of proposals. People want to borrow money, sell swimming pools, tennis courts, houses, everything. One bank actually suggested seriously they should take over the economy of the country and manage it for us."

"What did you say to them?" I asked.

His reply does much, perhaps, to enlighten the unwary. "We say different things at different times depending upon the mood.

People should realize there is enough intelligence here. After all, most of us have been trained in America, know the language, the culture, and the working habits.

"But we do not want that society here. We already have our own, and we will try to maintain existing values. That is quite the reverse of planning in a socialist country where they have a grand design for a new society. The problem in the West is that you misunderstand Islam. You think of it only in terms of religion. It is not like that. It is a social system which emphasizes strength—not weakness. You should work for the present as if you are going to live forever, and for the next life as if you are going to die tomorrow. People pray in the office once a day. It does not disrupt their work. We don't have a coffee hour, or go to the pub. Why worry about ten minutes' praying? The problem does not lie in the application of Islam, but in its understanding.

"We know we are not going to get over our problems in the short term. Every now and then we may face a crisis. Our basic knowledge is inadequate, our statistics are inadequate, but in twenty years' time we will be a productive and efficient society with tremendous self-confidence."

"Will women be part of this productive society?" I asked.

He looked startled. Like many nonroyal ministers, he has a foreign wife—Almira, a twenty-seven-year-old pediatrician. The establishment is not keen on such dilution of scarce Saudi blood, and special permission is required to marry non-Saudi women. "What is wrong with our attitude toward women?"

"They have to remain veiled outside the house, cannot drive a car . . ."

"But aren't there some women in the West who do not drive?"

"Yes."

"Well?"

"They are allowed to."

"What does that signify? More accidents. You must see the advantages of our attitude toward women. We have perhaps the lowest divorce rate in the world, the best family ties . . ."

"The divorce rate is low because you can have several wives without divorcing them."

"Yes, but polygamy is not necessarily the fashion these days. It is permitted—as it is by Mormons in the United States [a common misconception among Saudi Arabians]—but few practice it. It is no longer possible to maintain four wives, especially as Islam makes you treat each one equally. Anyway, to talk about women is raising the issue at the wrong time. There are women here—and men—who are not trained."

I met him a few weeks later in London, where he was giving a speech. Everyone else began, "Brothers, sisters . . ." The Planning Minister for Saudi Arabia hesitated, looked around his audience of which about a third were women, glanced down at his hands, coughed, and began, "Brothers."

The weight of tradition hangs heavy. It will take more than a few years of Western influence to change it.

13/THE LEAKING FURNITURE OF RIYADH

"It will probably take fifty years to liberate all the Arab women, and the Saudi men will be the last in the world to give in. But it's bound to come."

JEHAN SADAT (WIFE OF THE EGYPTIAN PRESIDENT)

"In no case may men and women commingle in the place of work or in the accessory facilities or other appurtenances thereto."

SAUDI LABOR LAW, CHAPTER X, ARTICLE 160

BY THE SWIMMING POOL of the Beirut hotel sits a beautiful olive-skinned woman, plump breasts cascading firmly into a small bikini bra, thick black hair falling on her slim shoulders, and a smile of gentle contentment on her face. Her back is stroked with suntan lotion by a British salesman.

She is a twenty-three-year-old Saudi Arabian who was married at fourteen to a cousin thirty years older, and comes to Beirut twice a year with her husband's approval to "relax." Few things are as they seem in the money rush, as the salesman has discovered. A brief affair with a raunchy married Saudi woman had been beyond his most outrageously optimistic thoughts.

They were discreet. Apart from mornings at the pool, they had been seen publicly on only one occasion. That was when Princess Misha, granddaughter of Ibn Saud's eldest surviving son, Mohammed (see Appendix), and her boyfriend joined them for dinner at a restaurant. Misha, also twenty-three and married, was a lively, pretty girl who seemed very much in love with her boyfriend, the cousin of a Saudi diplomat.

The salesman and the Saudi woman parted after three days to return to their different worlds: she to another spell of life enclosed behind four walls, allowed out only if she cloaked herself in black cotton more oppressive than a nun's habit, he to the self-generating frenzy of a business world where he soon forgot an unexpected fling in Lebanon.

Until January 1978. At London Airport on his way to Rome, he picked up a newspaper. A story inside made him tremble with shock. Princess Misha had been stoned to death. Her lover's head had been hacked off in the main square of Jidda by one of Mohammed's elderly retainers.

Adultery, sanctified within Islamic marriage by the convenient device of allowing a man four wives, and embarked upon with enthusiasm by Saudi men in parts of the world to which they now have access, is punishable by death under the barbaric hypocrisy which passes for God's law in Saudi Arabia. Although the Koran says heaven is at the feet of a mother, some men still say *Karram Allah* ("God forgive me") before even mentioning such a worthless subject as women in conversation.

Of all the tensions being detonated by the money rush, few will provide such an explosion as the emergence of women into real life. It is beginning, after thousands of years of inconsistency.

Even on flights within Saudi Arabia, young girls and women discard their veils with relief during takeoff and carefully cover themselves again before landing. On international flights, beautifully groomed girls board in London, Paris, or Beirut, flirt blatantly during the journey, and disembark in Riyadh wrapped in black indistinguishable from other "Guinness bottles," as they are known to foreigners. An adulterous wife has one advantage in Saudi Arabia: the garb she is forced to wear in public makes it impossible for her to be recognized. She can go from place to place in the knowledge that no one dares stop her, and no one can follow with certainty. Saudi Arabia is hell for private detectives. It is also hell for women who cannot accept archaic limitations.

"You must switch off as soon as you leave the plane," says the English wife of a prominent Saudi. "You have to. It is two separate worlds. And it affects not only women. My thirteen-year-old son goes to Millfield [a British public school]. I take him to England a few days before the start of term. The first day he is there, he will not take off his shirt in front of other children. After a day or two, he wears a T-shirt. But it takes a week before he will undress in front of his friends and feels happy to walk around in shorts.

"We have worked so hard here for fourteen years. We have spent so much money. But where have we gone wrong? Why does everyone try to leave so quickly and so often if Saudi Arabia is so wonderful? We are doing everything except developing a society and an environment which is pleasant to live in."

Some women are satisfied. Half the population cannot be kept subjugated without collusion on their part however much it is based on fears of change or the weight of tradition. It is sometimes impossible for Westerners to appreciate when they visit a Saudi home that the women scuttling in the background may have more "rights" than a lonely suburban housewife in the West. Saudi women retain their own name when married, keep their own money under all circumstances, and must be treated equally with other wives when divorced. If a husband divorces his wife and later wishes to remarry her, he faces restrictions which might surprise the most advanced sexual crusader in the West. The woman first has to marry another man and have intercourse with him. Occasionally the experience is more satisfactory than with her first husband, so she stays with the second man.

Surprisingly, even a few Western women find life in Saudi Arabia tolerable, although they need to have somewhat limited social ambitions. In Dammam, on the east coast, I met Muriel Smith, whose husband, Don, earns $20,000 a year working on the docks. They share a house with another English couple and have few complaints. "I miss a drop of whisky now and again," says forty-five-year-old Muriel. "But I reckon I go out here more than I did when we lived in Liverpool. We go to the airport every Thursday and Saturday. It's a beautiful airport. We spend a couple of hours watching the planes take off and land, and have a cup of coffee. It's ever so much fun."

Even Zaki Yamani's twenty-six-year-old wife, Tammam, a former biology student in Beirut, does not seem too bored. Her bookshelves are crammed with videocassettes and she can sit watching soap operas and detective films when her husband brings guests home. But no country overwhelmed by the money rush can afford to keep half the population unoccupied, cloistered, and ineffective, fluttering through life in Givenchy creations while they rot their bodies with chocolates, their psyches with frustration, and their minds with videotaped American pap. Already the flickerings of emancipation are beginning, discreetly and illegally. Saudi law, devised in unintelligible legal language by Egyptians, forbids women and men to work together, but in Dhahran I met twenty-nine-year-old Naileh Mousli, who is an oil engineer; a remarkable achievement for a Saudi girl who is one of twenty children. Her father had two wives, and she is the youngest of nine, in nine years, by his first wife. She works for Aramco and is married to a Lebanese who is also employed by the firm.

"My father is in real estate and my mother is illiterate. But she is very broad-minded and pushed us really hard. She wished she could have been something, and she knows how times are changing. I am very proud of her. When I started work I was criticized by some members of the family, mainly through ignorance. I had a very hard time trying to explain in simple terms what a petroleum engineer does. Some of the Saudis in the field don't like it. One told me he would not let his daughter be like me for anything. That doesn't make me feel humiliated because I realize their customs and I know what they think. I expect some people to be shocked because it is strange. A lot of people, even Americans, don't believe I am a Saudi.

"I find it tough at times because I am given all the opportunities to work here like a man, but when I talk to my aunts and other women, I have to think backwards, go down to their level, and talk about cooking, raising children—the things they care for.

"You cannot force change on people. You present it to them and make them aware. Then it is up to them. I am lucky because I have been to college and have the chance to know what I want. I don't like the way my mother was brought up, and I don't like the way she is living now. I am going to change that for myself.

"But it is difficult for a man who might feel the same way. He

has a role imposed upon him and cannot just drop everything
and tell his father and grandfather that he is not going to be a
male chauvinist any more. If he did that, he would be isolated,
excluded by his friends. That is why Saudi men who want to
change the situation marry foreign women. They know that if
they marry a Saudi woman, both his family and hers will impose
tradition upon them. If he marries a foreigner, at least he will
have peace from her side. If I married a Saudi and he did not
want me to wear a veil, my father still has the influence to insist.

"Westerners criticize our society, but they have never tried to
understand it. Maybe you are making more of an effort now because you need us. But you base everything on your own standards. Of course, we have not been able to update the customs of
our country quickly enough to match the new circumstances. It
is creating a lot of tension under the surface. Saudi men don't
feel comfortable in the presence of Westerners. They are suspicious, unsettled, and wonder what is going to happen to their
women. Well, that is the price they have to pay for Western
technology."

The price is too high for the *ulemas* (Muslim scholars, equivalent to Christian priests), who fight fiercely to retain their authority. The President of Girls' Education, Shaikh Nassar bin
Hamad al Rashid blacklisted a twelve-year-old girl from any
Saudi school for answering a magazine questionnaire that she
"loved" a popular singer. Her family had to move to another city
and change their identity.

In spite of his imposing title, Shaikh Nassar is not actually allowed to enter the schools for which he is responsible (he com-
municates with them by letter or telephone) because that could
compromise the pupils, although it is difficult to accuse him of
anything but the utmost propriety.

He is a tall, slightly stooped man. A full gray beard and the
habit of padding barefoot about his office gives the image of an
Old Testament prophet. As we talked one day, his secretary, a
small young man, watched intently, his dark brown eyes quiver-
ing whenever sex was mentioned, which was frequently, and he
shifted nervously as if expecting the devil himself to walk
through the door. The room was gloomy, full of heavy furniture,
and there was an atmosphere of fervent piety as Shaikh Nassar

began to explain to me his version of female sexuality and the advance of fundamentalist Islam.

"At first there was resistance here to girls' education because people thought it would be harmful. But when they realized responsible men—the *ulemas*—would be in charge, they changed their minds. The resistance to education came not from us, but from the people themselves.

"Why are girls segregated? *Sharia* law—and Christian—does not agree that boys and girls should be together until they are married unless they are brother and sister. They need one hundred percent concentration, and if they mix, they will not concentrate. As regards Christianity, I am referring to the Old Testament, which does not allow sex without marriage nor the causes which might lead to it.

"But there are other reasons why girls' are segregated. We want to pay attention to women, to be generous to them because they need more taking care of than boys. This is the only country in the world where women are given their rights. They don't honor women in Britain or America or the Soviet Union. We call it honoring a woman. What do you think?"

"I think it is patronizing, out of date, and is going to lead to trouble," I replied, such heresy making the secretary jump like a startled rabbit. Shaikh Nassar was urbane, amused at such Western incomprehension.

"We give women freedom, but within the limits of their religion. If they want to break away from their religious boundaries, that is all right. Naturally, education is a two-sided weapon. It is good if it is used for the sake of welfare, but bad if used for any other reason."

Many of the leading Saudis, like Shaikh Yamani, send their daughters to be educated abroad, particularly in the United States. Surely, if anything were going to corrupt a nation's youth, that would?

"You cannot judge a whole nation by a few people. Knowledge is a virtue and should be pursued everywhere except where there is vice," he replied obliquely.

"Like in the United States?"

"Like in the United States. For the welfare of the whole world it is important that Saudi Arabia's morals should not decline, and there should be at least one place in the world where good manners are important. There is so much bad behavior in the world, and it is all because of the Jewish influence."

"You must be joking," I said, although I knew he was not.

"The Jews are enemies of humanity, and their aim is to pull everyone down into materialism. They control the mass media, the banks . . . everything."

How strange that extreme godliness and prejudice should be such frequent partners, but we had wandered from the subject of sex segregation.

"There will never be coeducation in this country," exclaimed Shaikh Nassar. "In the last seventeen years we have had good control, and it is getting better all the time. Things may be different in Oman and Bahrain, but these countries were under British colonization, so new ideas were introduced. The hope is now that they are independent they will come to the right Islamic solution."

The smell became more intense with each step nearer the bathroom. It was like methylated spirits, but sweeter and more powerful, strong enough to bring a tear to the eye and an involuntary twitch to the nose. Outside, the temperature rose to 120° and the small subdivision of boxlike houses shimmered in the heat.

Most people slept as the sluggish afternoon drifted on. But in his bathroom, the senior executive of one of Europe's largest companies, a gastronome and habitué of prestigious restaurants, was dressed in sky-blue briefs and apron. One white handkerchief was tied round his forehead as a makeshift sweatband. Another covered his nose and mouth to keep out fumes which rose venomously from three pink plastic buckets on the floor. They were one-third filled with a colorless liquid, almost pure alcohol called *sediki* (Arabic for "my friend") to which he added water, stirred, tasted, grimaced, and spat.

In the kitchen his wife kept watch over two pressure cookers containing a boiling mixture of sugar and water, the basic ingredients. She looked nervously out of the window whenever a car drove along the unpaved road, and her relief showed when it passed by, obscured in a cloud of dust within a few seconds. Her husband was considered one of the leading brewers in the Arabian peninsula, his *sediki*-based gin and whisky sometimes indistinguishable from the genuine variety, and his wines compared favorably to some adequate French vintages. But if his ability were recognized by the Saudi police, the dismissal from his firm would be as instant as the humiliation of their immediate expulsion from a country where alcohol is allegedly banned.

Alcohol has always been forbidden to Muslims, but the first ruler of Saudi Arabia, King Ibn Saud, allowed foreigners to import it for their own use as the country developed during the 1930s. This concession stopped in 1952 when one of his sons, Mishari (see Appendix), shot and killed the British chargé d'affaires who had ordered him to leave a party for being drunk. Mishari is now a businessman, his life saved because the widow declined his head, which was offered by Ibn Saud, as well as blood money of $140,000. But after the tragedy, the King banned the importing of liquor as "the mother of crimes and the basis of all corruption." Now even boats are launched with bottled water from the Gulf.

The penalty for drinking or providing alcohol is severe—public lashings followed by imprisonment—but implementation is selective. A few days after I arrived, a Dutch tugboat captain had been sentenced to 200 strokes of the cane and ten months in prison for failing to seal his liquor cabinet on arrival at the Eastern port of Dammam, and two Britons were about to suffer the same fate for selling homemade alcohol to Muslims.

At the time, however, I was sipping a refreshing gin and tonic at Zaki Yamani's Riyadh home, served to me by his personal assistant Lord Patrick Beresford. (Old Etonian, former Royal Horse Guards officer, polo-playing friend of Prince Philip, brother of the Marquis of Waterford—all the gossip-column trimmings. Yamani apparently started a trend for hiring sprigs of the British aristocracy: King Khalid's boat captain is Sir John Onslow.)

Every day, Saudi Arabian airports are clogged with the paraphernalia of sophisticated Western domesticity: vacuum cleaners, refrigerators, deep freezes, videocassettes, blue movies, hi-fi sets of such impedance and ohms as to tax the hearing of the most acutely audiosensitive dog, sickly confectionery to glutinize the minds of educated Saudi women condemned to suffer sanctified humiliations, and boxes labeled simply FURNITURE. These are collected by the elite sometimes summoned discreetly to the airport by deferential customs officials with the warning "Your furniture is leaking," before the elixir from bottles of finest Glenlivet or Chivas Regal, unhappily broken en route, reaches the nostrils of the less fortunate.

Even foreign diplomats have to be careful. They dispose of empties by crushing them into small pieces and returning them in the diplomatic bag, or dropping them into the Red Sea during boating "picnics." Meanwhile, the "furniture" cartons have a more practical use as makeshift living accommodation for low-paid expatriate Arab and Pakistani workers who are forbidden to join a trade union and are flown home at the first sign of disruption.

For those unable to obtain whisky, or to pay the black-market price of $100 a bottle, *sediki* can be a pleasant alternative. It has been brewed in Saudi Arabia for centuries but achieved status when Western expatriates, worried about the lethally explosive potential of homemade alcohol, issued a 33-page booklet of instructions and diagrams known as *The Blue Flame*. This describes the setting up of a "sneaky home still which can be stored in a dresser drawer and yields an acceptable product in one run" to the more complicated "fractional distillation still" and has become a much-prized literary work unobtainable today. "The prohibition is sternly enforced, especially by adherents of the Islam (Moslem) religion. Hence, take care of this booklet and remember discreet handling is mandatory."

It provides recipes for everything from absinthe (136 proof), Cointreau 1 and 2, vodka ("pour 110 proof *sediki* into a vodka bottle"), wines, and Kahlúa ("mix one pound of drip coffee with 1¼ quarts of water. Boil and simmer slowly for forty minutes. Strain through cheesecloth. This will make about one cup of concentrate. Cool and add 1–1¼ quarts of 180 proof *sediki*, plus two ounces of vanilla extract"). The booklet observes that "those of us who have spent time in Saudi Arabia discovered that there was a generous quantity and wide variety of alcohol available, even though it was absolutely forbidden to possess, sell, carry, drink, or manufacture. Moreover, we discovered it was of excellent quality, nearly hangover-proof, and every ounce manufactured in almost any household kitchen. The preparation was a respected secret, yet eagerly shared with good friends."

The party that evening was a farewell to the managing director of an arms manufacturing firm and a number of prominent members of the European and American community had been invited, but no Saudis. A Lockheed executive observed, "We used to invite them to our parties, but they were always getting drunk and pushing each other into the pool. It was terrible. In all my time here I've only known one top Saudi who did not drink. You daren't invite them home, because they come only for the booze, and you can never get rid of them."

An ambassador added, "You have a lot of drunkenness and all the evils of Prohibition here, although it's not so bad as Chicago in the Al Capone days. Many of the princes would like a glass of beer after playing tennis, but whisky is much cheaper to transport, because of its size, and so they have that or nothing."

A side effect of state-administered asceticism is the character change it creates in those exposed to it. The "just a sweet sherry at Christmas" man starts to pant for a large whisky. The faithful husband lusts for the most bizarre offerings of Times Square or Soho. The casual eater will not rest until seated in front of the best the Tour d'Argent can provide.

Meanwhile, however, they creep back to the womb of a hotel and sit in the lobby drinking Pepsi-Cola (Coke is boycotted), playing chess, and listening to each others' exaggerations while they await the only live entertainment of the day: mealtime.

At least eight Pakistani waiters, immaculate in green or red jackets, hover, impatient to please. But only one man is qualified to take orders for the set menu of junk food—usually described as chicken or beef—and he wears a dinner jacket à la mode to give credibility to an otherwise undistinguished intellect. He has a large pad, numerous pieces of carbon paper, and scatters sheets to various waiters, keeping one for himself which he personally delivers to a man seated behind a dirty yellow curtain at the side of the dining room: the cashier.

Diners, invariably depressed by the day's events, clutch their bottled water ($2 a liter), or the more expensive Schloss Boosenburg ("alcohol-free sparkling grape drink, a product of Germany") and await something they have not ordered, followed by profuse apologies and much head striking from the headwaiter who appears terminally panic-stricken minutes after opening time.

One lunchtime, when the food was more than normally unappetizing and the headwaiter more than normally apologetic, he murmured, "Tonight you must have champagne."

Champagne? In Riyadh? Nonsense. Then I recalled a rumor, dismissed at the time, that Crown Prince Fahd, himself no stranger to Western delights, had hinted to hotelkeepers that perhaps, on occasions, guests could be offered a drink.

That evening, edgy with anticipation, I sat myself at a corner table, slightly hidden behind a pillar, and was greeted immediately by the headwaiter prancing with enthusiastic delight, who licked his pencil, wrote on his note pad, stood still, arched his back, and breathed "champagne" like the dying sigh of an orgasmic frog.

He toddled off, distributing parts of his note pad to bowing waiters.

The champagne arrived at the same time as the soup (an unidentifiable taste camouflaged with noodles), and had been poured into a large jug, half full of ice, and topped with a piece of lemon. This, presumably, was to avoid the scandal a genuine bottle would cause.

I smiled as I poured the first gentle drops, and I felt a temporary touch of guilt at not sharing my secret with the Texan electronics salesman who had two bottles of bourbon confiscated at the airport but still called everyone—including the waiters—"shaikh." The wine hit the glass, and bubbles sparkled upwards —slightly anemic, and there was a yellowish color, but I attributed this to the lemon.

A sip, swilling it around to let the taste buds appreciate fully this unexpected delight . . .

"Good?" asked the headwaiter.

"It tastes like apple juice," I said.

"Oh, no, sir. It *is* apple juice, but it has things added."

"What things?"

"Perrier water. Saudi champagne is Perrier water and apple juice."

I paid the bill—$10—and walked out of the hotel into an evening heat that felt oppressive as lukewarm blancmange. What I needed, I thought, was a call from the Chief.

14/WISHBONE AND JUNGLE JAP

"It works in the jungle, it works in the desert, it works every-where."   ADNAN KHASHOGGI, QUOTED IN FORTUNE, JUNE 1977

"I have heard disturbing reports that Khashoggi just bullshits you."
     STANLEY SPORKIN (DIRECTOR FOR THE SECURITIES AND EX-CHANGE COMMISSION ENFORCEMENT DIVISION)

THE TELEPHONE CALL came through to London just before mid-night on Saturday. "This is Bob Shaheen. Would you be able to see the Chief tomorrow morning at about ten o'clock?"

"Yes. Where?"

"In Cannes."

For Adnan Khashoggi, Saudi Arabia's most visible multina-tional entrepreneur, distance and time are irrelevant. He travels 60,000 miles a month in his green-and-white Boeing 727 (gold-colored—*not* gold-plated—bathroom fittings, Telexes, six color televisions with videocassettes, separate wardrobes for Cifonelli suits and gold-embroidered *thobes*), an updated Bedouin flitting from one continent to another arranging deals, smoothing prob-lems, allegedly bribing government officials, and surrounding himself and his clients with conspicuous symbols of status like yachts, expensive cars, beautiful women, and hospitality on a scale which impresses the most dour bankers as much as it alarms their blue-rinsed wives.

"People are hypocrites," he says. "They don't know how to

live. Many of them would like to live as I do, but they don't dare. They are afraid of what others would say. I enjoy living pleasantly. I can afford it. I have worked hard for it. Why should I deprive myself? In the beginning there was hostility in Saudi Arabia because they thought I was exposing myself too much. Now they have become used to it. I'm not afraid. I have nothing to hide. Whatever I enjoy, others enjoy with me."

After the first blast of Riyadh self-righteousness, he is a refreshing change. His uninhibited life-style, the basis for Harold Robbins's novel, *The Pirate*, is financed by a reputed $500 million in profits over the last few years ($200 million in 1977 alone) and makes him one of the few identifiable targets for snipers who lie along the route of the money rush, as well as a potential all-purpose savior. He nearly prevented British financier Jim Slater from falling to disgrace in a heap of debts. During a series of meetings in Beirut and Paris in 1975, he offered to buy Sir James Goldsmith's 20 percent holding in Slater Walker, plus a further 5 percent, for $14 million—enough to ensure the company's survival. However, according to Slater sources, he could not provide the $4 million cash needed to implement the deal and asked them to arrange financing, an impossibility for a firm already in a morass of difficulties. Khashoggi's aides have a different interpretation: asking for financing he knew would not be forthcoming was a tactful way out of an overpriced deal; it is a refinement on the usual method of polite smiles and promises for *bukra*.

As I flew to meet Khashoggi, he was reported to have "abducted" his five children from his wife, Soraya (née Sandra Jarvis-Daly of Leicester, whom he married when she was seventeen); and another newspaper was about to disclose "London's newest night club, *Le Privé*, designed to become the capital's most exclusive joint, opened last year. Fabled Arabian 'Mr Fixit' Adnan Khashoggi is said to be one of the names barred from membership. This might be because he is a flashy Arab!"[1]

It was mid-afternoon in September, the best time for the Riviera, and Robert Shaheen sat in his room at the Majestic Hotel in Cannes with all the curtains drawn and shutters closed. He wondered aloud, yet again, about criticism which always en-

velops his boss. Once he searched for a comparison. "It happened
to Caesar, to Jesus, and it happens today when a man has great
visions and dares to be different."

Five identical black briefcases with combination locks were
stacked on a dressing-room table. He used to travel with twenty-
six—one for each letter of the alphabet. In spite of the reduction,
he claims that within minutes he can provide any relevant information to Khashoggi, whom he calls "the Chief." "It sounds
more pleasant than 'boss,' less authoritarian, and reveals his character. The Chief is the most wonderful, kind person. He is wise,
and a true believer in the golden rule. Quite a guy—as you will
see. But you will have one problem. You are going to like him."

Shaheen is tall and immaculate in a three-piece, pinstriped suit
which he wears everywhere, including the desert. He feels such
formality indicates that he is always on duty—thus allowing the
Chief time to relax. "I try to be never in the way and never out
of the way."

An American of Syrian descent, he has been Khashoggi's
amanuensis since the early days, and he gives a deceptive impression of being an old-fashioned courtier who stretches hyper-
bole about his boss into the realms of fantasy. He is a yes-man
only in public, disagreeing and giving shrewd advice in private.

Like others in the Khashoggi entourage, he exudes "B" movie
bonhomie, but, for all the apparent openhandedness, he is cautious about publicity. Discussing an article on Khashoggi about
to appear in the *National Enquirer,* he mused, "I need something for the middle classes. They are apt to be misled by talk of
scandal." Employees now have to sign a four-page closely typed
contract agreeing not to disclose any information whatsoever
about the company—even the existence of the contract.

Shaheen, making telephone calls to all parts of the world from
his Cannes bedroom, taped some of them on a pocket recorder
"so the Chief can get the full measure of the conversation, and
not just a summary," and glanced through a book he was reading, Robert J. Ringer's *Looking Out for Number One.* "He hits
home in a few places."

He does not really need guidance on the subtleties of the
money rush, the gestures which separate winners from losers. He
has picked up a number of tips over the years. When Khashoggi

is entertaining at a restaurant, Shaheen excuses himself toward the end, nips round the back to settle the account, and then returns nonchalantly to the table. Lo, there will be no embarrassing rustle of paper money, no signing of credit cards or checks. It is a scrap of etiquette he learned from the Governor of Mecca himself, Prince Fawwaz bin Abdulaziz. "That's elegance . . . class," he explains. "That's what separates us from those who believe we are merely ostentatious."

The telephone rang. It was the Chief, checking a few details, fixing appointments, and making arrangements for a dinner party on board his yacht that evening.

"Go back to your room," said Shaheen. "You are now in a holding pattern."

The Saudi answer to the American dream was about to be revealed, for Khashoggi sees himself as spiritual successor to the pioneering hucksters of those long-lost days before uptight investigative journalists and messy international restrictions began to destroy the incentive of entrepreneurs. "We have the same opportunities now as the Rockefellers, Vanderbilts, and J. P. Morgan had in putting America together," he says. "But we don't have ten percent of the corruption that went into the United States at that time."

Well, now . . . his heroes may have been egomaniacs, not too fastidious about the finer ethical considerations in life, they may have been into extortion (for profit), and bribery or blackmail (for profit), and art (for tax reasons), and public relations (for transforming profit into charity) but . . . Khashoggi is hardly the Cinderella of the money rush, cruelly exploited by the ugly stepsisters of American capitalism and international big business.

His millions have been accumulated largely because arms manufacturers value his close friendship with members of the Saudi Arabian royal family. It is said that he has bought influence in the United States by political contributions of doubtful legality and accepted money which was meant for bribes. But he is at least prepared to defend his actions, and is far less squeamish about his image than Sir Shapoor Reporter or Iraj Sabet in Iran, or Mohamed Mahdi al-Tajir in the United Arab Emirates, or the phalanx of self-seekers serving the Sultan of Oman.

Khashoggi anticipated and set some of the rules of the money rush. "If someone says to me, 'I love you,' I have more suspicion of him than the guy who tells me, 'I hate you.' But for the guy who says, 'I just want to make money'—God bless him. That's the guy I want to deal with. We want profit-orientated thinking. With Western technology and Middle East money, we can go places in the new world that is coming."

As for sentiment: "We sell projects, but we try not to fall in love with them."

The family fortune was started by his father Mohammed who, as personal physician to King Ibn Saud, imported the first generator to Mecca in order to run an X-ray machine. He rented out the generator, which became the basis of an electrical company which still exists.

Adnan was sent to Victoria College, a British-style boarding school in Alexandria, where the "character-building" system of cold showers and early-morning runs did so much to inspire—or kill—the puritan spirit in those members of the Arab elite that it enriched, including King Hussein and Hisham Nazer. He learned the art of buying popularity, and spent half his pocket money entertaining classmates, thereby discovering information which led quickly to his first entrepreneurial success. He introduced the father of one classmate who wanted to import towels to the father of another who owned a textile factory. He received a gift of $400 "for doing practically nothing."

After Victoria College, he was sent to study petroleum engineering at the Colorado School of Mines, but arrived on the East Coast during a blizzard, hated the cold, and disappeared to San Francisco, where he enrolled in an economics faculty at Chico State University, lived in a cheap hotel room (which he divided in half with chairs and called a "suite"), and taught his friends that the essence of obtaining credit was to create confidence. Usually they learned this valuable lesson with their own money. Once he borrowed $5 from a classmate to buy a pack of cigarettes. "Keep the change," he told the shopkeeper to the horror of his friend. Adnan explained, "My bill is due tomorrow, and I don't have the money. If I tip nearly five dollars, it means I have plenty of money, and they won't ask for immediate payment."

Traditional education was of little use to a man of such imagination. He left Chico State, went to Stanford for a term, and then returned to Saudi Arabia. "I was very excited about the possibilities. I wanted to industrialize Arabia overnight, but found it difficult. No banks would talk to me. A local entrepreneur lacked credibility and experience in what is called 'packaging.'"

Nevertheless, through friendship with Prince Mohammad bin Saud, then Minister of Defense, and contacts made in the United States, Khashoggi was asked to supply Kenworth trucks for the army. His commission of $245,000 helped him win a contract to service Dhahran air base. He denies that royal connections are any use. "Royal princes have many friends and personal relationships, as in any free, civilized society. However, these intimacies are never the basis of personal benefits or grants to privileged friends."

Later, to Pentagon officials, he was even more emphatic. "Prince Sultan does not need Adnan Khashoggi. If he wants $10 million, all he has to do is take it from the government. Adnan Khashoggi will never offer Prince Sultan money—that is like a beggar offering riches to a king."

His first company, however, the Alnasr Trading and Industrial Corporation, was backed financially by King Saud who also gave him a fifty-year monopoly to develop Saudi Arabian gypsum deposits.

Foreign firms, impressed by Khashoggi's contacts and anticipating the money rush, scrambled to be represented by him. It was not always successful. In 1962 he became agent for Marconi. "If anyone wants to do business in Saudi Arabia, he must have first-rate contacts; otherwise you can spend an awful lot of time just hanging about waiting for appointments," says S. E. Clark, Marconi's director of overseas operations. "However, we never got a penny piece out of him. We found that he was so busy and so great were his ambitions that we could never get hold of him."

Khashoggi's typically Saudi reply conceals more than it reveals. "They failed in the most important virtue of business—patience."

Meanwhile larger companies were on the horizon. Two years

later, when he was twenty-nine, Lockheed paid him $2,000 a
month "to research the market," and as chairman Don Haughton
explained, "teach them the customs." It was an association that
was to lead to Lockheed's acute embarrassment and fees of $106
million for Khashoggi.

Ironically, the arrangement was initially dismissed as futile. "I
met the American ambassador, and he told me I was wasting my
time being Lockheed's agent because Saudi Arabia would never
buy any sophisticated weapons. He said that all Ministry of Defense contracts were mere show to satisfy the pomposity of Saudi
officers. I returned to Riyadh, wrote to the late King Faisal mentioning the conversation in detail, and presented it to him personally. After reading it, the King threw it aside in anger and
said, 'I am afraid the Americans will never understand us. Do they
want us to send our youth to America for training, and to graduate from the highest American aviation school, and on their return make castles in the sand?'"

The answer was no, and in the next few years Khashoggi
made a fortune proving it. Apart from Lockheed money, he received a commission of $45 million from the sale of French
tanks, another $2 million from a British helicopter company, and
so on. In the last ten years, he has been involved in about 80 percent of all arms sales to Saudi Arabia, but he claims this represents only one third of his company's interest. "Are we in the
arms business? You know—guns, bullets, bombs. I think not. We
supply the military with technical support systems. We are not
like Mr. Sam Cummings with his machine guns."

In the United States, he began to create goodwill for himself
by contributing to Richard Nixon's campaign funds. The exact
amount remains speculative. Some estimates say it was $1 mil-
lion, but Adnan denies it. "I met Nixon in Paris in 1967 and we
had dinner at the Rasputin Restaurant. We became friends, the
way you sometimes do when you have a drink with a man and
there is a pretty girl between you.

"When I went to New York, he gave a cocktail party for me,
but when he was running for President, an Arab businessman
with big ideas suggested to me, 'Let's give him $50,000.' I said
Nixon could not appoint any of my men as ambassador, so why
should I give him money? Instead, I suggested we finance a cam-

paign record, and split the profits 50-50. They never paid back the money. My friend wanted to sue those guys for it."

By 1973 Lockheed was becoming disenchanted with its representative, particularly as his commission on the sale of Hercules transport planes which cost $2.5 million each, had risen from 2 to 8 percent, in addition to a $200,000 "marketing contingency" payment per airplane. According to Lockheed, this was for "under-the-table compensation to Saudi officials: but we really have no way of knowing if the so-called 'under-the-table' compensation is ever disbursed to Saudi officials, or stops at our consultant's bank account."

Khashoggi was still popular in government circles, though, and David Alne, a former director of the Pentagon's International Sales Negotiations, called him "an inexpensive aid program for the United States." The following year, the U.S. embassy in Jidda recommended him as "an excellent contact for U.S. firms."

Then came the Northrop "problem." The company alleged it had given $450,000 to Khashoggi to bribe two Saudi Arabian Air Force generals—Hashim and Zuhair. The generals were code-named Trumpet and Geranium in Telexed messages between Northrop's headquarters at Century City, Los Angeles, and Khashoggi's Riyadh office, where he was known as Wishbone. The money, according to Northrop chairman Tom Jones, was to ensure the success of orders for twenty Tiger fighter airplanes. Khashoggi admitted receiving the money, but said he kept it for himself because "I knew it would threaten to terminate Northrop's relationship with Saudi Arabia if it was delivered."[2]

He had not "stolen" the money, he claimed, but had credited it against Northrop's account. The vagueness of his various explanations was intentional: "What do you tell stupid people like that? I play games with them."

Khashoggi was not willing to play games with the Securities and Exchange Commission, however, who ruined a trip he made to the Sands Hotel, Las Vegas, in March 1977, by trying to subpoena him. He flew to Barbados the next day and did not return to the United States for over a year. "Is American morality suddenly to become the basis for world morality? We're not doing anything naughty. I have no need to pass bribes in Saudi Arabia.

I took my fees, and they were large, but so were the deals I helped put through for America. The more you produce, the more you earn. That, after all, is the basic element of the United States free-enterprise system."

He has about $50 million in United States banks and companies, and thirty of his fifty executives are American. He owns property—Texas, Florida and Arizona, steak houses in San Francisco, is developing a $250 million industrial park in Salt Lake City, and owns two banks in California. There was a rumpus when he tried to buy a third, and he was defended by Prince Sultan. Allegations against his friend were "part of the Zionist campaign aimed at distorting the Arab image," he claimed and added, "Hell broke loose when Arab interests wanted to invest only $25 million in San Jose banking operations, but nobody seems to be complaining against a $25 billion rip-off of the American taxpayer by Israel."

Adnan's multifarious businesses operate under the umbrella of Triad Holding Company, based in Liechtenstein. A few trusted aides have been with him for years: Bob Shaheen, Sabih Deif, an Egyptian lawyer who writes the single copy of the balance sheet in longhand, and a former Lockheed man, Louis Lauler. His brothers, Adil and Essam each own 10 percent of the company. His father, Mohammed, was honorary chairman until his death in 1979.

A Korean bodyguard, Keel, and a valet, George, accompany him everywhere. Each morning while George shaves him in a special chair, replicas of which he has in his residences throughout the world, he sits and reviews his operations in thirty-eight countries: financial management, banking, a travel firm, a furniture factory, an insurance company in London, a fashion house in Paris run by Kenzo Takada, who markets clothes under the Jungle Jap label, interior design, property development, hospital management, elevator production, cranes, ship chartering, beef slaughtering in South America, a cattle ranch in the Sudan, hotels in Tahiti, Fiji, New Zealand, and Australia.

Not all the results are successful. He planned a $600 million tourist resort near Cairo, but the contract was canceled suddenly in the summer of 1978 after reports of questionable land transactions and environmental objections had given the project the nickname "Pyramidgate." A $200 million loan he arranged for Sudan from a consortium of thirty banks (earning his own company $1 million commission) has been so mismanaged by the government that it has resulted in increased inflation and balance-of-payment difficulties. Khashoggi cannot be blamed for that, but in 1974 the management consultants McKinsey & Co., told him his own investments had been haphazard, and management chaotic.

He has a dozen homes: three in Saudi Arabia, two in London, one each in New York (the forty-sixth and forty-seventh floors of Fifth Avenue's Olympic Tower; the top floor of this $3 million extravaganza holds the swimming pool), Sardinia, Rome, Beirut, Paris, and Cannes. A $44 million yacht with helicopter landing pad was still under construction, so I prepared to meet him on the 200-foot cruiser he was making do with for the season.

Not bad for a forty-three-year-old flashy Arab.

The short trip was a misery for Bob Shaheen, nattily attired in his working suit. He doesn't much like the sea, and he ducked as the speedboat zoomed through the harbor exit, heading over the choppy Mediterranean to where the cruiser lay at anchor a few hundred yards away.

Khashoggi is small, portly, with soft brown eyes, and a gentle manner, immediately relaxed and relaxing, tactile and confiding, a salesman whose face betrays none of the tensions involved in his exploits. His fifteen-year-old daughter, Nabilia, and thirteen-year-old son, Mohammed, were on board preparing to go to school in Geneva the next day. High-spirited and friendly, they did not look abducted, although I was to read the next day how they had—at that very moment—been on the telephone in tears to their mother.

"You have to accept personal publicity like that," says Khashoggi. "It's like losing a leg. There's nothing you can do about it. Okay, if you want to see me early one morning, dancing at a nightclub with a blonde, God bless you. If you want to see me on my big boat, you are welcome. I don't want to be an Onassis, or anything like that, but it's disastrous for an individual to become mysterious.

"Let people see us as normal human beings, playing around as they do, enjoying life, doing business, having children. We are a mystery only because we came out of the desert, but we are not from Mars. It will take many years for you to understand us, and us to understand you. I am afraid the average person will not understand.

"I was treated well by the West when I started but when I became exposed—through Lockheed and the San Jose bank—I became a star in orbit, ready to be shot at. I have worked hard to build credibility.

"My fees are high, but whoever thought when I started that the amounts would be so large? Why the fuss? You don't say to David Rockefeller at Chase Manhattan, 'If it's a billion dollar transfer, don't take your commission of one-tenth of one percent.' And banks do nothing except print paper. Some of our deals take ten years with overheads of millions. Only one in five materializes, and we face a lot of problems. We need a large intelligence network in order to anticipate the competition. A lot of intrigue goes with it. You don't just do our work in a white shirt and tie."

So, I suggested, you have to bribe, and cheat, and generally comply with the rules of the money rush which make kung-fu seem like Girl Scout volleyball?

"It depends who you are talking about. Everyone is living with the problem of bribery. It exists in the U.S. Congress, in the House of Commons. How do people get contracts with the Pentagon? You have proved that there is corruption in your societies.

"In Saudi Arabia, we are fighting Western corruption. Lockheed wanted a decision in a hurry, and were willing to pay for it. They met a general, and he complained 'Adnan Khashoggi does not pay me,' at least clearing me of corruption, but the company was angry. They wanted to know what I did with the money. I told them it was none of their business.

"When you choose a man and he does things for you which seem to be a miracle, you pay him. Why grumble? If you want to be pure, ask him to write 'I have never bribed.' At least then you will have purified your soul. That is my recommendation to the Western world. If you know he paid a government official, that is corruption and is between society and his conscience with

God. In Saudi Arabia the official would lose his job in the morning, and be in jail in the afternoon. I was glad when the Church investigations began. It ended with Lockheed looking guilty, and me innocent.

"We try to be a really organized, professional marketing organization, and we have a few big contracts. Of course, there is no justification for a man getting five or ten percent on a contract worth $100 million, but if you are sitting in the middle of the desert, not knowing what to do, you will be more than happy to pay someone for professional advice. You could do it on your own because Saudi Arabia needs things, but you will frustrate yourself.

"Some intermediaries happen to be a friend of a prince, and maybe the poor prince enjoys playing cards with them. One day the intermediary says, 'Please, Your Highness, will you see so and so?' The prince sees him, has a cup of tea—does that make him guilty of anything? There are princes in business, but their influence is equal to everyone else. It was proved when the son of the Crown Prince was humiliated to zero over the telephone contract. That's a good example.

"Of course there are people who put out their hands because they have no money—like customs officials. If you have nothing to declare, but the officer is going to be naughty, unpack all your bags, and make you wait for two hours when you are tired and want to go home—maybe you give him money. In some eyes, that is a facility for comfort. In others, it is a bribe. How many are like me, able to complain about such treatment? Others have to submit to these weak people."

As we sat on deck watching the sun go down, his children were in the makeshift cinema on board, servants were laying gold tableware for dinner, and some exquisite girls from Paris were scenting and chiffoning themselves for an evening of pleasure. Along the Croisette, envious glances were turned toward the boat. Those stern mausoleums—the Majestic, the Splendid (without a humiliating post-Concorde "e"), *Le* Claridge for *the*—built so British Victorians could stroll in the sun and imagine they were still in Bournemouth, now have a different clientele brought by the money rush. Arabs and Persians abound.

"Look at it this way," suggests Khashoggi. "The gods are kind, and have distributed things around. If *we* had all the sea, the good weather, and so on, these poor people here would not benefit. The British, at their peak, used this as a playground. Now we do.

"At the moment in Saudi Arabia, we are at the crossroads between dependence upon the West and trying to understand ourselves. Our country is a cocktail of many things. You have a Ph.D. from Oxford, next to someone with a big position in government who hardly knows how to write his name. You see wealth side by side with poverty. But the poverty is by choice. Ninety percent of the population is not educated, and they reject certain forms of development.

"Our tradition causes misunderstandings. Women, for instance, cannot go unveiled in Saudi Arabia. But in Mecca, during the pilgrimage, they *must* open their faces. Religion calls for equal treatment of women, and it is sad that we are destroying half our society by selfish desires to keep them down and behave in the same way as our grandparents. It will definitely change.

"There is, too, a type of hypocrisy over drinking. It is the same in certain American states where there are laws against the easy access of alcohol. People are allowed privileges if they make the effort to do certain things—but you cannot give your full blessing because that would lead to overnight corruption and an uncontrollable society.

"If you are a religious family, you have to tell your children how to behave. You might be the worst father in the world, chasing girls, drunk all night, gambling. But at least when you face your son, he wants you to be perfect. That is a rule of life.

"I would not like to see the basic things in our society destroyed—the family unit, faith in Islam, which is practically the same as Christianity. Money can corrupt if you don't know how to make it enter the system slowly. What will happen if we go quicker? Look at Kuwait. All those educated people with nothing to do.

"It may be happening to an extent in Saudi Arabia, but if they don't work hard, inflation will take everything away.

"There are those who think that religion is a hindrance. I believe it is a safety valve. If you don't have a belief, you become immoral, and there is no hope for you. I am a strong believer. I cannot go to bed at night until I have prayed because it is something I was brought up with."

"It must be awkward," I said, "having to pray five times a day."

"I am lucky about that," he replied smiling. "There is dispensation for travelers. They have only to pray twice a day."

Truly the gods are kind—to some.

For me it was back to Riyadh, and the muted delights of watching a camel race with King Khalid and his guests.

15/HEDGING BETS ON THE FAMILY FARM

"The hand you cannot bite, kiss it."
BEDOU SAYING

"Last night, in bed, I was twice bitten by a marauding mouse."
JOHN WILTON, BRITISH AMBASSADOR TO SAUDI ARABIA, IN A LET-
TER TO THE TIMES, NOVEMBER 11, 1977

THE JOCKEY CLUB in Riyadh is not one of the most elegant set-
tings for the sport of kings, but it is an essential location for
money-rush supplicants. International protocol insists that state
guests are entertained at some form of spectator sport, and it
would be indelicate to invite them to a public stoning or mutila-
tion. As there are no facilities for opera, ballet, and theater, the
choice is limited to soccer or horse racing. On balance, in spite of
the millions being spent to create a national football team,
horse racing is likely to be the less boring.

Today King Khalid's guest is the Sultan of Oman, ruler of the
second largest country on the Arabian peninsula, and guardian
of what is in effect Britain's last colonial outpost in the Middle
East.

It is a meeting of some piquancy, as if an aristocratic spend-
thrift down on his luck was obliged to seek money from the village idiot who had accidentally stumbled on a fortune. Omanis
consider themselves, not without justification, to be the pa-
tricians of the Arab world. Their royal family stretches back two
hundred years, and, although the country is little known, they

feel they have developed an attitude to life based on the civilized virtues of old Britain.

Unfortunately, their oil is limited, and the Sultan is extravagant, building himself lavish palaces and giving generous gifts to foreign advisers. One is said to have received a Christmas present of £1 million in cash. Now, alas, the country is running out of money, which is why His Majesty is in Saudi Arabia (and why I was to see him a few weeks later in Iran)—apart, naturally, from the official reason: to congratulate King Khalid on his remarkable recovery from surgery in London.

In the recent past, the Saudis, with American help, have tried to claim land which the Omanis, with British backing, say is theirs. Taking advantage of this delicate dispute between two Western powers, and capitalizing on dissatisfaction within Oman, the Chinese and Cubans backed a ten-year-long civil war in the country. The Sultan, whose army has been controlled by the British Defence Ministry, sought help from other Arab countries and Iran. The Shah immediately saw the possibility of extending his influence in Arabia, as well as providing his troops with invaluable battle experience, and sent 3,000 of them. At first they made the distressing mistake of shooting each other rather more frequently than the enemy, but they improved, even though they are still known to the British as "Geraniums" because of their sensitive attitude toward the more rigorous aspects of fighting. The civil war ended officially in 1977, but embers simmer.

Except for Jordan, the Arab states did little to help. It took them several years to realize the dangerous implications of a strong Iranian presence in Oman. Now they are worried. And there is another problem: Oman controls the Arab side of the Straits of Hormuz, the potentially vulnerable 25-mile-wide gap between the Gulf and the Indian Ocean through which most of the world's oil is transported. The Sultan has to be supported. So today he is an honored client, and the Saudi elite sit in rows on the clubhouse balcony awaiting his arrival.

En masse, dressed alike in their gold-threaded *thobes*, they look indistinguishable. The faces have a pudgy, effete petulance, accentuated by the headdress, and are reminiscent of eighteenth-century European aristocrats—before the deluge. It is not surprising they look the same. The majority are the result of one man's remarkable virility and uninhibited use of *droit de seigneur;* a man who had forty-three sons (see Appendix), an unknown number of daughters, admitted to marrying 135 virgins and "hundreds of others." Perhaps understandably, he still thought the world was flat when he died in 1953.

King Abdul Aziz bin Abdulrahman al-Faisal al-Saud—known to the world as Ibn Saud, to his own people as Abdul Aziz, and to President Roosevelt's Secretary of the Navy, James Forrestal, as "Eben Sihudo, whatever his name is"—united the country which takes his family name by a combination of ruthlessness and religion which his sons and grandsons now emulate in trying to control the impenetrable problems of the money rush.

Their success is limited, but they do at least influence the world. As Prince Sattam, fortieth son, aged thirty-seven, deputy Governor of Riyadh, told me that morning, "Anything that affects us will be felt in New York, Moscow, and London. But we have only just started. I remember when we had one road and two schools. Now look at the changes, and imagine what is happening to us. It is something else."

Like most of the younger princes, he was educated in the United States and acquired a smattering of vernacular although not accompanied—as with Iranian students—by an American attitude toward democracy.

"What is democracy? It is a way of saying you have a vote and a parliament. But in England and America you can buy votes. Politicians say what people want to hear—not what they *should* be told.

"Foreigners find it difficult to understand, but we have a proper democracy here. There is no difference between a prince and a Bedouin, rich and poor. Anyone can see me without an appointment. They don't use my title. They shout 'Sattam' or 'Son of Abdul Aziz.' I shout back at them. Even the name of royalty comes from abroad. We don't have a king, we have a ruler.

"Now that we also have money, we use it to help others. All right, some of the people to whom we give think we are stupid, and people here complain we are too generous. But should we be like the Americans? Look what they do. They have all kinds of food, and then they throw away wheat at the same time as thousands of people in India are naked, starving. They are dying. Why does that happen?

"We think of the best for human beings wherever they are—even in Israel. It is the Americans and Russians who don't really want to solve the problems in the Middle East. They need to keep everyone busy—as in Vietnam. They went in there to test their weapons, and had to continue from an economic point of view. We can use our money to try to prevent it happening here, but if we carry on like this for much longer, we are going to have a war.

"Of course we are also concerned about the problems in Saudi Arabia. We have everything, including drunken driving, but we have much less crime than anywhere else in the world."

"That," I said, "is because your punishments are medieval."

"You say we are savage. Well, what do *you* do if someone comes to your house and kills your children? You say he's crazy and put him in hospital. That's not good. We have proved here that you are more secure in your house than anywhere else in the world. When we kill one person, we do it on purpose so that a million others will be thinking not to murder.

"If someone steals, we cut off his hand. It is not barbaric. He has to steal three, four times. It depends. If he is hungry and steals food, we don't cut. But if he comes to a bank, breaks down the door, and takes the money, we do cut. That will continue forever, I hope.

"There will be changes though. We need more people— 1,200,000 for projects on which we are working over the next five years—so we cannot close our doors. Everyone must come to see us, and that makes difficulties. They are not coming for a holiday. They want to make money, and they bring their problems from A to Z—traffic, residence, security. But the biggest problem is they have a lack of understanding about us. People won't tell the facts about our religion, our history, our way of life. . . ."

It is, indeed, easy to mock the progeny of Ibn Saud[1] as they sit twiddling their worry beads awaiting their guest and greeting members of the clan—cousin, uncle, brother, son, who knows? Who knows, too, if they can survive the unimaginable changes taking place around them? They realize, perhaps too late, that patriarchy is dangerously outmoded, that a country can no longer be run like a family farm. They sip their orange juice and look vacantly into the distance, thinking perhaps of London hookers and other daydreams made possible by the money rush.

"People won't tell the facts. . . ."

But where are the facts? Nobody bothered to write them down because few thought them important. The story of how the sons of Ibn Saud became pawnbrokers to the world is a classic of muddle, ignorance, and farce.

There is time, before the King arrives, to start with Round One.

Round One

Ibn Saud was born, for official purposes, on November 26, 1880. No accurate date can be ascertained because records were not kept, his mother was illiterate, and he was one of many children born into a family in decline.

A hundred years previously, the al-Saud were one of the most powerful tribes in the unprepossessing semipagan Nedj area of central Arabia. In about 1740, their leader Mohammad had been convinced by a preacher, Mohammad ibn Abdu Wahhab, that it was necessary for Arabs to return to a literal interpretation of the Koran and rid themselves of idolatry and influence of foreigners like the Ottoman Turks. Together they attempted to bludgeon others into the same belief and had a few successes. Eventually, in February 1807, their followers reached Mecca.

"At the sight of this torrent of armed and naked men, everyone fled in order to leave them the street, which they filled completely," wrote a contemporary traveler.[2] "I watched a column march past which seemed to be composed of five or six thousand men. As they marched, some gave shouts of holy joy, others in a loud voice confusedly recited prayers, each one in his own way.

"Tumult succeeded confusion. One saw them at last, like a swarm of bees moving without order around the Ka'aba, and in their tumultuous fervour smashing with muskets, which they carried on their shoulders, all the glass lamps which surrounded the House of God.

"They destroyed all the mosques consecrated to the memory of the Prophet and to those in his family; also the tombs of saints and heroes held in veneration. Constables for the punctuality of prayers were ordered to shout, to scold, and to drag people by the shoulders to force them to take part in public prayers five times a day."

Such purity may have had its reward in heaven, but on earth the al-Sauds were defeated. They eventually had to seek exile in what is now Kuwait, in order to escape from their rivals for control of the Nedj, the Rashid family.

It was from there, in 1902, that Ibn Saud, financed by the Emir of Kuwait, led a raiding party of forty men against Riyadh, which the Rashid family had made their headquarters. They attacked at night, capturing the harem, and waited until the following morning for the head of the family to return from the fort where he deposited himself overnight for safety.

Ibn Saud described what happened: "I struck him first on the leg, and disabled him; quickly after that I struck at the neck; the head fell to one side—the blood spurted up like a fountain. The third blow was at the heart. I saw the heart, which was cut in two, palpitate like that." He illustrated with a shiver of his hand. "It was a joyous moment. I kissed the sword."

After the battle, he began to convert the numerous wild tribes of Arabia by sending missionaries, called *ikhwan* (brotherhood), to develop an agricultural policy and spread the word of Wahhabism. Their slogan was "Back to the Koran and the Land," and Ibn Saud managed with some subtlety not to arouse the jealousy of either the tribes or the *ulemas*. "You owe nothing to me," he said. "I am like you, one of you. But I am appointed to direct the affairs of our people in accordance with the Book of Allah. Our first duty is to Allah and to those who teach the Book of Allah, the *ulemas*. I am but an instrument of command in their hand. Obedience to God means obedience to them."

When subtlety failed, executions were substituted, as they are today, without trial or any possibility of an appeal and became memorable events "the talk of caravans hundreds of miles away." Philby witnessed several. "In a matter of seconds after the three men had been placed in position, the first head was off, rolling in the dust, while the body fell forward with blood spouting from the neck. The second man instinctively turned his head to meet the coming blow, with the result that the sword just failed to sever the head from the trunk as the victim toppled over. Then a few rapid steps and a backhanded sweep of the executioner's sword did their work so cleanly that the headless corpse of the third criminal remained on its knees spouting blood upwards. The execution was over, and the police proceeded to lash the three corpses, each with its head by its side, to the railings. The proceedings had been rapid and efficient, without fuss or noise, and it was only the curious goggling crowd of pushing, jostling sightseers that created a slight feeling of nausea. Faisal [Ibn Saud's son] remained seated for a few moments after it was all over, till the executioner came up to report the completion of his task. "God bless you," said Faisal simply, adding for my benefit, "It is as well to commend them for doing their duty, so that they may do it better next time."

There was one additional method of persuasion, more diplomatic and presumably less hazardous, which Ibn Saud used to consolidate his influence: marriage. He started with the Rashids, marrying the widow, and later the granddaughter, of the defeated leader. But he did not break God's law. He never had more than four wives at a time, and restricted himself to two new ones a year as he became older.

Each wife had a house of her own, which he visited in rotation. His own home was run by four favorite concubines, and he also slept with four slave girls, on different days, as well as numerous others (sometimes not even removing their veils), who were then passed on to privileged courtiers.

"He has Christian girls, also. Ask him for one. He will present one to you," a visitor, Ameen Rihani, was told. His Finance Minister recalled, "He once presented me with a Georgian girl. She was brought to him from Buraidah, and after he had entered her —one night only—he gave her to me. Never in my life have I seen or heard of such august beauty.

"Her skin—white as alabaster. Her hair—like cataracts of melted gold. Her lips—red as pomegranate seed. Her forehead—lofty and glowing like the dawn. I sat before that image of beauty, like a child, and I felt shame upon me. I was ashamed to touch her. I got up and walked out of the room. And on the following day, I sold her to a man from Kuwait for 400 rials. Only 400."

(The Finance Minister did not always receive such perks. One day, when he was in his sixties, he made an error over some trivial matter. Ibn Saud ordered him to walk barefoot from Riyadh to the east coast, a distance of 200 kilometers. The minister was away for two days before he was rescued and brought back to Riyadh.)

Ibn Saud was a good-looking, tall, impressive man, much given to dousing himself with perfume, with a virility confirmed by the numbers of his children but perhaps exaggerated by stories that he had a different woman every night from the age of eleven until he died in 1953.

Nonetheless, at least one visitor claims he could set his watch by the mounting anxiety as harem hour approached. At 4:00 (equivalent to 9:00 P.M.—he was on Muslim Sun Time), Ibn Saud would finish whatever he was doing and depart for the house of one of his wives. "What do you folk know about love, who take one wife and then sleep in different beds? Why, the longest winter night is all too short for me. Even when I settle down to rest, I wake from time to time to embrace my companion. And sometimes I do it in my sleep," he boasted.

His interest in women was uniquely pelvic-oriented, and he allowed himself to be shocked by Western morality—dancing, adultery, even dining in mixed company. For years he never saw a woman eat or drink, including his own mother, and although Princess Alice, Countess of Athlone, established a notable precedent in 1938 when she attended a state banquet in Jidda, his sons and grandsons remain much influenced by his attitude. "When a technocratic minister invites you to dinner, you meet his wife and can pretend you are in a civilized country," says a diplomat in Jidda, "but the royal princes hardly ever bring their wives."

Their father had strong ideas. "It is permissible for women to read the Koran and scriptural literature," he declared, "but ordinary reading, and especially writing, is an accomplishment regarded as unsuitable in a woman, although not forbidden."

As a devout Muslim he looked forward to Paradise, where, he believed, God normally allowed each man seventy whores and up to four wives. He wanted to take six, and told friends that he thought God might allow this dispensation in view of his rather unusual marital status. His first wife, Bint al Fiqri, who died within six months of their marriage when Ibn Saud was fifteen years old, remained a fond memory throughout his life. But his most powerful liaison was with Hassa bint Ahmad al-Sudairi, whose seven sons (see Appendix) provide the most influential clique in Saudi Arabia.

During his lifetime, Ibn Saud allowed few of his sons any authority, and he treated them like children even when they were well into their thirties. As the country became more wealthy, they had little to do but indulge themselves, and it is not surprising that a family of such diverse cross-breeding sustains more sexual and social quirks than the average two-child household.

It contains within it extremes from the late voluptuary King Saud to the priggish Vice Minister for the Interior, Prince Ahmad, but the most powerful member is Crown Prince Fahd, the senior Sudairi, and effective ruler of the country. His chief rival is Prince Abdullah, Commander of the National Guard, whose mother was from the al-Saud's traditional enemies, the Shammar tribe. Now, too, the eight sons of King Faisal (in particular, Foreign Minister Prince Saud), and some of King Saud's estimated fifty-two sons, begin to clamor for attention. As the leader is chosen in family conclave, and is not automatically the eldest son, these antagonisms, temporarily swamped by the money rush, provide seeds for future conflict. They have already made the ailing Khalid a compromise King.

Time out to pay respects as he arrives at the races.

Outside the Jockey Club, soldiers of the National Guard stand to attention as a black Rolls Royce glides to the door. There is polite applause, but little excitement, as the King and his guest disembark and go through the clubhouse and onto the balcony.

The King is stooped, and walks with the aid of a stick. He looks more frail than usual standing next to the tall, full-bearded Sultan, who is elegantly turbaned and accompanied by a swarm of young aides and a few smooth-looking Lebanese gentlemen dressed in Savile Row suits who clutch black Samsonite briefcases. Some of the younger Omanis carry paper bags and boxes, which they hide discreetly under their chairs. They look as if they have just visited the January sales in Oxford Street.

In front of the clubhouse there are a few pieces of wispy grass, but the racetrack itself is of hard sand which, when loosened, drifts with the wind into the stand, caressing everyone with a film of dust. The King and his guest sit together at a wooden table on which is placed a silver cup and a massive pair of binoculars which they use from time to time. An endless tide of liquid refreshment is brought forth—tea, water, orange juice, and more tea. The King sips water.

As there is no betting, emotions are muted, and the finer qualities of racing are admired. The King has banned the import of foreign horses, believing the local variety to be superior, and indeed every thoroughbred racehorse in the world is descended from one of three Arab stallions imported into Europe between 1687 and 1729.[3]

Today one of the King's horses is running. It will win. More proof, he thinks, that Arab horses are still best. He is in for a shock.

Round Two

In the early years of the century, Ibn Saud carried his family's revenue in the saddlebag of his camel. It soon became insufficient to provide for the wives, mistresses, and children he gathered with immodest haste as one tribe after another succumbed to his *ikhwan*. Moreover, the Rashids were being financed by the Turks, and the feud with them was rekindled.

At the start of the First World War, Ibn Saud was virtually bankrupt, and therefore gladly signed an agreement with the British to remain neutral in return for $120,000 a year, four machine guns, and 3,000 old rifles. One of his enemies, the Sherif of Mecca, Hussein, became more actively involved. Promised support for an independent Arab state after the war, Hussein fought against the Turks (helped by his liaison officer, T. E. Lawrence). He did not know that the British and the French had already agreed on a secret postwar carve-up of the Middle East which would suit their own ambitions and rivalries regardless of traditional Arab aspirations, and would be the basis for suspicions which today determine the results of the money rush. Ibn Saud's domain was left independent because no one really wanted it.

His battles with the tribes continued, culminating in victory after which he proclaimed himself King of the Hijaz. On September 23, 1932, the new nation of Saudi Arabia was declared. He still had no money, but now he had potential and could aspire to become less of a client and more of a partner to the Western nations who had been competing for his as-yet-unrecognized favors.

British and French tactics after the First World War seemed to indicate an attitude of postcolonial aggrandizement which irritated and alarmed America, so the world's first energy crisis was manufactured. In January 1920, a United States Geological Survey reported that the situation "can best be characterized as precarious," and claimed that within five years America would be totally dependent upon Britain for oil supplies.

Although this was not true, the British eventually agreed to split up the Turkish Petroleum Company, formed in 1914 by Armenian financier Calouste Gulbenkian. In a new consortium renamed Iraq Petroleum Company (IPC), Gulbenkian retained his famous 5 percent, Esso, Mobil, and Gulf had a 23.75 percent share, as did Compagnie Française de Petroles. Anglo-Persian and Royal Dutch Shell kept 47.5 percent. There was one condition: the British and Gulbenkian insisted the partners should not compete against each other anywhere within the Ottoman Empire.

But where *was* the Ottoman Empire?

It had been broken up by the First World War, and simple oilmen could not be expected to understand the complexities of international boundaries. They met to discuss the problem, and spent hours in inconclusive bickering until Gulbenkian produced a red pencil, drew a circle round most of the Middle East, including Saudi Arabia, and announced, "That was the Ottoman Empire which I knew in 1914, and I ought to know. I was born in it, lived in it, and served in it. If anyone knows better, carry on."

Thus the major oil companies excluded themselves from the world's largest bonanza, although neither they nor Ibn Saud realized it for many years.

In 1922 Ibn Saud was in a tent at Al-Hasa, an uncomfortable oasis in the east of his territories, awaiting the arrival of the British High Commissioner to Baghdad, Sir Percy Cox. Sir Percy brought money, but he was already three days late. A lavish tent, away from the Arab encampment, had been provided for him, equipped with a bathroom, Johnnie Walker whisky, cigars, and other luxuries which Ibn Saud thought a gentleman might require. "Let us have a little civilization," he suggested mockingly as he waited, and ordered tea with milk to be served in large cups rather than black coffee in small bowls as was his custom.

"This is civilized tea and the English drink it not as we drink our coffee, like this," he said, slurping, "but without noise, like this." And he sipped gently. "You see, we are not very far from civilization—a few steps, only."

Sir Percy arrived at last, and behaved in fine colonial fashion, dressing in a dinner jacket (he had an excuse—the dining room was furnished with elaborate decorations from Bombay, London, Paris, and Havana), and scribbling notes in pencil to Ibn Saud demanding a written guarantee of "friendship" in return for the annual $120,000.

"We have had too much of civilization," said a disgusted Ibn Saud to Ameen Rihani one evening as he left Sir Percy's tent. "Who are the Arabs? We are the Arabs. The trouble with the Arab is that he will not do anything in which his own interest is not paramount. We have discovered treachery among the closest of our allies. Two fundamental things are essential to our state and our people: religion, and the rights inherited from our fathers.

"People think we are receiving large sums of money from the English, but they have only paid small sums considering our services on their behalf. What we have done for them during and after the war, no other Arab could do. And yet, see what they have done to me. They spin nets for me.

"When the English want something, they get it. When we want something, we have to fight for it. I will put my seal if Great Britain says, 'You must.' But I will strike when I can, not in betrayal, but in self-defence. When I cede my rights under force, I will get back when I have sufficient force, *insha'allah.*"[4]

Ironically, the man who was to be an indirect agent of revenge was only a few yards away. Major Frank Holmes, a rough New Zealander posing as a butterfly collector, had in fact been sent by a London syndicate to acquire oil concessions in Arabia, and arrived a few days after Sir Percy. The High Commissioner was appalled that such a man dared to intrude on Britain's chaps in the desert. It was like a tramp entering one's club and making a pass at the hatcheck girl. He warned Ibn Saud that any agreement with Holmes was a breach of contract and the subsidy would stop. But Ibn Saud, taunted that he was being blackmailed by the British Government, humiliated by the haughtiness of Sir Percy, and determined not to lose any more of his coveted independence, sold Holmes the concession anyway—for $4,000 a year, fair price for what he considered to be a useless 60,000 square miles of sand.

At first it seemed Ibn Saud was correct. Holmes found no oil, was unable to sell his concession to any of the American companies, stopped paying the rental, and left for the island of Bahrain twelve miles off the Saudi coast. There he was more successful. He found some indication of oil and sold the concession to Gulf for $50,000 (after it had been turned down by Esso). Gulf, however, could do nothing on their own because Bahrain was within the "Red Line," drawn by Gulbenkian, and Anglo-Persian refused to participate because its geologist did not consider it a feasible risk. So, in 1928, Gulf sold out to the Standard Oil Company of California (SoCal), which had turned frantically to the Middle East after losing millions of dollars in unsuccessful prospecting in Ecuador, Alaska, Venezuela, and Mexico.

No one warned SoCal that Bahrain was yet another British sphere of influence, and only British companies were allowed to operate there. It took nearly two years to overcome this problem by registering a subsidiary in Canada (Bapco—the Bahrain Petroleum Company), setting up an office in London, and appointing a British, albeit a colonial, representative in Bahrain: Major Frank Holmes.

Meanwhile, Ibn Saud was increasingly debt-ridden and frustrated. Although he had used the fanaticism of the *ulemas* to help establish his own authority, he found their missionary fervor tiresome. They made his capital Riyadh into a morgue where it was hazardous for ordinary people to walk down the street looking happy for fear of harassment by religious police. Their power over superstitious nomads was absolute—which is why he had used them himself—but now he needed to progress, and to do that he employed tricks.

The introduction of the telephone was his first opportunity. The *ulemas* naturally opposed it because telephones were not mentioned in the Koran. "Do you think," he asked them, "that the devil would carry the words of God?"

Of course not, they replied.

"Very well, then, I will read some verses from the Koran over the telephone."

After that, they had to accept grudgingly a network of wireless stations on which the King spent large amounts of money, as he did on water supplies and his even more elaborate personal household. He bought motorcars by the dozen, although he could hardly use them because of lack of gasoline, and he still had to bribe enemies and placate the poor. "As the long returning procession of cars approached the palace, the road on either side was lined with black-veiled women and children, old men, and cripples from the town and neighbouring villages, all hopeful of royal bounty," wrote Philby. "One of the two bodyguard slaves, always in attendance on the king in his outings, and standing on the running-boards of the car, would leap to the ground as the car slowed down and receive the sack of silver from the royal hands for distribution of its contents among the waiting suppliants."

The pilgrimage trade was declining because of a world slump and the British would not increase their handout, Ibn Saud's only other source of income, without considerable restraints and rigorous conditions. There was only one practical source for new income: Russia. The Soviet Government had been first to recognize the Wahhabis in 1926, thinking them a progressive regime in a backward area. They upgraded their consulate and sent a Muslim minister to Jidda. Ibn Saud was not keen on Russians because, he had been told, they slept with their mothers and sisters. But now, in 1931, he had to accept their offers of aid. His debts had risen to $800,000, he had stopped paying bills, delayed the salaries of officials, and declared, "If anyone would offer me a million pounds, I would give him all the concessions he wanted."

It was, at the time, an absurdly inflated hope. The major companies had far too much oil, and their disinterest in discovering any more was so complete that Ibn Saud had to rely on the generosity of an American philanthropist, Charles Crane, who visited Jidda in February 1931. Crane, who had previously been in the area studying date culture, inherited a fortune from his family's bathroom fixture business and spent his life trying to promote peace and understanding between Arab nations and the West. He agreed to pay for a geologist, Karl Twitchell, to examine the country's mineral resources. Delighted, Ibn Saud presented Crane with two pedigreed stallions. Crane, equally delighted, gave Ibn Saud the most exotic and unusual gift he could imagine: a $1 box of California dates!

Twitchell immediately saw the high potential of Saudi Arabia and tried unsuccessfully to involve the major oil companies before he was approached by SoCal, whose discoveries in Bahrain encouraged the company to look toward the mainland. SoCal also hired Philby, whose commitments, although less ostentatious than the King's, were causing financial hardship at a time when his income from a Ford dealership was static. He had three daughters to support, and a son, Kim, at Cambridge. He signed a secret agreement with SoCal which paid $1,000 a month for advice, $10,000 if SoCal won the concession, and $25,000 if oil was found in commercial quantities. At the same time, he contacted the opposition, writing to a friend in Anglo-Persian, Martin Lees. "Financial stringency is beginning to open the doors of Arabia to industrial exploitation," he said and implied that he might represent the company.

Anglo-Persian decided, instead, to send their own man, Stephen Hemsley Longrigg, to battle with SoCal's Californian lawyer, Lloyd Hamilton, who arrived in Jidda in February 1933. Philby acted as intermediary between them and Ibn Saud who insisted, at first, on a down payment of $200,000 in gold.

This was twenty times more than Longrigg was authorized to pay, and, he confided to Philby, the company did not really want the concession. It was more concerned in keeping out the Americans. After some persuasion, Anglo-Persian increased its offer to $20,000, but payment could not be in gold—that would suggest the pound was unreliable. From then on, Anglo-Persian was out of the race.

Hamilton, who had brought his wife on what he assumed would be a quick business trip, is the first recorded Western victim of the IBM syndrome. Talks dragged on until April 20, when it was finally agreed that SoCal would pay $60,000 immediately, a further $40,000 in eighteen months, and $10,000 a year rent. Payment would be in gold.

That day, in the United States, President Roosevelt banned the export of gold without Treasury permission because there had been a series of bank failures. In Jidda, frantic bargaining resumed, while SoCal requested an export license for gold worth $170,327.50, and Washington bureaucrats took time to study and ponder the issue. The delay seemed endless. Ibn Saud became restless and pressed for payment within three months of signing an agreement on May 29.

Finally, in July, a desperate SoCal representative went to London, bought 35,000 gold sovereigns illegally, and transported them to Saudi Arabia by ship where they were counted and accepted by Finance Minister Shaikh Abdullah Sulaiman. Two days later, SoCal at last received a reply from the U.S. Treasury, signed by Undersecretary Dean Acheson. It regretted that they could not have an export license for gold.

By now, though, the Americans had won the round, in spite of punching in the wrong direction and being almost tripped by their own supporters in the closing seconds. The pace was quickening, and the next round would see international duplicity of a more spectacular kind.

In the interval after the fourth race, one of King Khalid's aides handed boxes to the Sultan and members of his entourage who were sitting in the front row of the balcony. Hurriedly, the Sultan's young men reached under their seats for the plastic bags from which they took several small leather boxes. These were passed reverently to King Khalid and senior members of his government amidst much applause and apparent delight, although the ritual exchange of gold commemorative medallions on every conceivable occasion must by now benefit only Western jewelers with an aptitude for such work.

Spontaneous generosity is endearing when not overdone, but the Saudis' reputation is such that some Western guests now sit, waiting, in the expectation that every meeting with a prince will end with a Piaget. That used to be almost true, but the gifts are now more restricted to wandering statesmen or visiting ambassadors and their wives, causing unexpected financial anguish on return home. Ambassadors are not required to pay customs duty on such gifts, which can sometimes mount up to thousands of pounds, but their wives are. Many a London jeweler has watches sold to him by the wives of ambassadors who could not afford the duty.

But . . . to the racing. The King's horse is running, a fine specimen which duly wins against competition from European thoroughbreds, much to his delight. "There you are," he tells friends. "We can do it." It is the first time he looks happy that afternoon.

"Of course, of course," say those around him, smiling and clapping.

It takes a brave man to tell him, later that evening, that his horse, a present from a member of the family, is imported from France. But nothing is ever as it seems in Saudi Arabia, as so many people are discovering.

Round Three

SoCal drilled nine dry holes in the next five years and had almost decided that the expense, already $30 million, was too great for further exploration, when engineers returned to a previous well in the rocky hills overlooking the Gulf port of Dammam. They drilled deeper, and, on March 4, 1938, struck oil at what became known as Dammam Number 7. The foundations of the Saudi Arabian money rush were irrevocably set, although again it did not seem so at the time.

A year later, Ibn Saud pressed a valve on a pipeline, was presented with another car, and his country had begun oil exporting—only to find it limited a few months later when World War Two broke out. At the same time, there was another drop in pilgrimage traffic, a drought killed crops and dried up the water supply, and Ibn Saud—once more broke—asked SoCal for a loan.

"We believe that unless this is done, and soon, this independent kingdom and perhaps the entire Arab world, will be thrown into chaos," the company wrote to Roosevelt in an attempt to have Saudi Arabia included in the Lend-Lease program.

But there was no legal loophole to allow this, so the American Government prevaricated—what were a few desert Arabs in relation to their own war preparations?—and Roosevelt asked his Federal Loan Administrator, Jesse Jones, to "tell the British I hope they can take care of the King of Saudi Arabia. This is a little too far afield for us!"[5] The British, although gentlemen, can be devious when self-interest is involved, and it took the Americans two years to realize they were being duped. Almost $33 million of their money, given in the form of Lend-Lease, was used by the British to buy popularity with Ibn Saud.[6] At the same time, a geological expedition of 500 from London, disguised as a locust-control squad, investigated the oil potential.

"It's one of the few things you can be sure," fumed Navy Secretary James Forrestal, in a telephone call to President Roosevelt, "you can say today it is one of the great, important stakes for this country . . . that stack of oil is something this country damn well ought to have, and we've lost a good deal of our position with this Shaikh—Eben Sihudo, whatever his name is—and we are losing more every day."

Roosevelt decided, "I hereby find the defense of Saudi Arabia is vital to the defense of the United States," and began to lend money direct—$28 million in the next two years, which was frittered away on extravagances—and sent his personal representative, Patrick Hurley, to see Ibn Saud. "I found many manifestations of [his] confidence in America," reported Hurley, "and of his eagerness that American interests rather than those of any other foreign power, so often instrumentalities for political penetration, should assist the Saudi Arabian Government in the development of the natural resources of the country."

Now the two Western leaders, Churchill and Roosevelt, preoccupied as they were with everyday death and destruction, began to shadowbox in preparation for the future.

"There is apprehension in some quarters here that the United States has a desire to deprive us of our oil assets in the Middle East on which among other things, the whole supply of our Navy depends," Churchill cabled Roosevelt.

Roosevelt replied, "I am disturbed about the rumor that the British wish to horn in on Saudi Arabian oil reserves."

After further "friendly" exchanges, Churchill added, "Thank you very much for your assurances about no sheep's eyes at our [!] oilfields in Iran and Iraq. Let me reciprocate by giving you fullest assurance that we have no thought to trying to horn in upon your interests in Saudi Arabia. My position is this as in all matters is that Great Britain seeks no advantage, territorial or otherwise, as a result of the war. On the other hand she will not be deprived of anything which rightly belongs to her after having given her best services to the good cause—at least not so long as your humble servant is entrusted with the conduct of her affairs."

American diplomats now felt it was time to stop the British habit of tying innocent undeveloped countries to contracts and treaties which made them dependent forever. On the last day of the Yalta Conference in December 1944, President Roosevelt casually said that he would see Ibn Saud before returning to the United States, an announcement which infuriated Churchill and caused him to "burn up all the wires" in vain attempts to arrange a prior meeting, according to U.S. Minister in Jidda, Colonel William Eddy.[7]

The King left Riyadh in magisterial fashion, with 200 cars carrying his harem and members of the court, for Jidda, where the U.S. destroyer *Murphy* was waiting to take him to the meeting on board the U.S. *Quincy*, at Great Bitter Lake, just below Suez. The *Murphy*'s captain, horrified at the sight of such a retinue, said he could accommodate only the King, four advisers, and eight servants. A compromise was reached: forty-eight men altogether.

On board, the Saudis erected a tent and set up a throne. They refused the ship's distilled water, sent ashore for a local brand, and then asked permission for eighty-six live sheep to come on board so that food could be prepared according to Muslim rites. Another compromise: ten sheep were allowed.

President Roosevelt, sick, tired, and dying, was less demanding of his own traditional comforts when the two leaders met on board the *Quincy*. A chain smoker, he restricted himself to a few puffs in the ship's elevator so as not to offend his guest with even a hint of tobacco smoke. The men had an immediate rapport. Roosevelt discussed farming, as he had with the Shah, and gave Ibn Saud his spare wheelchair after the King, arthritic from battle wounds, admired it. He cherished the gift, although it was too small for him, as he did the official present of a DC-3 Dakota which became the foundation of Saudi Arabia's somewhat chaotic national airline, Saudia.

In their discussions, Roosevelt promised to do nothing which could be considered hostile to Arab interests. Two months later, he was dead, and Ibn Saud, who did not understand the realities of American democracy, was about to feel hoodwinked again.

After meeting Roosevelt, the King was driven incognito through Egypt, via Cairo (the first large city he had ever seen), to a hastily evacuated Hôtel du Lac in Rayum, where Churchill awaited. It was an inauspicious occasion. "A number of social problems arose. I had been told that neither smoking nor alcoholic beverages were allowed in the Royal Presence," wrote Churchill.[8] "As I was host at luncheon I raised the matter at once, and said if it was the religion of His Majesty to deprive himself of smoking and alcohol I must point out that my rule of life prescribed as an absolutely sacred rite smoking cigars and also drinking of alcohol before, after, and if need be during all meals and in the intervals between them. The King graciously accepted the position. His own cup bearer from Mecca offered me a glass of water from its sacred well, the most delicious that I have ever tasted."

The exchange of presents was also embarrassing, and left a niggardly impression after Roosevelt's generosity. Churchill gave Ibn Saud $200 worth of perfume bought in Cairo. The King reciprocated with diamond-encrusted gold swords and a large box of jewels which he presented to Sarah Churchill "for your womenfolk."

"It appeared that we were rather outclassed in gifts," said Churchill, "so I told the King, 'What we bring are but tokens. His Majesty's Government have [*sic*] decided to present you with the finest motor-car in the world, with every comfort for peace and every security against hostile action.'"

An armor-plated Rolls Royce was duly delivered, but it had right-hand drive and remained unused because the King liked to travel in the front and would not sit on the left side of a chauffeur because, at that time, it was considered demeaning. There was one consolation for the British taxpayer: under government rules, gifts received at a state occasion have to be given to the Treasury. Money raised by selling the jewels "for your womenfolk" paid for the Rolls.

America's domination of Saudi Arabia was consolidated after the war despite vigorous competition from British and French arms firms and help given to the National Guard by soldiers imported from the British Army. Everything was done to satisfy the increasingly profligate and rapidly multiplying members of the ruling family. Oil royalties were sent direct to Ibn Saud himself—$38 million in 1949—and when he complained it was not enough and that Aramco paid more in U.S. tax, accountants devised a new system whereby part of the tax went to the King. This satisfied everyone, except perhaps American taxpayers who increasingly subsidized Saudi Arabia. But they were not told.

By now Ibn Saud was in decline. His life had spanned too many changes, too rapidly, for him to comprehend the complex maneuverings of the postwar world. It was a traumatic journey from hacking off a rival's head with a jeweled sword to defending himself against ruthlessly competitive arms salesmen; from swapping dirty jokes with cronies in the desert to discussing the finer points of Oligocene-Miocene formations with buttoned-down Ivy League geologists; from bullying by the British to sycophancy from international con men.

He sank into a shell, ignoring the excesses of many of his sons who, released from the danger of his frightening displeasure, turned every night and day into party time, with imported whores (some of whom still live in Riyadh unseen and forgotten), alcohol, and colored electric light bulbs to add final twinkling touches to the vulgarity of their gimcrack palaces.

Their father, depressed and disillusioned, dyed his hair with henna to ward off visible signs of age, but could do nothing about the famed tumescence now activated only by the sight of a fresh young virgin. On one of his few overseas visits—to see King Farouk in Egypt—he murmured wistfully one night, "There are some nice girls in this country. I wouldn't mind picking a bunch of them to take back to Arabia—say $200,000 worth of the beauties." He was a sad man now, swindled by relatives, deceived by advisers, let down finally by his own body. His genius had been to create a united country from a group of traditional enemies. It was for others to build a nation, to provide schools, hospitals, and homes for a poverty-ridden peasant society. Ibn Saud died of a heart attack on November 9, 1953 and was succeeded by his eldest surviving son, Saud, who built himself a homestead suitably in keeping with this new honor: the $25 million al-Nassariyah compound, which included a palace for each of his four wives and thirty-two mansions for concubines. Half of Riyadh's electricity supply was used on its air-conditioning system.

Saud's epic debauchery was manipulated skillfully by the CIA, who provided him with boys and girls, and overlooked by Aramco—now a consortium of SoCal, Texaco, Esso, and Mobil—which created an isolated, American-style encampment near the oil fields in Dhahran. They understand the perils of becoming involved in ideological arguments with the King—they would be thrown out of the country—and their program of building schools, hospitals and a railway link between Dhahran and Riyadh was described several years later by Management Developments Director Mel Lafrenz as "simply a realistic appraisal of what we ought to do to stay here as long as we could. We did not do this to be Big Daddy.[9] The British agreed. They said that every time the King sneezed, Aramco built a new hospital.

In 1972 the Saudi Government bought a 25 percent holding in the company for $500 million, later increased to 60 percent in preparation for total nationalization. Americans still hold 3,500 of the 22,000 jobs, but will become less active as tax laws make working abroad uneconomic. "An American would not leave home for the sort of money you can pay the British," says an Aramco director. "Also, they won't come here on bachelor status, which the British will." The company continues to initiate progress—sometimes unlawfully, as I discovered previously—but in the early years, caution was essential.

King Saud was fortunate. Although the money rush which was to give new agility to Saudi Arabia's apologists had not yet begun, he lived in an era of paranoid anti-Communism. As President Eisenhower proclaimed in 1957, before inviting him on a state visit, "The existing vacuum in the Middle East must be filled by the United States before it is filled by Russia."

For altruistic reasons, of course.

At the time, Saud was receiving $350 million a year, but he still managed to run up debts of $500 million. It was clear to members of the family that he would have to be deposed, but such action was anathema to his chosen successor, Faisal, as religious as his brother was riotous, who insisted on sanction from the *ulemas*. When this was forthcoming, Saud was paid off with a $3 million a year pension, and exiled. A new era in the short, seesaw history of Saudi Arabia began.

"We are a simple family," explained Faisal to the credulous, as he declined exotic trappings and drove to work in a Chrysler. He married four times (one dead, two divorced) but lived with his favorite, Iffat, for forty-two years (four daughters, five sons). After the excesses of his brother, honest banality was a welcome change, and he illustrated his vaunted simplicity with a remark about the twin devils, Communists and Jews. "Never forget Karl Marx was a Jew." But at least he pushed the country forward— although it still needs a shove.

Faisal abolished slavery by buying nearly 2,000 slaves from the shaikhs for $2,000 each and setting them free. Against strong *ulema* opposition, he introduced girls' education in 1960 and television two years later, innovations which may seem modest in the West but caused uproar in a country where women are biological playthings, and Koranic interpretation of idolatry is so fundamentalist that heads are removed from human figures on imported road-crossing signs. The ensuing riots ended in deaths, and, indirectly, his own assassination.

On March 25, 1975, Prince Faisal bin Musa'id, a twenty-six-year-old nephew, walked into the King's *majlis* (conference room) and shot him in the head three times. At first, it was thought this could be a plot by other Arab countries—Libya? Yemen?—to foment revolt. In fact, though, Prince Faisal was the brother of one of the men shot by police during the television-station riots, and he was merely seeking traditional bedouin revenge.

The feudal farm has many shareholders, and those who understand families will realize why that alone is enough cause for the al-Sauds to be nervous, the Americans to be protective, the Russians to be covetous, and the Iranians amused. "If I was in Saudi Arabia, Billy would be Crown Prince," President Carter joked in Washington, an observation which brought a wan response from Crown Prince Fahd. He has quite enough nouveau riche nincompoops in the family.

All that, without the additional perplexities of power they did not seek, authority they do not deserve, and a money rush with which they cannot cope.

Camels are now racing at Riyadh Jockey Club, lurching around the track in ungainly fashion, a young Saudi perched behind the hump looking as if he might fall off at any moment and thrashing the beast with a stick in gallant but hopeless attempts to make it trot faster. The scene recalls grandmothers in an egg-and-spoon race: no one denies they can do it, but the aesthetic, intellectual, or even veterinary fascination is not immediately obvious. Perhaps it is an acquired taste, like cricket.

The sons of Ibn Saud and their sons and their cousins, watch the visitor from Oman stony-faced. How much has he been given this time, and how long will the King scatter money to buy off the greedy, inept, and politically vulnerable? Saudi Arabia donates at least one-seventh of its income in aid, forty times more than the proportion given by the United States.[10] There is financial support for most Arab countries, the PLO, and a variety of miscellaneous items ranging from mosques in Regent's Park and Geneva to a $15 million sports stadium in Bahrain, $500 million for Jordan's Hawk missiles (the cash is sent direct to Washington, lest it be dissolved by King Hussein's enthusiastic overspending on nonmilitary projects). Sometimes the generosity has unexpected results. Many Yemenis, who provide more than a million of the labor force, returned home when Saudi money enabled their own countries to develop.

North and South Yemen, with their opposing political loyalties and strategic location at the entrance to the Red Sea, are particular targets for Saudi blandishments. Historically, the Yemens are one country, but they have rarely been united. South Yemen, known as the People's Democratic Republic of Yemen (PDYR), was the British colony of Aden for over a century until 1967 when it began to become the first Marxist state and Russian foothold in Arabia. In order to discourage its support of an uprising in neighboring Oman, Saudi Arabia offered $800 million "aid," a gesture which led indirectly in July 1978 to the execution of moderate President Salem Robei Ali and his replacement by a stronger pro-Soviet regime. The continuing buildup of Cuban soldiers and East German civil-service "advisers" is a problem which can no longer be solved with money.

North Yemen, also known as the Yemen Arab Republic is more susceptible. It received a down payment of $600 million and a continuing commitment of at least $100 million a year to thwart Russian influence. But it remains one of the world's least stable countries, with tribal and religious differences making a perfect target for "destabilization," and close ties with Saudi Arabia do not provide adequate life insurance for its leaders. Two presidents were murdered in nine months between 1977 and 1978.

Charity has another price, too. "Everyone becomes very religious in the presence of a Saudi," explains a diplomat in Jidda. "When King Khalid went to Kuwait in 1976, he told them they must do away with pork and porn. Go back now and see how easy it is to buy bacon or a tit magazine. The thing is, you don't pick your nose in front of your rich aunt. You wait until she is round the corner and not watching."

Also, you try to pay an annual visit to demonstrate your affection. Pilgrims, so important to Ibn Saud, are roused in their millions by the money rush (nearly 2 million in 1978), so that a fifth of Mecca will soon be covered with parking lots and roads. Jidda, the world's fastest-growing city, has increased its budget 270 times since 1971. A few years ago, it had no proper roads and no piped water. Now it has a Dior boutique, jewelry shops, Henry Moore sculptures, Italian street lamps, decorative gardens, and such high rents that a property owner recoups his investment in two years. The road from the airport to the center of town has not changed for centuries, however: it still sells high-priced junk, with mediocre Persian carpets a specialty.

Whenever the grandsons of Ibn Saud return from studying abroad (one out of every thousand Saudis is educated in the United States), they see physical changes undreamed-of only five years ago, but the old taboos remain the same. Prince Faisal bin

Abdullah, twenty-nine, was a student at Stanford and bought a 264-acre ranch in the Portola Valley, California. He spends six months there, and six months in Riyadh. "I miss the freedoms when I return home, but I really do believe that at the heart of it, there is a lot of superficiality in the West.

"In our world money is the name of the game, and you can destroy life with it. We have to ask ourselves why we are doing things and where we are going. The main thing that worries me is the concept that people who have come from nothing are going to act too grand because of a stroke of luck. Sometimes I really pity ourselves."

Surprisingly, nearly all the students do return. Unlike Iranians, half of whom stayed abroad, according to private estimates made by former Prime Minister Amouzegar, the Saudis seem content to sacrifice intellectual luxuries of Western democracy for the tedious conformity of their own country. Are they mad? Are they anesthetized by cascades of money into a belief that the pampering and self-indulgence of private life amongst the elite in Riyadh is a substitute for real life? Or are they so mesmerized by the rapidity and confusion of the money rush that radical feelings are suppressed because they fear that any political change will be catastrophic?

That most famous "simple Bedouin," Shaikh Zaki Yamani, who can be a little too "simple," a little too charming, a bit too smooth and smug, adds in his slow, well-modulated Arab-American accent, "There will be great changes in the next few years as people return from university and some of our projects are finished. Our great challenge is not to lose our muscle. Look what happened to the Kuwaitis. They have gone all soft. None of them work. That must not happen to us.

"We must keep positive things like our democracy. Yes, this is a real democracy. Anyone can go to the King and say, 'Look, Khalid, this is not right.' Can you imagine people telling the Shah what was wrong with Iran? That's the difference between our societies."

It is true that the offices of the family farm are open to all, yet Saudi Arabia is incubating revolution. "The evil day is inevitable," says a banker. "If you pay everyone enough, all you can do is postpone it." And when it comes, the only hope is that it will be bloodless because the armed forces are too incompetent to use the extraordinary numbers of lethal weapons which are being swapped for oil.

The military provides the country's best vaudeville. As King Khalid leaves the Jockey Club, members of the National Guard, eager to assert their patriotism, cram into blood-red jeeps and cars to provide a cavalcade. There is much crunching of gears and squealing of tires and shouts of unintelligible enthusiasm combined with alarm when it is thought too many are clambering into the same vehicle. The King, swaddled in his huge Rolls Royce, is already being driven off.

Crash, kerthump . . . One jeep, its occupants anxiously watching the departing Rolls, shoots backward by mistake, neatly scraping a staff car containing assorted top brass. The soldiers, caught off guard, stumble and fall over each other, cursing the driver whose look of intense determination is turning to bewilderment. "Perhaps he thought it was a camel," says an onlooker.

Never mind. It has been a good day's racing, and Sultan Qaboos is well pleased. He has been given $100 million for "civil development" in Oman, a final lurking place of the British Raj, where changes in the last few years have been even more rapid than in Saudi Arabia. Yet there is worry on the family farm that their indigent neighbor may be the first serious Arab casualty of the money rush.

Part Four
Oman

16/GHOST OF THE RAJ

"The sinner who goes to Muscat has a foretaste of what is coming to him in the other world." PERSIAN PROVERB

"One reads about groups around the world assassinating people, kidnapping, hijacking. We have to be careful if we want peace and security so our people can enjoy freedom and wealth." SULTAN QABOOS OF OMAN

IT WAS THURSDAY midday in Muscat, capital city of Oman, and the weekend exodus had begun. Outside the new police station, Superintendent John Eggleton, lately of the Northumberland constabulary, rocked back and forth on his heels in the sunshine and watched traffic building up on the only road north to fishing villages on the picturesque Batinah coast.

"It's a wonderful way of life here," he said. "Unspoiled country, beautiful scenery . . ."

Had he looked at it another way, he could have seen beauty already marred by unplanned urban sprawl reminiscent of Santa Monica, although roadside billboards have an inspirational rather than commercial message: FORWARD OMAN UNDER THE GLORIOUS LEADERSHIP OF H.M. SULTAN QABOOS. GOD IS BEHIND YOU.

But after twenty-seven years in the British police, Superintendent Eggleton did not regret coming to this, the last corner of Arabia. Until a few years ago, Oman was the most backward country in the world, ruled by a preposterous despot whom the British finally exiled to Claridge's Hotel. It is now being dragged into the twentieth century. A strategic coastline covering 1,800 kilometers of the Indian Ocean and entrance to the Gulf, and proximity to Russian footholds in the Middle East and Africa, give it a vulnerability which ensures finance and flattery not only from the Saudis but also from Western governments and neighboring Arab countries whose leaders tend to refer disparagingly to the Sultan and his father as "those Indians." The money rush makes all participants mutually dependent, however much they despise the differences between each other.

Oman is run largely by foreigners,[1] particularly British deposited in postcolonial tristesse from Aden or India to create a society where permissiveness will not strike and where respect for old values and authority remains a virtue. "The Omanis are such wonderful people," confides a grande dame at a chic cocktail party. (Compared to Saudi Arabia, Oman is a paradise for the self-indulgent.) "They are submissive without being presumptuous."

It wrecks a spirit of enthusiastic self-awakening to dwell too much on submissiveness, so nations do not boast about their role in Oman's development. America sends millions of dollars via Saudi Arabia,[2] a bookkeeping exercise abstruse enough to confuse the most diligent economic sleuth, and the ubiquitous CIA has met Qaboos to plan closer links between the two countries at the expense of the British, whose altruism toward Oman has a two-hundred-year history. It is not officially disclosed how many men were provided by the elite Special Air Service (SAS) for the British Army Training Team (BATT). Soldiers themselves were forbidden to tell even relatives when they were sent there. They were withdrawn early in 1978, leaving 62 British officers and 54 men on loan service with the Sultan's forces and about 400 others who are on individual contracts. There is also a secret security force commanded by two members of the SAS and directly responsible to the Sultan.

Now that they have given the Communist chappies in Dhofar the old heave-ho (well, almost) British Army folk can cultivate those other military occupations: empire building and bitchery. "There is continuous rivalry between us and the men on loan," says a senior officer who, having retired after thirty years' distinguished service in the British Army, finds himself earning

$32,000 a year tax-free "trying to weed out the Sultan's forces" miles away from the pleasant Home Counties cottage to which he returns for a few weeks each year.

"My life is hell," he continues. "I am a bloody mercenary. Would I be here if it wasn't the money? All I am trying to do is carry out the Sultan's orders to produce a jolly good Navy, first-class Air Force, and a super Army, but the continual harassment and aggravation from officers of the British Army would be considered mutiny anywhere else.

"Lots of English are on the take, and it makes me very ashamed. The rip-off is twenty-five percent. It used to be seven percent. Only a few months ago, we had to get rid of someone who had taken $2 million in backhanders from contractors who built runways during the civil war. He was given cash payments, so nothing could be proved. Now he is living in America.

"One part of my job is to see that the Sultan buys the correct weapons. The trouble is that if he sees a nice-looking tank, he thinks he needs it, and the British Defence Ministry encourage him. They want to keep control over the country, even if it does mean we have far too many sophisticated weapons. Anyway, they could stop a serious aggressor only for about three minutes if there was anyone competent enough to use them, which there is not. No doubt it is good for British arms manufacturers, but if the Sultan had not been so indoctrinated, he would have got rid of the British years ago."

The officer, who claimed that his life had been threatened in two anonymous telephone calls, mentioned several times during the conversations which took place over four days, that "I shall deny I ever spoke to you, of course." Such cloak-and-dagger melodramatics are an integral part of life amongst those who have lived in Oman several years. Whispered confidences and hushed condemnations which they dare not speak aloud come from the most unlikely sources—bank managers, auditors, company chairmen, diplomats, as well as senior Army officers. Some of the allegations are true, but others derive from a sense of frustrated self-importance characteristic of old colonials. They are flotsam of the empire who have lived their adult lives abroad and could never return to the Britain that first inspired their loyalty because, in their eyes, it no longer exists. So they come to rest finally in Oman, where benevolent paternalism is appreciated, and they find to their despair that the money rush creates new attitudes amongst the natives and attracts a different class of Britisher into administration. It isn't cricket, and it isn't fair, and it certainly isn't democratic.

"Democracy," said Superintendent Eggleton, and the word drifted dreamlike through the torpid atmosphere as if its very enunciation was its own condemnation. "Democracy? Well, there are all sorts aren't there? The one in England is undesirable and is ceasing to be one. Here, they have an excellent type of democracy and can probably get away with it. I hope they do."

Had he looked at it another way, he could have said that Oman has no parliament, no elections, no free speech, press censorship which makes Iran seem liberal, and travel restrictions which make Saudi Arabian visa requirements seem no more arduous than embarking on a day trip to the coast.[3]

But he said simply, "It takes a few months to adjust."

He earns $1,800 a month tax-free on a three-year contract, is provided with a cook and houseboy, and welfare shop where he can buy goods on credit at reduced prices. The police also have their own stadium—the only one in Oman with real grass, flown in deep-frozen from South America. It is part of the Sultan's policy, learned from the British and perfected with advice from his hero the Shah, to create rival power blocs in order to diminish the threat of a strong single-minded opposition. The armed forces are now split into a Navy, Army, and Air Force, each with its own commander. He has competitive secret services and has allowed the police to become a much-envied paramilitary force with its own separate air wing. The Ceylonese-born commander, Felix da Silva, is British, and so are the head of immigration and the intelligence chief. Communication between the various groups of armed authority is restrained and leads to the sort of bureaucratic muddle so common to civilized societies: an international arms dealer in Europe was surprised by an order from the Oman police for 400 Lee-Enfield rifles. Two days earlier he had bought some weapons from the Army: 400 Lee-Enfield rifles.

Felix da Silva has ingratiated himself with the Sultan to an extent that the police are all-powerful. Until recently the British and American embassies were not informed if one of their citizens was in trouble, and people were deported within twenty-four hours without any form of trial. The Shell subsidiary, Petroleum Development Oman (PDO) paid the fine of a secretary badly hurt in a car crash. "She was convicted on drunk driving. But she wasn't drunk, and she wasn't driving," said a colleague. "The other car was driven by a policeman, though."

Magistrates are appointed by the police. "Who else is going to do it?" asked Eggleton, and he added reassuringly, "We choose good, erstwhile people with a public conscience. In a developing country, you cannot have the whole complicated business we have in the West. We are trying to be simple about it, and I would say it works better than the English system. I was always frustrated there by holdups, shilly-shallying back and forth. Here people get a very quick, fair hearing. The Omanis have very strong ideas about fairness. . . ."

Just then all the traffic at the intersection of the road from Muscat to the airport was halted, and roadblocks set up.

"Don't worry," said Superintendent Eggleton. "It won't be more than half an hour. The Sultan is going to see President Numeiry off. Anything else you want to ask?"

"Wasn't one man hauled into prison because he accidentally cut an electricity cable with a plow?"

"It's important to take a serious view of that sort of thing. Electricity is vital here. Besides, as I said, the magistrates are very fair."

All traffic on the main road was now being hustled into the nearest turnoff.

Under *Sharia* law, which operates in all the money-rush countries except Iran, women are barred from court and have to testify through an open window. A man's word equals that of two women. Superintendent Eggleton explained that women did not actually commit crimes in Oman, so it was academic liberalism to suggest the tradition was archaic. He continued with his thoughts about justice: "The British go on the facts of the case and are blind to everything else," he said. "The biggest villain unhung can get off. You are not allowed hearsay evidence, which I often thought was very unfair because it does not give the judge the right idea. Here it's much more normal. If someone has done wrong, he is the first to admit it, and that makes it much easier for the police. I had to fight in England to keep a relationship between the police and the public."

Half an hour passed. Superintendent Eggleton remained unperturbed. "Won't be long now. We've just heard they have left the palace."

Earlier in the year, his sixteen-year-old son had been out to Oman, and loved it. He was going to join the British Navy.

An hour passed.

A few weeks previously, the Sultan hired a circus from England for about $400,000, to perform on National Day, November 18, which is also his birthday. The police were in charge of the organization and unfortunately charged so much—from $10 to $24—that very few Omanis could afford to attend. The tickets were reduced to between $2 and $14, and then replaced by free shows.

"It was a great success," recalls Superintendent Eggleton. There is always something prestigious on National Day—the opening of a new television station, dropping candy on children from an Air Force airplane, fireworks displays (organized by a British company) and military bands whose tunes symbolically merge Oman's past with its present: "Skye Boat Song," and "I'm a Yankee Doodle Dandy."

Two hours passed.

There was surprisingly little obvious complaint from Omani drivers who had been waiting in the 100° heat. Some were out of their cars and sat on the roadside. Many Europeans and Americans who only wanted to cross the main road—a matter of a few yards—swore and cursed as they saw their weekend arrangements wrecked. "We'll never be able to get away now."

"Not long to wait," Superintendent Eggleton said happily.

Occasionally a police car came into sight, lights full on and siren flashing, leaving dust in its wake and a silence which seemed eerie and improbable with so many people delayed for so long for no apparent reason. It was as if they had been sedated, and perhaps they had been by the heat. Such passivity would be inconceivable in most countries.

Suddenly, at half past two, there was activity at the crossroads. Police began to talk urgently into their pocket radios and positioned themselves at strategic positions.

A few people who had now been waiting nearly three hours ambled nearer the edge of the main road. In the distance a clatter of helicopter blades could be heard, then the wail of police sirens still far off but coming closer.

"He's on his way," said Superintendent Eggleton. "A few more minutes."

An Army helicopter appeared over the horizon, dipping low into the hills, followed by two police Bell 205s which crisscrossed the roads, fluttering hither and thither with machine gunners at the ready. Then, cruising at 75 kilometers an hour in the middle of the road came three police cars, followed by two Mercedes full of security men, six Cadillacs, one of which was flanked by a dozen motorcycle outriders so it was impossible to see who was inside, then the Sultan's personal ambulance, and twenty-five other cars brimming with functionaries of one sort or another.

"It was the best day in the history of this country when that man came to the throne," said Superintendent Eggleton as he watched the departing cavalcade. "He's a wonderful man. The people here love this sort of thing, you know. They don't mind the waiting. They expect it. It's part of their tradition."

It was with no feeling of revenge, or even a desire to satisfy tradition, that I later kept the Sultan waiting an hour and a half. I was having a leisurely talk at the American embassy prior to walking a few yards to the $6 million pink confection which the Sultan uses as his palace during his increasingly infrequent visits to Muscat, when I was told our meeting would be at Sib, his more exotic $18 million palace forty kilometers away.

I assumed the last-minute change of plan had been made either for security precautions vital to every autocrat or because His Majesty was playing on his garden lake with the electrically controlled toy boats which had lately become his favorite hobby.

A guide and driver provided by the government whisked me away and ignoring strictly imposed speed regulations, we arrived at Sib half an hour after the scheduled time. Guards lolling against the gate were pleasant, hospitable, and delighted to talk to someone. His Majesty, though, was in Muscat so far as they knew. Back we sped, the guide and driver arguing, sweating, hurling tearful recriminations at each other followed by sullen accusations until they turned to reassure me. "No problem, no problem," they said, and started arguing once more.

There was no problem. The Sultan, hearing of the dilemma, had rescheduled a few ambassadors so our discussion could take place when I arrived: a gracious honor from a man who is also Prime Minister, Foreign Minister, Defense Minister, and the fourteenth hereditary successor to one of the oldest regal dynasties in Arabia (see Appendix).

He is an impressive-looking man dressed in long Arab robes enhanced by a vivid colored silk turban, and a *khanja* (curved dagger) at the waist: tall, full-bearded, with alert, intelligent eyes. His lips give a hint of sulkiness, of quick temper, or determination, and it is easy to believe he was only just dissuaded by British Foreign Office pressure from bombing Aden in 1976 and precipitating a quick end to his own particular money rush. Yet, when I saw him later in Iran, he was dressed in a Western suit and looked less impressive: slightly balding and nondescript, too meek to cope with the eighteen wives ascribed to him inaccurately by a British newspaper.[4] Americans, too, have found him ineffectual and nervous on his trips to Washington. He is more relaxed with his Lebanese or British aides, one of whom had dressed in a dark gray civil service–type suit to be present at our discussion.

"Throughout our history," said the Sultan, "we have been friends of Britain. I admire the British because they are loyal. Secondly, it is a nation which takes things rather quietly. The British don't shout, and that is something I admire. They have a very calm way of doing things. As long as we need assistance and the British are prepared to give it, we will have it. We rely on them, and they are very welcome, but our people are being more and more trained, and Omanization is taking place."

It may not seem that way, with British running the country, Iranians defending it, and Saudis paying for it.

"We share the same interests as Iran, and perhaps look at things in the same way. It is wholly right that we should help each other. Financial help from Saudi Arabia is very much welcomed, and there are no ties attached. It is like a brother who helps a brother."

That is an unusual occurrence in Arab history, which is replete with stories of brothers killing each other, of family feuds which span generations. The Sultan himself was put under house arrest by his own father, whom he called "headstrong and bigoted," and whom he eventually overthrew in 1970 with the help of the British.

"That was a big decision, of course. But there are two kinds of loyalty: loyalty to a father and loyalty to the country. I had been brought up to believe loyalty to your religion and your people is greater than to family, and that loyalty should prevail. My relationship with my father was very formal. It was the Sultan and the Prince. I had to call him 'Your Majesty.' It was very formal. . . ."

Sultan Sa'id bin Taimur was a man of strong convictions intent on ignoring the twentieth century in the hope—largely realized—that it would ignore him. He forbade his people to play music, wear sunglasses, carry dolls (a religious prohibition against idols), use gas stoves, or buy tractors. This last regulation may have been a sensible precaution. In the early days of the money rush, several combine harvesters were sold to nouveau riche desert-dwelling Arabs. Omanis were not allowed to leave their village, repair their houses, or buy a car without written permission from the Sultan. Those caught smoking were given a public lashing. There were no newspapers, telephones, television, radio, or hospitals, and only three elementary schools. "The British lost India because they educated the people," he explained. Theoretically, Omanis could be educated in Britain, but only with the Sultan's permission, which he naturally never gave. Some went to Russia, and many more to Egypt and the Omani possession of Zanzibar.

Medical care was practically nonexistent. "We do not need hospitals here," said the Sultan. "This is a very poor country which can support only a small population. At present, many children die in infancy, and so the population does not increase. If we build clinics many more will survive—but for what? To starve?"[5] Some causes of infant mortality which still exist were horrifying, according to missionary Beth Thoms, who worked in

Oman during the 1950s. She described a condition known as atresia, where normal vaginal muscles become inelastic scar tissue. "When this condition exists, the child cannot be born. The woman in labor suffers agony, for in her body the irresistible force of birth contractions propels the fetus against an immovable barrier of rigid scar tissue, which has closed the birth canal like a purse string. Suddenly everything rips open.

"How was the scar tissue formed? The answer is that it results from the packing of rock salt into the vagina after the birth of the first baby to contract the vagina lest the husband, not deriving the satisfaction from his wife which he experienced before delivery, should divorce her."

The Sultan ruled without benefit of secretaries or clerical staff, simply giving orders on his radiotelephone (the only such device allowed in the country) to his expatriate British officials. He lived most of the time in Salalah, the green, monsoon-swept southern part of the country famous for its frankincense, and not in his capital, Muscat. As he told the commander of his armed forces, Colonel David Smiley, "If I go to Muscat, I will be surrounded by suppliants, all asking for money. I have no money to give them, and so they will go away discontented. Therefore it is better if I stay here in Salalah."

Officials occasionally made an appointment with him to discuss one abuse or another, and they found he would chat amiably about cricket scores, quote from Shakespeare, ask about contemporary events in London—and ignore the purpose of the visit. Sir Hugh Boustead, the archetypal colonial appointee of impeccable rectitude, whom I was to meet later in his desert hideaway, was sent to administer a development program to which the British contributed $500,000 (military aid at the same time was between $2 million and $4 million). He recalls, "It was the Sultan's habit to call me down to Salalah periodically to discuss plans which were in hand. We would sit on the sofa together in his very charmingly appointed drawing room in front of a low table, and I would go through all our points. It shook me to find that letters sent to him asking for an early decision had not even been opened. I always felt he was not really interested in development.[6]

"One of the earliest health centers had to wait for over a year and a half while the Sultan and the Treasury discussed who was to pay for the builder. The Sultan, of course, won, and the Treasury paid. I used to wonder greatly over all these matters since I knew that only recently the state of Gwadar in Pakistan, which had belonged to Oman, had been sold by the Sultan to the Pakistan government for $6 million, the interest of which was accumulated in Swiss and American banks."

Another adviser, complaining to the Sultan that his judges were corrupt, was at least given an honest answer: "I know they take bribes," he said. "But if I stopped them, I would have to pay them more."[7] He used torture, including the rack, and prisoners were thrown into a dank Portuguese fort, Jalali, without trial and until he remembered to release them. "It was horrible," says Colonel Smiley describing one of his visits. "Prisoners were shackled, the fetters around their ankles connected by a heavy iron bar. When any of them had to go outside to relieve himself, he lifted the bar by a piece of cord to take some of the weight off his feet; but most of the time they lay on the hard stone floors of their long barrack rooms, without mattresses or even straw to rest on. Worse than the discomfort and the miserable diet was their lack of water, which the black-hearted governor deliberately withheld from them; whenever I visited them—a regular part of my duties—they would crowd round me, trailing their shackles and gasping piteously, 'Water, sahib, water.'

"Among the prisoners there was at least one who should never have been there—a harmless old lunatic. He would spring to attention, as smartly as his fetters allowed, whenever I appeared, and shout 'God save the King!' with a pathetic attempt at a salute. In any civilized country, he would have been at large."

Having been educated at the British-run College of Princes in Ajmar, India, the Sultan learned early the niceties of political reality and appreciated the importance placed by career colonials on "honor" and "duty," not to mention subservience to the titled—however spurious the honor and barmy the holder. "There is no doubt he was thoroughly deceitful and used us," says a diplomat still working in the Middle East. "I remember there was a religious uprising in Tanuf, a village behind Nizwah, that could have been difficult. It was in about 1956. Well, our boys went in and blew up the place for him."

The Sultan paid almost manic attention to his own security, and had parts of his Salalah palace designed independently by several firms of British architects so no one but he would know its exact design.

Spies were everywhere. The late Sir William Luce told me of an occasion when, as British Political Resident in the Gulf, he visited the Sultan for a two-day meeting. "I was a very heavy smoker at the time, but managed to last twenty-four hours before I found it essential to have a cigarette. I crept to my room, locked the door, shut myself in the toilet, drew the curtains, and had a hurried, reviving puff. Carefully I put the ash down the toilet, followed by the cigarette, and flushed it twice.

"Two minutes later, and I swear it wasn't more, there was a knock on the door and one of the Sultan's slaves was standing there. He said simply, 'A cigarette has appeared,' and then he went away. I didn't know what was going to happen. I could not understand how they found out unless there was a chap permanently posted at the end of the pipe to see what came out.

"That evening I had dinner with the Sultan. He did not mention it directly, but we eventually got on to the subject of smoking. He had a very quiet voice, and he said, 'You know, if we find people smoking here in the streets, we flog them. Oh, yes, we have to flog them.' He left it at that."

17/TILL THE END OF TIME

"Your master is the Sultan. But if he should give you any order contrary to British interests, you have the right to appeal to me, and through me to the Foreign Office."

SIR BERNARD BURROWS, POLITICAL RESIDENT IN THE GULF, AD-VISING COLONEL DAVID SMILEY ON HIS APPOINTMENT AS COM-MANDER OF THE SULTAN'S ARMED FORCES IN 1958

"If we were in trouble before, we could say 'The Royal Air Force will come.' That is not true anymore."

SULTAN QABOOS EXPLAINING TO THE AUTHOR WHY HE SPENDS SO MUCH ON WEAPONS

WHEN THE MONEY RUSH began, it was assumed that Oman had always been closed and poverty-ridden, an impression not discouraged by successive British administrators, many of whom did far too little for a country they were "helping." In fact, Oman once had the largest empire in Arabia and in 1833 became the first Arab country to have diplomatic representation in the United States. It is their historical achievement so often aborted, but now, by the grace of God and the money rush, being rekindled, which makes Omanis feel more grand than other Arabs.

In the early centuries A.D., Oman was part of the Persian empire. It became one of the first to adopt Islam and provided a refuge for former supporters of Muhammad's son-in-law, Ali. The Omanis fought the Persians for mastery, and after a number of uneasy compromises, their leader, called an Imam, controlled the interior (known as Oman), and the Persians held the coastal towns around Muscat.

At the beginning of the sixteenth century, rival European powers realized the strategic importance of the country to trading routes and in 1507 the Portuguese explorer Affonso da Albuquerque invaded Muscat, destroying all the ships in port and ensuring the discipline of his prisoners by slicing off their ears and noses. The Portuguese remained in control for over a hundred years until retaliation began in 1622 with the British East India Company evicting them from Hormuz. A few years later, in 1659, the British tried to arrange a treaty with Oman for a naval base but their negotiator, a commercial traveler named Colonel Rainsford, died before it could be signed.

For Oman it was a relief, and the next hundred years provided the country's greatest achievements. The Omanis built the strongest non-European fleet in the Indian Ocean and conquered Portuguese territory on the East African coast from Mogadishu to Cape Delgado and Zanzibar. For a time they even held Bahrain to the north, and as a bonus, they attacked and defeated British ships, consigning the crews to slavery. Gradually, though, the country disintegrated under the pressure of internal jealousies until Ahmed bin Sa'id, founder of the present Sultan's dynasty, made himself influential by playing off the British against the French—particularly as Napoleon needed his support for a planned invasion of India. Eventually the British won and formalized their victory in an agreement signed on October 12, 1798, between the Sultan, "whose grandeur be eternal" and the British East India Company, "whose greatness be perpetuated" which stated:

> Whereas frequent applications have been made, and are still making, by the French and Dutch people for a Factory, i.e. to seat themselves either in Maskat or Goombroom [now Bandar Abbas], or at other ports, it is written that whilst warfare shall continue between the British company and them, never shall, from respect to the Company's friendship, be given to them throughout all my territories a place to fix or seat themselves in, nor shall they even get ground to stand upon within this State.

Two years later, on January 18, 1800, an even stronger pro-British treaty was signed in order that "no opportunity may be offered to designing men, who are ever eager to promote dissensions, and that the friendship of the two states may remain unshook till the end of time, and till the sun and moon have finished their revolving career."

The British now controlled Oman, although it was never given the official status of a colony for fear of antagonizing the French, and there was another period of stability and prosperity until 1856, when Said bin Sultan died after a fifty-year reign and his two sons quarreled over the inheritance. The British mediated, and one son, Thwaini (who was to be assassinated ten years later by his son) kept Muscat; the other, Majid, took Zanzibar and agreed to pay his brother compensation of 40,000 Maria Theresa dollars a year. When he failed to pay, the British took over responsibility under the Canning Award of 1861 and paid the equivalent of $13,000 every year until 1970.

Family dissension coincided with other events which further destroyed Oman's position. British ambitions in Africa inhibited Omani expansion, the slave trade basis of her wealth was suppressed, the opening of the Suez Canal made the country less strategic, Muscat's population fell from 55,000 to 8,000, and medievalism and dependence from which it had raised itself was reimposed. It was not very British. One sultan had two cages at the door of his palace. First offenders were kept in one, and a lion in the other. Recidivists were put in with the lion at feeding time.

There was the occasional viceregal visit, performed with ceremonial perfection only to be expected. For his appearance in 1903, Lord Curzon had a red carpet laid on the sand from water's edge to the steps of the imposing consulate building, bought thirteen years earlier for 5,000 Maria Theresa dollars (about $1,600). To prevent his feet from getting wet, he was carried from boat to carpet on a sedan fashioned from a kitchen chair. It was most proper, and Curzon complimented Oman on being like a "royal feudatory of the British Crown rather than that of an independent sovereign." The whole coast, he added, had been saved from extinction. "We have not destroyed your independence but preserved it. We are not now going to throw away this century of costly and triumphal enterprise; we shall not wipe out the most unselfish page in history. Your independence will continue to be upheld, and the influence of the British Government will remain supreme." (See Appendix.)

The following year, realizing the importance of the Straits of Hormuz, Curzon insisted that three flagstaffs be erected on its narrowest part at the Musandum Peninsula to deter Russian advances. But which flag should fly? Not the Union Jack—the land was not legally British. The Foreign Office suggested the Blue Ensign of the Royal Indian Marine. But, explained the horrified Admiralty, we might have to defend it. Unthinkable, said the Committee for Imperial Defence. So the flagstaffs were removed. No one in Whitehall realized that they could not be seen from the sea anyway, and the inhabitants of Musandum would not be overly impressed either. They were the Shihuh tribe of troglodytes who communicated by making barking noises, had the curious habit of standing on one leg, and were known for their savage unfriendliness.

In Muscat, meanwhile, successive sultans tried to raise money by levying taxes on tribes in the interior. In retaliation, the tribes reinstated the title of Imam, dormant for many years, and elected a leader to oppose the Sultan's power. The British sent a gunboat to prevent an uprising and referee between tribal leaders lobbing cannonballs at each other from one Portuguese fort to another. Then the British bribed the Sultan with 100,000 rupees to sign an agreement banning the import of arms. The tribes were furious because gunrunning to India provided a large part of their income. They rebelled again and were once more "discouraged" by the British, who sent 700 Indian troops to Muscat. Finally, in 1920, with the British Political Agent in the Gulf as chief negotiator, the Treaty of Sib was signed and kept secret for fifty years for no apparent reason other than endemic melodrama (see Appendix).

By the time the present Sultan's father succeeded in 1932 at the age of twenty-one (*his* father was "encouraged" by the British to abdicate, and went to live in Bombay), the country was bankrupt and had a total budget of $100,000 a year. Sa'id bin Taimur resolved never to get into debt and to keep his country as independent as possible in spite of the British. His first test began in 1949 when Saudi Arabia, supported by the American Government, which wanted to reduce British influence in the area, and Aramco, which was prospecting with enthusiasm, claimed nine villages of the Buraimi oasis lying between Oman and the Gulf which were administered jointly by Abu Dhabi and Oman. Before oil was discovered, there had been no necessity for internationally defined borders, but now it became a critical issue. Britain was asked to negotiate, and after talks had dragged on inconclusively for three years, the Saudis attacked on August 31, 1952, with arms and transport supplied by Aramco.

The Sultan mobilized an army of 8,000 tribesmen and prepared to defend. He was joined by a slightly bewildered British soldier, Colin Maxwell, then thirty-six, formerly of the Palestinian police and the British Army. "I wanted to get back to Arabia, and the F.O. [Foreign Office] mentioned a job in Oman," he told me.

"It sounded exciting, so out I came. I arrived at Sohar, where the Sultan was encamped. It was real Lawrence of Arabia stuff— terribly exciting. They were all on camels about to go off to fight the Saudis. We waited five days while the British and Americans tried to defuse it."

The British were worried because, as a diplomat later explained, "The Americans were so mixed up in it all. Suppose the Sultan had gone in under our auspices and some idiotic American geologist had got himself killed: There'd have been hell to pay. It just wasn't worth the risk. We couldn't let them do it."[1] So the Consul General was dispatched from Muscat. He arrived at Sohar, stiff with cramp, and told the Sultan and his tribesmen to go home.

The dispute went to international arbitration in Geneva, where talks began in September 1955 but broke down when the British accused the Saudis of trying to bribe anyone with influence. The Americans retorted that the British were annoyed because they knew they were about to lose. It was, according to Foreign Secretary Harold Macmillan, "a new and irritating problem which required immediate attention. The Buraimi oasis was vital to our oil interests. Our only course was to support the local ruler, whose rights we accepted, and to occupy the area by force. In all the circumstances, I thought it wiser not to consult the United States or even the old Commonwealth territories about our decision. This operation was successfully carried out on the morning of 16 October and the House of Commons duly informed. When I told Dulles what had happened, he did not seem unduly disturbed, although a day or two later he complained that the State Department was upset because they had no prior warning. I explained that this was due to anxiety to avoid involving him in any accusation of complicity, and with this explanation he appeared satisfied. The charge of bribery was fully justified, for when we occupied the area a Saudi police detachment was found in possession of sums of money far in excess of their requirements."[2]

There was uneasy peace for two years, and then the Saudis encouraged the Imam to form a breakaway government with offices in Cairo. The Imamate issued its own passports and sold stamps, printed in London, which showed flowers, nude women, and various sporting activities. They eventually became collectors' items. Harold Macmillan, now Prime Minister, was asked again for help by the Sultan. "We had a moral duty," he said this time.[3] "Since British friendship and support had been afforded to the Sultan for more than a century, to have withheld our assistance at this critical moment would have involved a grave loss of confidence. Moreover, although no oil had yet been proved, two companies were actively carrying out exploration throughout this area. We had, therefore, an additional reason to support our ally . . . yet for the British Government after the events of 1956 [Suez] to embark single-handed upon a further military enterprise seemed at first to some of my colleagues hazardous and even foolhardy."

Nevertheless the RAF, the Cameronian Highlanders, the Trucial Oman Scouts, and a squadron of SAS flown in from Malaya, managed to defeat the rebels while the Americans behaved "outrageously" and "once again we had to operate without full American assistance," according to Macmillan. It was the last Anglo-American war, and the Buraimi dispute is still not settled.

For Colin Maxwell, "It was rather a risky enterprise, coming so soon after Suez," but he has stayed in Oman, becoming a Brigadier and Deputy Commander of the Army. He plans to retire there and write a book about the history of the Sultan's

Armed Forces. When people reminisce today about the British empire—its triumphs and deceits, its achievements and exaggerations—it is fashionable to ridicule characteristics which were considered admirable: unquestioning obedience to authority, abstemious stiff-upper-lip commitment, pugnacity. Often these qualities hide a sentimental and genuine philanthropy, a lively imagination pruned by duty at a British public school so that it finds satisfaction in deserts or jungles rather than boardrooms or fleshpots. It is cruel to suggest that it is unnecessary—even harmful—to try to pin such elusive ideals on people who really don't need them, don't understand them, and would perhaps be far happier muddling along in their own un-British way. Those who try are easy to mock, but behind the caricature real people emerge, with genuine idealism and courage. Like Colin Maxwell.

Maxwell's life has been threatened on many occasions, and he has faced death with aplomb and imagination. When commanding the Sultan's forces against rebels, it was rumored he would be assassinated by a man dressed as a woman. One afternoon, while swimming naked in a remote lake, he noticed a black-robed woman approaching slowly and with apparent menace. He jumped from the water, exposing himself on the assumption that a genuine woman would be so horrified by the sight that she would run off. The figure came nearer and passed by. She was a woman. But blind.

Brigadier Maxwell, a pink-cheeked bachelor whose clipped military moustache adds sternness to an otherwise jovial face, has seen the world into which he was born disappear, and only the faint echoes remain in Oman. "I was at school in England, of course—Radley and Cambridge. I came out here on spec, but in a very short time decided it was where I was going to stay. I am fascinated by the country—its environment and its people. It is magnificent. It has a mountain range down the middle, and the people all have different characteristics. It's extraordinary how nostalgic we become about Oman. It's the people, the terrain, and the extraordinarily happy life we have had here.

"I like soldiering, and we've had quite a lot of skirmishing. It has been some of the most wonderful old-fashioned soldiering in the world. The Omanis are now battle-hardened, and they have gained a lot by their training.

"The only threat to this area is communism. It has always surprised me that the Arabs, who are not particularly in favor of communist doctrine, can be attracted and become indoctrinated to be pretty hard communists. We know that some of our students go to Libya and do rebel training. I suppose they are well paid, but they don't go in sufficient numbers to worry about yet."

Each year he returns "home" to England for a month's holiday with his sister. "I see some signs of decline in the country, I must admit," he says wistfully. "I blame a lot of it on the present government."

After the 1958 trouble, Harold Macmillan sent his Undersecretary of State for War, Julian Amery, to Oman to help the Sultan organize more reliable armed forces. Amery in turn contacted Colonel David Smiley, an old friend, who was planning to retire to a farm in Kenya. "Sit down, David, I have a job for you," said Amery, producing a large folder. "You can read all about it in there."[4]

"What is this job? And where?" asked Smiley.

"I want you to command the Sultan's armed forces in Muscat. We give him help. We sometimes give him advice. But"—and here Amery gave a knowing smile—"we do not give him orders." The message was clear. The Sultan had to do as he was told if he wanted British money. Meanwhile, the British could disown any responsibility for the brutality and backwardness of the country because it was "independent."

Trouble between Oman (as the interior was called) and Muscat continued, and the Sultan retired to his palace at Salalah, in the Dhofar region, 800 kilometers to the south. Every so often, the RAF transported him and a few slaves to London for a holiday at the Dorchester, but at home opposition grew in the form of the Dhofar Liberation Front and culminated in an assassination attempt on April 28, 1966. One of his bodyguards shot at him from a few yards, and missed. Publicly emulating the nonchalance of his advisers, the Sultan went to the nearest Army headquarters and told the British officer, "We seem to be having a little trouble down at the palace. I wonder if you would be so good as to come down." Privately, he was terrified, and for the next four years he stayed inside his palace, which he equipped like a madman's fortress with 33 tons of weapons worth

$3,000,000: machine guns, Bren guns, mortars, antitank guns, CS gas, 2,000 Lee-Enfield rifles with 600,000 rounds of ammunition. He had 500 slaves (upon whom he practiced his marksmanship by making them swim in the sea while he fired at nearby fish), and 150 women who were hidden in rooms no one knew existed.

At the instigation of the British, his only legitimate son, Qaboos, whose mother is a Dhofari, was sent to Sandhurst when he was eighteen. His roommate, Tim Landon, became a close friend and has risen subsequently to remarkable heights (Brigadier) and wealth (houses in London and Athens) in the Oman Army. Qaboos studied local government with the Bedfordshire County Council, spent a year with the Cameronians in Germany, developed a taste for Gilbert and Sullivan, traveled round the world, and returned to Oman where he was immediately put under house arrest by his father and engaged, sight unseen, to the daughter of one of the family's traditional rivals, Shaikh Ahmad bin Mohammed al-Harthi.

But even without imagined rivalry from his son, Sa'id bin Taimur could not withstand the first rumbles of the money rush which were combined in Oman with stirrings of Arab nationalism stoked by communist support from South Yemen. "The Communists chose Oman as their route to the Gulf's oil wells, and a starting base for future control of the region," said Sultan Qaboos later. "Communist control of Oman would inevitably lead to control of oil resources without which Western industry and civilization cannot survive." The Dhofar Liberation Front went through several name changes including PFLOAG (Popular Front for the Liberation of Oman and the Arabian Gulf) before becoming simply the PFLO (Popular Front for the Liberation of Oman). A colonial war smoldered with British "advisers" often killed in action.

"Just think what I can do for my people when we have oil," said the Sultan to penniless American explorer Wendell Phillips as he gave him the concessions.[5] And when oil was discovered in 1967, he showed his delight in a surprising way. Julian Amery recalls an occasion in Salalah when the Sultan rang a bell "and to my surprise a servant brought in three decanters. I wondered what on earth had happened—because the Sultan never offered alcohol to guests. He said, 'Give me your hand.' I did so, and he poured the contents of one of the decanters over my hand. It was the color of whisky, but it was in fact oil."

"I just wanted you to know," said the Sultan, "that we now have it."

For about half an hour the two men sat there, rubbing their hands in the three different grades of oil which the decanters contained.

But in fact the Sultan was unable to use the wealth brought by the oil. Parsimony was so ingrained in his nature that he hoarded the royalties and did little for the country. By 1970 the situation was so bad that the British Government made it clear to the Sultan's "advisers" that a takeover would not be opposed, particularly as they planned to withdraw from the rest of the Gulf in 1971 and any upheaval in Oman could incite rebellion elsewhere.

Accordingly, on the afternoon of Thursday, July 23, 1970, Shaikh Braik bin Mamud bin Hamid al-Ghafari went into the Sultan's study and asked him to abdicate peacefully. Sa'id's answer was immediate. He took a pistol from his desk drawer and shot Shaikh Braik, wounding him. The Sultan himself was shot in the leg and buttock, but refused to surrender except to a British officer. This done, he was put on a RAF plane for Bahrain and then England. Three days later, the Omanis were told what had happened.

"It was a most tear-jerking experience," said Colonel Hugh Oldman, the Defense Secretary. "There was incredible happiness. There was overt joy and sheer jubilation." Some of the former Sultan's slaves were paraded for the press. "Some had been forced, under pain of beating, not to speak. As a result they had become mutes. Others stood with their heads bowed and eyes fixed on the ground, their necks paralysed: The slightest glance sideways had resulted in a severe beating or imprisonment. Others had incurred physical deformity from similar cruelty."[6]

A trembling twenty-nine-year-old Qaboos was flown to Muscat, the capital he had never seen, where an exultant welcome was arranged by British officers. He had few Omani friends and none he could trust. All his compatriots who hoped for a future had left to study and work abroad. He took over a country in the middle of a civil war with no plans, no government, and very little money. But a new era was beginning. He was a young man untarnished by scandal, uncompromised by family jealousies. The money rush was about to provide an unparalleled opportunity and challenge to create from nothing in a few years an Arab society which was also a modern state. It could be done. The omens were good.

The first thing Sultan Qaboos did was offer an amnesty to those who fought against his father. He paid former rebels $300 a month, gave them each a rifle, and formed them into vigilante patrols called *firqats*.

The second thing he did was run the country so near bankruptcy that international banks declared his credit no longer acceptable.

Now, what he might do inadvertently, is to make Oman a stepping-stone for the disintegration of the money rush.

18/SWEETS FOR THE CHILDREN

"Be reasonable and choose the right path: either an honourable life under Qabus, or death and decay with Godless communism."
LEAFLET DROPPED BY OMANI PLANES OVER DHOFAR IN 1973

"It is difficult to find a man to feed the child's mind. A teacher can be a dangerous man."
OMANI MINISTER OF EDUCATION, AHMED GHAZALI

"PEOPLE MAKE MISTAKES," admitted the Sultan as we sat in his Muscat palace, "and mistakes were made, but not to the extent that others imagine. We went faster than perhaps we should have done in normal circumstances, but we were fighting a war at the same time as trying to develop a country."

Development was begun by an Interim Planning Council, presided over by Defense Secretary Colonel Oldman, which immediately transferred a road contract from a German to a British firm, planned a new town in an airless, waterless valley miles from anywhere except Army headquarters, and summoned Qaboos's uncle Tariq from Germany where he had been since 1958 in amiable, self-imposed exile with a German wife (two Omani ones stayed at home) to be Prime Minister, and thus prevent him from becoming a focus for revolt.

Fortunately, the Al bu Sa'ids have outgrown the traditional Arab ruling family's obsession with slaughtering each other, and Sa'id bin Taimur's four brothers, each by a different mother, are uncompetitive. The eldest, Majid, is half black and considered far down the social scale. As Governor of Mutrah, he is content to be as helpful as possible. One day he arrested some gold smugglers and proudly exhibited their loot in his office until requested to return it because the smugglers were influential. "Majid is all right," says Tariq. "He is not corrupt in the normal way."

Tariq, the brightest, has a Turkish mother and was educated in Turkey and at Heidelberg University. In the Second World War he served in the Indian Army, good training for battling against the rebels in Dhofar when, equipped with two retainers carrying his personal Bren gun, he followed troops on maneuvers. Unfortunately Sa'id kept him so short of money that every Christmas he had to present himself at Salalah to be given a cash gift. This became increasingly niggardly, so he bought a couple of broken-down army trucks and set up as a contractor, eventually moving to Germany after a series of disagreements. He enjoys music, but his main loves are bridge and gambling—to such an extent that one of his friends alleges he put his last $2,000 on a single number at roulette. It came up, giving him $70,000 profit.

He had never met his nephew Qaboos, and was alarmed to discover that they trusted each other slightly less than they trusted the British. Qaboos refused to let him have access to any financial details, because, he said, the oil concession was in the name of the Sultan. So they both sanctioned projects without consultation, Tariq spending vast amounts in an unsuccessful attempt to force Qaboos to reveal how much was available. When Tariq resigned, frustrated in December 1971, a number of companies realized why they had not received written confirmation of oral agreements. Tariq left hundreds of letters unopened and wrote to no one because he did not even have a secretary.

The rift between uncle and nephew did not last and Tariq, who now calls himself the *éminence grise,* was made chairman of the Central Bank and his daughter married Qaboos. The former putative, or actual, father-in-law is under house arrest in Salalah.

In spite of initial problems, the Sultan was determined to create a proper government, and he began to make all the appointments that a Bedfordshire County Council would presuma-

bly consider necessary. He asked an oil company executive to be
Minister of Social Services and Labor.

"What are social services?" asked the aspirant minister.

The Sultan thought for a moment and then replied, "I don't
know. No one has ever asked me that before."

At least he tried, and in some ways the country is more liberal
and progressive than its neighbors. An ecological balance in the
south which has not been disturbed for two thousand years is
being preserved. Ministers are often young and enthusiastic. Alcohol is allowed, although it is controlled by a police permit
which costs $30 a month.

But the most noticeable difference between Oman and other
Arab countries in the money rush, except Iraq, is female emancipation. Less than a decade ago, Omani women were as shut off
as their Saudi counterparts are today. Colonel Smiley, former
head of the Sultan's Army, recalls, "On one of my visits to Sohar,
I had to bring back in my airplane a fourteen-year-old girl with
the face of an angel who had been shot in the stomach by her
brother 'for looking at a man.' She lay silent and uncomplaining
on her stretcher and died before we landed. Her brother went
unpunished."

Anomalies still exist—a girl traditionally "belongs" to the son
of her father's brother and he must give permission if she wishes
to marry someone else—but prejudices are being obliterated within a generation, and working women are accepted and encouraged. Lyutha Sultan al Mugheri, a thirty-year-old television
and radio director, says, "We couldn't suppress women here now
because everyone is needed to help develop the country. I have
a lot of men working for me, and they are proud that there is a
woman who can actually do something."

Most Omani women are unveiled and take part in normal life,
frequently becoming senior to men. They are provided with sex
advice columns in local newspapers which would make Saudis
froth with indignation. "Shy wife and happy sex," says one headline. "A thirty-two-year-old woman, mother of two children aged
thirteen and ten, came to me with a strange problem. She
confided that she has lost all sexual desire. Her husband felt her
emancipation was the cause of their sexual disharmony." There
are pictures of women's football teams with a promise that soon

such wanton entertainment will be a normal part of Omani life. "The day is not far off when in every country women will work and play side by side with males as equal members of society."

The Sultan's wife still appears veiled in public. He says, "She is new on the scene. I am sure she will do things in her own time. There are no obstacles to women's progress. I think we should let things take their natural course without shouting about it too much. That might create different attitudes and perhaps make it more difficult."

The pressures caused by dramatic change in a society like Oman produce inevitable contradictions and an innocence which is likable and can be harmless if it is not disillusioned too soon. Ahmed Ghazali, the thirty-year-old Minister of Education, emanates optimism with all the energy of an idealistic young schoolmaster. His family left Oman for Zanzibar when he was nine, and he has only just returned.

"As we are modernized, we are in danger of throwing away our traditions, so I am trying to make students understand that to be modern and educated does not necessarily mean they have to overthrow. Many of our students think they have to wear trousers, drink, and smoke in order to become modern. In our schools, they must wear the *dishdasha* [white gown worn by Arab men]—even foreigners. There is nothing wrong with traditional clothes.

"Education isn't everything, and who says it gives you a good life? In England over half a million well-educated people are unemployed. What is the point of education if that happens? In this office, for instance, I could get a computer and do things quicker and cheaper. But I would throw three hundred people out of work. Where would they go? When people are unemployed they sit and think, and what do you expect them to do? They destroy things.

"We can't protect our students from the bad side of modern life. You can't stop movies or television, but we can make them work in a helpful way and we can choose what we show. There are good American detective films, taken from police records, which can help. So much Western material is unrealistic. You see, for instance, a man walking down a street. He meets a girl, and two days later they marry. These things never really happen, do they? I don't like to see kissing in the streets. I was in Paris and saw a boy and girl kissing at traffic lights. It's terrible. It's not the place and it doesn't have the mood. I try to be strict in making our students behave well. It's better to be ignorant and polite than educated with no manners.

"I hope the mistakes we make will be new ones of our own because we are trying to experiment for ourselves. We are building a new generation to take our place, and we know that the pen can lead them to a prison or a palace. It is for them to choose, and if we don't make them right, then one day they will destroy us. I am sure of that."

The money rush nearly did. It hit Oman as the country was struggling to develop and seemed like a miraculous remedy for every bottleneck and delay. Income rose from $226 million in 1973 to $1.02 billion the following year, most paid direct to the Sultan who distributed it to ministries according to his own preferences. Oil revenues are still paid direct to him, and the amount is a closely guarded secret. In 1978 he received about $1.5 billion.

The bonanza was followed by massive overspending and uncontrolled extravagance as ministers realized that the way to increase their budget was to tempt the Sultan with a prestige project and promise it could be finished as a birthday present by National Day. A television system was introduced in 1974 at far greater cost than necessary, although the TV station in Muscat remains a source of great pride and is a ritual stop for state visitors. (The German engineers disappear to the background during these occasions, and Omanis are seen to be in control.) A pipeline worth $50 million was ordered and left to rust because there was no available project, and no one could decide what to do with it. A desalination plant estimated at $57 million, was rushed through on the promise that it would be ready for National Day 1975 and would provide the Sultan's garden at Sib with 1,000,000 gallons of water a day. Eventually the cost was $300 million; it had to be closed down for technical reasons, and water and power in Oman are about five times as expensive as necessary. Electricity costs the average household about $100 a week during the hottest months of the summer. The *falaj* system (underground waterways), built painstakingly by the Persians nearly 2,000 years ago, and still in use elsewhere, have been neglected, and boreholes were sunk indiscriminately without thought for the future.

There were so many crooks in the planning office that the same land was sold several times to different buyers, some of whom found they had no access except through other people's gardens. Contracts were signed willy-nilly, and, as in other money-rush countries, there was something for everyone. A Japanese firm unsuccessful in competing for a television station in Salalah suggested they organize the fishing concession instead. Experience was unimportant, and corruption was part of everyday life. "The Sultan refers to it as 'sweets for the children,'" said one bank manager. "On some road-building contracts there is a fifty percent markup for commission. Naturally it is always denied and is done carefully enough to be unprovable in law, but protestations of innocence from Arabs leave me unmoved. As a banker you see these things. Everyone is involved, including British advisers."

The Sultan is more circumspect. "One can't be a hundred percent sure there is no bribery. Maybe one in a hundred puts something in his pocket. I would not swear it did not happen, but not in a big way. And people know here that if they do wrong they will be punished. There is no doubt about it."

The biggest extravagance was military. The Dhofar rebellion became more intense as the guerrillas were backed by Cubans and trained in China, and it did not end officially until April 30, 1976. The Shah promised a squadron of Phantoms, in addition to troops from the Imperial Iranian Task Force, but insisted on a proper airfield. A 4,000-meter runway was constructed at Thumrait within nine months, regardless of expense. Cement was flown from Alaska at a total cost of $145 million. The Iranian Air Force used it once during the following year.

In 1974 the Sultan ordered Jaguar aircraft and a Rapier guided-missile system, both considered beyond Oman's needs by military experts and even by the British who sold them. "The early-warning system might hold up the Shah, or whoever, for five minutes," says a senior British diplomat. "However, everyone's got this sort of stuff, and I'd much rather they had our version than the French one."

The Sultan, like a fifteen-year-old boy about to drive a Formula One racing car, does not agree the equipment is too sophisticated. "If you look at things militarily, what you use today will be obsolete in two or three years' time," he says. "It's better to buy something really up-to-date so you can use it for the next ten years. If you get anything less, you will soon be far behind." Nevertheless, in a tacit admission that he was too extravagant, the Sultan restricted government spending in July 1974—only to commit a further $400 million to his air defenses two months later. He is proud of his military knowledge and takes his authority seriously. When he announced that he was dividing his forces into three separate branches, a colleague joked, "I suppose you will have uniforms made as Admiral of the Fleet, Marshal of the Royal Air Force, and Commander-in-Chief?"

"I already have," replied the Sultan gravely.

The RAF left Masira, a base they had established as an emergency landing ground in 1932, on March 31, 1977. The Sultan gave them a tea party to celebrate and denied he was letting the Americans take over to monitor Russian movements in the Indian Ocean. He began to establish links with the Chinese, though, and is determined to appear independent and strong—hence an armory which takes at least 40 percent of the country's budget and phony statistics which boost the population from a reliable estimate of 500,000 to nearer 750,000 in official pronouncements.

The stockpiling of weapons is paralleled by nervousness about his personal safety, for which the Sultan takes precautions of a less tangible nature. Superstition forbids him to travel on certain days of the week—it used to be Friday, now it is Wednesday—and a woman from the interior with claimed psychic powers was paid an undersecretary's salary, given a Mercedes, and interpreted his dreams. His mysticism is at a more primitive level than the Shah's and therefore easier to manipulate. One senior minister, closely associated with a British contracting company, wears armbands with "magical" symbols designed to "protect" the Sultan. Although such devoted service is appreciated, he also travels with a number of bodyguards, once taking twenty-four to a private dinner party. When asked why he needed so many, he replied, "They say I need them."

"They" were Robert B. Anderson, a former Secretary of the U.S. Treasury and Deputy Secretary for Defense, Yahya Omar, a Libyan entrepreneur on the diplomatic lists in Germany, Britain, and the United States, who, according to some sources, has made $400 million in commissions since 1970, and an unidentified former CIA man. The polite tussle between America and Britain for control of the Sultan's section of the money-rush course continues while he gratifies his own truncated authority by personal extravagances which do not equal the vulgarity of some Saudis or Gulf Arabs, but do provide a tempting target for have-nots in other parts of Arabia.

Sitting in a putrid refugee camp in Lebanon, it must be galling to hear about "that Indian" ordering himself two dinner services worth $100,000 each, specially built thrones from Essex, ultrasophisticated electric organs, and building lavish air-conditioned sheds for his beloved Jersey cattle which he then allows visitors to watch through a one-way mirror as they are milked. His more ostentatious shopping sprees are not publicized in Oman, but a number of well-educated young Omanis are not thrilled to discover that in one day he spent $1.5 million at a Chicago firm buying six Cadillac Sevilles, one Eldorado, six Mercedes, two Porsches, a 25-foot speedboat, 1,255 pieces of luggage, eight refrigerators, a gas range, three grapefruit trees, and two La-Z-Boy reclining chairs. He is also criticized for buying hundreds of silk shirts at a time.

Some misunderstandings arise from a puritanical assumption in the West that extravagance is not a fit subject for jokes. Anyway, Arabs are humorless, so what they say must be taken literally. Ordering $36,000 worth of perfume at Harrods, the Sultan was warned by a salesgirl that it would evaporate. "Don't worry, it's for the bath," he replied. And when his private VC10 was delayed on the runway for three hours during a strike at London's Heathrow, he relayed a message to the control tower asking how much it would cost to buy the airport. These were not meant as serious remarks, but they were reported as such and given credence by the genuine arrogance with which the Sultan sometimes disguises his feelings of inferiority. "I am Sultan. I can do what I like," he told an adviser and was nonplused when this sort of remark was passed on to the Jordanians. When he went to thank them for their help during the Dhofar war, a senior official said, "We wanted to see you in order to find out if you really were mad."

The Shah was much more amenable, perhaps because he shares an enthusiasm for heritage. They see themselves as a couple of aristocrats amidst the parvenus, and when the Sultan went to Persepolis, he was acknowledged as a real king, compared to the Gulf rulers, who were treated like Arabs. Both the Sultan and the Shah have a love of dignity, military parades, and a regal life-style which demands numerous residences. The Sultan has a $1.6 million Georgian manor house in Britain, and a 4,000-acre estate near Berchtesgaden, which he bought for a trifling $4 million. The latter is a surprising location for such a self-proclaimed Anglophile, but he sends his wife and mother there for the summer. Occasionally, as in 1976, he appears to "forget" to recall them, and they await his pleasure while the snow begins to fall. In addition, he has three palaces in Northern Oman and two in Salalah, most of them bristling with closed-circuit television equipment, and decorated opulently with a touch of the Indian bazaar and 1930 Hollywood kitsch. "It took Louis XIV years and years to build Versailles," observes a diplomat, "but modern techniques are quicker, and he seems to be making full use of them."

"I don't have many palaces," says the Sultan. "This one [in Muscat] is the Palace of State, not my personal one. You must have a suitable place to greet visitors, otherwise we would be accused of being Bedouin and not knowing how to entertain people. I inherited Sib, and in Salalah I have the so-called castle, which is also government owned."

It is indelicate to point out that he is in fact the government. When he disappears to Salalah, as he does for increasingly lengthy periods, checks are not signed for months, causing even the largest multinational firms temporary cash-flow problems. Maybe there will come a time when Oman is "ready" for democracy. What does the Sultan say to that?

"We should think of democracy as people having a greater say about what goes on in their own country and being free to express the way they feel. We are preparing ourselves for this, but we are not going to import a particular form of democracy. I think that is very dangerous. We read about India, where everyone said that British democracy succeeded. . . . Look at what happened. No. I think we should adapt democracy to our country, rather than try to import someone else's version.

"Our hopes for the future are great. So far, the things we have done with oil money are nonproductive. We had to develop fast. Now we are concentrating more on industry and agriculture and soon we will be able to feed ourselves without imports. We have fisheries, mineral resources, and so on. We have an endless source of limestone from one end of the country to another. So oil is not everything.

"But I think the biggest jewel of the last few years has been our progress in education. We are educating everyone, and that is a question of guidance. We don't want people to forget their religion or their traditions. We don't want them to think that everything in the past is bad. In some places this has happened, and people have fallen into the modern world without guidance. They thought everything new was good and everything old was bad. Well, we are steering our ship.

"Revolution? In the modern world it is something which attracts some people. But revolutions function only when there is a base. I don't think there is a base here. A few people will try to put ideas into the heads of others, but the Omanis will not be attracted to such ideas, so long as they are satisfied with their ruler."

At present they are. But the money rush builds expectations which it can never satisfy and creates a desire for freedom incompatible with the Sultan's autocracy. Unlike the Saudis, his capacity to bribe the opposition is slipping away with his rapidly decreasing oil reserves, and he is not strong enough to deter the Russians who bide their time with covetous menace in South Yemen.

For Oman the money rush may be a chimerical glint in a long history of foreign oppression, and its gentle people may once more be buffeted by the turbulence of international politics.

Sometimes the Omanis think they might make their country a tourist center so they can be independent of oil money. The world's most expensive Holiday Inn squats waiting on the ocean sands at Salalah, and more hotels are planned. Yet tourism means unrestricted entry, a thought that appalls the Sultan's instinct for self-preservation as much as it offends his people's sense of tranquillity. A group of Egyptian businessmen came to Salalah one day to meet local dignitaries and spend the whole lunchtime waxing enthusiastic about how they could turn the picturesque and peaceful coastline into a resort just like La Baule in northern France—hotels, fun fairs, chalets, and restaurants. They were not well received.

Some intrepid tourists have already arrived. As I left Muscat to visit the money rush's richest self-made man, I met an American couple who had been diverted to Oman from a package tour of the Middle East. They were anxious to rejoin their group, but, as happens frequently, the plane was delayed and tempers were frayed. "I wish those damned niggers behind the counter would get on with it," muttered the woman, while her husband stood stolidly looking out of the airport window. Suddenly the woman gave a shriek and rushed to her husband. "My God," she said. "Look over there. In our seat. By our baggage." The husband glanced to where he had piled their belongings. Sitting nearby was an Arab with a falcon tied to his wrist.

"Yes, dear?"

"There's a damned nigger in our seat with a parrot on his arm!"

Part Five

The United Arab Emirates

19/THE AMBASSADOR IN HIS LAIR

"One billion, two billion, I am worth much more than that."
MOHAMED MAHDI AL-TAJIR (AMBASSADOR AND BUSINESSMAN)

"If an old-fashioned moralist arrived in Dubai by mistake, he would find more crooks here than anywhere on earth, with the possible exception of San Quentin."
AMERICAN BUSINESSMAN

His EXCELLENCY the Ambassador of the United Arab Emirates to the Court of St. James's, Mohamed Mahdi al-Tajir, is not a crook. He has merely used the education provided for him in Bahrain and at Preston Grammar School in England, the experience acquired as a customs officer in Dubai, and hard work to become one of the world's wealthiest men.[1] His methods, sanctified by the money rush, but questioned by many, including senior diplomats, international bankers, and company directors, have made him richer than Adnan Khashoggi, more sinister than the Shah (with whom he shares Persian ancestry), more swashbuckling than Sir Shapoor Reporter (with whom he shares a reputation as a "fixer" of distinction), and as elusive to serious scrutiny as his position as a diplomat allows. Not for him the bold self-justification which might be expected from an honorary citizen of Texas, one of the few accomplishments he sees fit to mention in *Who's Who*.

He has been ambassador in London since his country was formed in 1971 from seven once-independent shaikhdoms: Abu

Dhabi, Dubai, Sharjah, Ras al-Khaimah, Fujairah, Ajman, and Umm al-Qaiwain. During that time his business interests have entwined the world: a fettucine of interlocking companies and nominee shareholdings which provide riches beyond avarice. He is one of the five really influential men in the Middle East and possibly the most important individual financier in the world. Those who aspire to honors in the money rush forbear to comment on how difficult it is for His Excellency to earn so much money while complying, as he surely does, with Western ethics.

An almost eighteenth-century figure, he takes his chances in a world where it was once considered proper—indeed, almost obligatory—for a government official like himself to be successful in trade, but where now there is an atmosphere of spurious morality inspired by those who can not possibly understand the simple rules of commercial life. As well as being a distinguished diplomat, His Excellency is an entrepreneur of many talents. Entrepreneurs take commissions. If a legitimate commission is branded as a bribe . . . well, marriage might just as well be called prostitution. In some cases, possibly, it is. But His Excellency the ambassador has never accepted nor offered a bribe. Like his friend Adnan, he does not need to. The commission is more than adequate.

But he is not flashy like Adnan. He prefers to use some of his money to become a cultural hero, purchasing stately homes that the British can no longer afford, thus saving exquisite buildings from the mortifying shame of becoming girls' boarding schools, museums, or even croupier-training establishments for Playboy Club bunnies. "We want to preserve Britain," he says. "We like your beautiful houses. After all, we can afford them."

He began his British sojourn by living at Windlesham Moor, a 54-acre estate near Sunningdale which had deteriorated, socially speaking, from the first home of Her Majesty Queen Elizabeth II and His Royal Highness Prince Philip to become the residence of a vacation-camp purveyor, albeit a knighted one, Sir William ("Billy") Butlin.

The great years of the ambassador's personal acquisitions were between 1974 and 1976, when according to some estimates, he paid $60 million for British property. He bought a 20,000-acre shooting estate in Scotland for $4 million, a Mayfair office building for $1,600,000, Dropmore House in Taplow (formerly owned by Lord Kemsley), a Regency house in Rutland Gate, Kensington, a mansion in Bagshot, the Park Tower Hotel, eighteenth-century Mereworth Castle (former home of the Dukes of Devonshire), a $1 million home in Majorca ("I go there occasionally"), and land in Wales which he was delighted to find so cheap that he resolved to go on buying it. He considered purchasing Mentmore Towers, complete with valuable antique contents, after the British Government declined to buy it from the owner, Lord Rosebery, for $6 million. But by then he had enough homes to make Adnan seem like a vagrant—and he also developed a sense of humor befitting an English country gentleman. After paying $1 million for Mereworth, he remarked that he needed somewhere appropriate to hang his paintings. More seriously, he is a rude reminder of money-rush impetuosity. "I saw this castle, liked it, and bought it just like that," he explained as casually as if it had been a rather amusing objet d'art picked up cheap in a flea market. "The Arabs like beautiful things. Art, painting, anything that is beautiful. Women, for example, although my wife would not think much of me filling the place with other women like a harem."

In addition to his English property, Mahdi al-Tajir owns a number of houses on the Avenue Foch, Paris, as well as farms in France, shares in African mines, an oil well in Texas which provides 400 barrels a day, and a bank in the Cayman Islands. He plays the London and New York stock markets. "I have never really bothered to find out how much I am worth," he tells the curious with laudable disdain. Money, like sex, is a vulgar topic of conversation to those who have enough, however riveting it may be to the deprived.

For the rich, it buys the artifacts of style, such as clothes, and the ambassador has become acknowledged as one of the world's most elegant men, whether he is lounging Mata Hari–like in a silk *thobe* on a sofa in his Dubai beach house or being soigné at a London dinner party. He spent $60,000 in two years at one of his three London tailors, buys five $4,000 vicuna coats at a time, and has his blazer buttons monogrammed tastefully in silver. His sons go to Harrow, of course. "When I wanted the best education for my children, I sent them to Britain. I know they share my love of the country."

His admiration is eloquently expressed in neo-Churchillian terms at every opportunity. "I am confident Britain will recover because it has the greatest asset of all—its people. They are the same people who built the greatest empire on earth, and they can overcome the crisis. All they need is the will," he announced to the *Daily Mirror* in May 1975.

Fine words, and a welcome change from the cynicism which blights so much of the money rush. It seems churlish to ask how and why the ambassador amassed his fortune. "I do not do business just to make money. I have enough. I do not need any more. It is not the £1 million I make in a deal and put in the bank that is important. It is the friends I have made and whom I continue to see."

He is suitably indignant about that most lucrative prize of the money rush—arms sales. "You cannot create a world by flying in guns and Phantoms." And he does not wince when embroiled in muckraking suggestions that he received commissions of $6 million from Boeing or $15 million from Lockheed. "This is not the first time I have been subjected to such accusations. Just as I did not reply in the past, so I shall not reply now," he asserts. One of the senior financial advisers to his country's President, Shaikh Zayed, told me, "We bought some Boeing aircraft for Syria and I looked at the cost very carefully. Maybe Mahdi had his cut, but we paid exactly the same for the planes as British Airways. That makes you think, doesn't it?"

But next to the King of Kings in Iran, His Excellency the ambassador has the money rush's least enviable reputation. There are numerous stories. It is believed by many in the Gulf that Shaikh Zayed once asked al-Tajir how much it would cost to settle the border dispute with Saudi Arabia. "Thirty million dollars for Kamal Adham [former head of Saudi intelligence]," he is alleged to have replied. Zayed agreed on the figure, paid the money, but it was—some believe—kept by the ambassador. More prosaically, a senior director of BP expressed an opinion heard frequently in private, although publicly it is not yet seemly to antagonize so powerful a man.

"There is the most scandalous case, and it has spread like a cancer through the lower Gulf, of our friend Mahdi Tajir. One hears one is not able to do anything in Dubai without paying him a commission—and that is an absolute fact. We have refused to do so on numerous occasions and are living with the consequences. I would have loved a new piece of land at Dubai Airport to give us a bigger and better aviation depot, but we make do with what we have because we wouldn't pay Mahdi Tajir for the privilege of getting it. He charges so much for changing a comma in an agreement, and so much for a period.

"We have operated in the Middle East since 1909 and to the best of my knowledge we have never, in our oil business, made a payment there to anyone. All right, you know that the man responsible for getting passports and visas slips the odd present to a customs official. But that's petty cash, part of the business of living. If you want a driver's license, you have to make sure the application gets to the top of the pile, but I know of no money paid by BP to any government official on the oil side.[1]

"In the Middle East now, as I understand it, the authorities have taken the view that commission is a way of spreading the oil revenue. What does it matter, they say, if a contractor bids for a job and his agent adds so much on top? The government is willing to pay so that the lads develop as entrepreneurs. In Kuwait, they did it by giving away bits of desert and buying it back at exorbitant prices. You have to have some mechanism, other than the dole, for pushing money around. It is not considered wrong in that part of the world, and now everyone is saying, 'If Mahdi can get away with it, so can we.' It's gummed up the whole works so far as we are concerned."

Mahdi al-Tajir arrived in Dubai twenty-five years ago, aged twenty-two, having been encouraged to leave Bahrain, where he was one of ten sons of a prominent carpet merchant, because his family's political activity unsettled the self-satisfied British colonial administration. "I was just told I was an undesirable person," he recalls, and adds that he thought the British Resident, Sir Charles Belgrave, was a fool.

In the fifties Dubai was a small enclave of semiliterate traders, ancestors of dissidents from the Bani Yas tribe who had left Abu Dhabi in 1833 to form their own community and continue the traditional part-time activity of interfamily slaughter. Those who

lost and lived were usually banished a few miles down the road
to Sharjah and, apart from occasional eye gougings and assassinations, had a gentlemanly, almost sportsmanlike, attitude toward the activities.

They were unable to buy weapons in pre-money rush days, so
made do with 300-year-old cannons which they plugged with
rags and loaded with pistons stolen from hijacked cars. "Cannonballs generally were in such short supply that a truce was declared after sunset prayers every night to enable both sides to
comb the battlefield for old balls that might be used again the
next day," an observer told author David Holden.[2]

A wide-open sewer euphemistically called a creek, separated
the town from a rival village, Deira, which had been established
a hundred years earlier by merchants seeking refuge from a
plague in Dubai. There had been continual arguments about
who should collect customs revenue from the *dhows* which navi-
gated the creek, so, one day in 1939, Shaikh Rashid of Dubai accepted an invitation to dinner and ordered his men to attack during the festivities when his hosts were unprepared. He later
excused his abuse of Arab hospitality as a necessary preventive
action: if he had not done it to them, they would have done it to
him. His victory was consolidated by marriage in the normal
way. As Rashid himself has only one wife, a canny move designed to prevent vicious squabbling amongst his own four boys
and five girls, he allowed his brother to marry the thirteen-year-
old daughter of the Ruler of Deira, Shaikha Sana. It is a union
blessed with children, protective family liaisons (her daughter is
married to Rashid's eldest son), and excitement: Shaikha Sana,
an unusually high-spirited Arab woman, shot and wounded her
husband's fourth wife, a former slave girl, and warned police
that she would shoot them too if they tried to arrest her. They
did not. Although she still wears the *burqa* (black mask) out of
tradition, she has built herself a thriving business consisting of
apartment buildings, taxi fleets (a fashionable occupation for
Gulf women), and an agency for importing Pakistani and Indian
construction workers. "I have lived in hell and I have fought my
way to paradise," she says. "I was nine when I saw them kill my
family. And four years later, I was made to marry the man who

killed them. If I am a strong woman now, it is because of such experiences."

Shaikh Rashid succeeded his father as Ruler in 1958, although he had in fact been in control for the previous seventeen years, and began to develop Dubai with a shrewdness which has made him one of the most respected rulers in the Gulf. He borrowed $800,000 from Kuwait in 1961 to dredge and narrow the creek so the water flowed faster, and then he married his daughter Miriam to Shaikh Ahmad of Qatar, a profligate car collector (he is said to have had 452 at one time) whose Byzantine family disputes make Dubai seem as docile as Pleasantville on a Sunday morning, but who was wealthy enough to give Rashid $400,000 to build a bridge across the creek.

Next, a harbor was needed. Rashid's advisers said that four berths would be sufficient, but he ordered fifteen, anticipating the unprecedented demand that the money rush would create. "You could never tell him what to do," says a former British Political Resident for the area. "With Shaikh Zayed it was different —a few stern words, and he did as he was told."

In spite of the development, Dubai was still a very small town when Mahdi al-Tajir arrived. It had few amenities, only one bank, and was known to seamen as "The Light" because of the solitary electric illumination over the offices of Gray, Mackenzie, the British shipping agents. Customs fees, the only income except handouts from his son-in-law, were $70,000 a month.

The main trade was "reexporting" gold to India and Pakistan, where its importation had been banned since 1947. The gold was ordered through the British Bank of the Middle East or the First National City Bank of New York (Citibank) and was supplied by Mocatta and Goldsmid, Samuel Montague, or the Swiss Bank Corporation. It was sent to Dubai legally in 10-tola bars (3.75 ounces) where it sold for $35 an ounce, and was then taken by *dhow* 1,200 miles across the ocean and smuggled into India, where the price was $68 an ounce.

A couple of years after al-Tajir's arrival, Dubai was importing 4 million ounces of gold, watches worth $15.4 million (enough to supply each inhabitant with at least two dozen), and 5.5 million ounces of silver. Customs duty was 4.625 percent, providing revenue of $6 million in 1958, and $140 million twelve years later.

Shaikh Rashid ensured that al-Tajir was suitably rewarded for his conscientious work, and soon Dubai was dealing with goods from ninety-four countries. As well as gold and jewelry, there were textiles from the Far East, canned food from Eastern Europe, rocket launchers from Northern Ireland routed deviously and presumably secretly to Southern Ireland, rifles sent to China, "pharmaceuticals" (although everyone denies any connection with drugs), construction and electrical equipment. The gold trade declined after Indira Gandhi's emergency powers, which were in force until March 1977, effectively stopped smuggling, although gold is still plentiful and relatively inexpensive.[3] Some shops can sell 30 one-ounce gold bracelets a day (a kilo) with a markup of 20 to 30 percent, compared with 300 percent in Western Europe and the United States.

Other bargains reach Dubai in a curious way. A Japanese electrical company had one million $25 transistor radios for sale at $1.50. They went first to Iran where they were treated with acute suspicion and found no takers. They increased the price in Dubai to $5.50, formed a joint partnership with a local businessman, and sold the lot. It was no trick. The radios had not been popular in Japan, so the manufacturer held a lottery with the transistors as a prize. The lottery raised $8 million—the cost of production. As the winner preferred cash, the firm bought back the radios for $1 million and would have been satisfied to make a modest profit by selling them at $1.50 each.

Throughout the rest of the Gulf, Dubai became known as a pirate's lair—unfairly, according to Bill Duff, an Englishman sent from the Kuwait Finance Department seventeen years ago to become Shaikh Rashid's financial expert. "It is not a smuggler's paradise at all. Nothing becomes smuggling until it is three miles, or whatever, off the Indian coast. People use Dubai as a supermarket, stock up here, and away they go. Whether they smuggle or not you cannot possibly tell."

Mr. Duff is one of several British advisers—police chief Jack Briggs is another—who have served the Ruler for many years. Their integrity is unquestioned, much to the occasional chagrin of British embassy officials in Abu Dhabi who complain they will not even do a favor for a fellow Brit. "I'm Rashid's man," Duff tells them.

The first thing Duff did when he arrived was provide himself with a title: General Inspector of Ports and Customs. "It is a job which should never have been mine," he says. "It's about time a local did it, but I've been saying that for sixteen years. It's been very nice, really. Half the joy of Dubai is you can live normally. You needn't think you are away from home, so to speak, and you don't have the feeling you are wandering through a *souk* [bazaar], as you do in other Arab countries."

Every year he spends six weeks in England, either at his home in Christchurch, Hampshire, or at his Kensington house in chic Walton Street. His office in Dubai is on the top floor of the customs building overlooking the creek and next to the Ruler's helicopter landing pad. "Wealth has made a difference here, of course, but I don't think morals are worse than before—although the sins are probably more sophisticated ones now. People here are very tolerant and don't regard money with much awe. Rashid thinks it's very nice stuff, and the more you can get the better. He doesn't throw it away on government. This must be the cheapest-run place in the world. There has been no increase in any of our setups, unlike in Abu Dhabi. As soon as you ask an Englishman or an Egyptian to organize a government, the first thing he does is put all the top dogs behind secretaries whose job it is to keep people away. Rashid never liked secretaries, and he is too experienced in the old style of ruling to try to keep people away.

"My job is to record. I'm an auditor, that's all. But we are always short of one figure because the Ruler keeps his oil income completely separate. In a way it is unimportant because we know it's there, and too many people are in on the secret to start fiddling."

Shaikh Rashid receives about $1 billion a year, paid in quarterly installments by the oil company and dispensed by the Department of His Highness the Ruler's Affairs and Petroleum Affairs, cable address PETROLEUM. Since 1963, the director of his Affairs has been His Excellency Mohamed Mahdi al-Tajir. "He has been the Cardinal Richelieu of the place," says Duff. "Before he came there was a haphazard customs collection, and the amount of business was not enormous. Everyone hated his guts at first. They always have done because he's so successful.

Nowadays, though, everyone is so rich it is not really that important.

"His capacity for dealing with foreigners is immeasurable. He takes them by the tail and twists it round them. He has computer reactions. He can compute automatically in his mind when he has got as much as possible from a deal."

There are those who feel that the ambassador's influence as the Ruler's most trusted long-term adviser gives unfair advantage to well-established firms at the expense of others.

They cite Costain which, between 1967 and 1973, did 80 percent of the civil engineering work in Dubai: a $70 million cement factory (the largest in the Gulf), a $20 million tunnel under the creek, an international airport, the original fifteen-berth Port Rashid, and, in a joint venture with Taylor Woodrow, a $240 million twenty-two-berth extension. Another Costain/Taylor Woodrow project is a dry-dock complex for tankers up to a million tons. The original $162 million contract, awarded in 1973, increased in price to $330 million in 1976, and had risen to about $400 million by 1978. It is probably one of the most spectacular money-rush white elephants; it has to compete with an OAPEC-sponsored dry dock in nearby Bahrain, and has the added problem of finding enough specialized employees.

The ambassador's role is open to speculation. His representatives are said to have a 50 percent interest in the dry-dock company, and American State Department sources have few doubts that his influence secured the contract. A confidential memorandum written by Nat Howell, former commercial attaché at the United States embassy in Abu Dhabi and signed by chargé d'affaires Philip J. Griffiths, entitled CONTRACT AWARDED FOR DUBAI DRY DOCK. IT'S HOW YOU PLAY THE GAME THAT COUNTS, says in part:

> It seems apparent that there was never any intention of putting the scheme out to competitive tender. The contract, valued at $162 million was awarded to two British firms, Costain Civil Engineering Ltd., and Taylor Woodrow (International) Limited after reported infighting among local participants in the venture. The entire story will probably never be told for obvious reasons. Several independent and

reliable sources in Dubai have, however, provided the reporting officer with the following outline of events.

A letter of intent for the construction of the Dry Dock, as originally planned, was handed to a representative of Taylor Woodrow on about January 6, 1973. Subsequently the letter was revoked and a meeting of January 8, 1973 took place. It is not clear whether or not a decision was taken at that time regarding the award of the contract. What does seem clear is the fact that subsequent developments stemmed from the eleventh-hour entry of Mahdi Tajir, a long-time adviser to Shaikh Rashid, into the ranks of the project's proponents.

The first indication that Tajir had been converted to the Dry Dock cause came as late as January 10 when he signed the agreement for financing with Lazard Brothers on behalf of the Dubai Government. According to the general view in Dubai these days, Tajir returned to Dubai shortly before that meeting and insisted that the contract was awarded to Costain. As a result, the tentative agreement with Taylor Woodrow, the firm supported by Abdul-Rahim Galadari who owns 25 percent of the Dry Dock company, was withdrawn. The resulting award to both Taylor Woodrow and Costain was a compromise designed to partially satisfy both Tajir and Galadari. Tajir was apparently somewhat mollified by the estimated $5-8.1 million that he will receive as a kick-back. He has reportedly also submitted a list of his approved subcontractors, thereby raising the possibility that he can yet increase his take.

Costain Civil Engineering which recently completed the Dubai Port, has been snapping up every Dubai project in sight. While the firm is very competent, its phenomenal success is probably not based on its expertise alone. So far as we can determine, it has never undertaken a project such as the Dry Dock.[4]

Costain denies the ambassador is its agent or that it has paid money to him. It will not disclose details about a former director, Mohammed al-Fayed, who some say is the ambassador's nominee and business partner. Mr. al-Fayed, who is a brother-in-law of Adnan Khashoggi, bought a 20 percent stake in Costain in 1974 from Slater Walker Securities for $8 million. He later sold his shareholding to Lonrho and bought it back for $22 million in 1976. A year later, in May 1977, he resold it to a group of fifty different institutional investors for $30 million, "removing one football which has been kicked around for quite some time," according to Costain's finance director, John Wells.

For an independent view of the ambassador's activities I sought a man of unimpeachable integrity who had been a Political Resident in the Gulf, the British Foreign Secretary's Personal Representative in the Middle East between 1970 and 1972, Middle East adviser to Inchcape, as well as a director of several banks and firms with direct involvement in the area: Sir William Luce. He had known the ambassador since 1961–"an amiable rogue, but less attractive than he used to be because he has become arrogant. He worships money, of course," he told me when we met at his Wiltshire home shortly before his death in July 1977.

"But corruption? It depends what you mean. It is the British who are peculiar about this, not the Arabs. We still have different standards of behavior from anywhere else in the world. They don't call this sort of thing corruption. But the fact remains that the commission business has become too much of a good thing. I think that when the standard rate went up to 25 percent even some Arabs thought it was a bit high. They get jealous when an individual like Khashoggi or Mahdi amasses hundreds of millions. I haven't the details but I know what he made on the dry dock."

"I heard it was nearly £3 million," I replied.

"Oh no, it was much more than that. The contract is now for about £140 million. We are talking more in terms of £35 to £40 million. It simply goes on the bill. Shaikh Rashid pays it."

This comment clearly distressed Mr. David Newell, managing director of Costain International, when I asked him if there was any truth in it. He left the room without comment or explanation. When he returned fifteen minutes later, he said he had been to see his chairman. "That figure of £30 million sent me up the wall. It is an absolute absurdity. How could we bury that amount without it becoming totally obvious?"

He refused to confirm that Costain pays commission in Dubai. "You don't expect us to say if we do, do you?" And clearly the firm would never become involved in underhand behavior. It is even possible that if they pay commission, which is perfectly proper, they are unaware of its eventual destination. As Sir William Luce explained, "It is a difficult thing. British firms don't like doing it, but what else can they do? If they don't, the Americans or Japanese will. But payment should not be concealed so far as the accounts are concerned. It must be shown as an expense and part of the contract. I am not sure of the mechanics of how it is actually done. I think commission is added to the contract and becomes part of the estimate. It is an astonishing racket, but I suppose it all adds to our foreign exchange."

The realities of business contradict official pieties spoken for public consumption, and now that the backwaters of the Gulf have been hustled into prominence by the money rush they bring a laissez-faire attitude to life which is easy to misinterpret. In the ambassador's lair itself, images blur into a kaleidoscopic pattern which wise contestants do not attempt to unravel lest by doing so they are confronted with a vision of morality inappropriate to their aspirations. Blink once, dream of a fortune, and hope the fairy godmother is in a benign mood.

Today she is not. It is difficult to see such a busy and important man as the ambassador. In London his aides and secretaries frequently appear uncertain of his whereabouts, and in Dubai there is a similarly haphazard approach. He still has his headquarters in the customs office, a dilapidated, fly-infested white building on the edge of the creek which swarms throughout the day with *dhow* captains whose scruffy appearance gives little hint of the prosperity brought to them by the money rush. It is an unlikely place for His Excellency, and he does not often visit his second-floor office, leaving details to Oscar J. Mandody, a sleek, affable Indian and Jane, a pretty English secretary whose solitary telephone bleats with importuning salesmen. She is energetically cheerful, sympathizing with those whose appointments have been canceled at the last minute, solicitous to claimants with an "introduction," and helpful to those who in desperation sit in the office . . . and wait.

A man from Wisconsin is there today with an idea and a deteriorating conviction that he has reached the end of the rainbow. He is a partner in a medium sized air-conditioning company, and at the end of a closely scheduled two-week visit to the Gulf, having made initial contacts through embassies in Washington. He started in Bahrain, received polite interest and no orders, and then had his schedule disrupted by a typical seven-hour Gulf Air delay to Kuwait. His meetings elsewhere had been characterized by endless cups of black coffee and little else. Dubai was his final opportunity to prevent a humiliating return home without a single tentative—never mind signed—order. It hurt to think of the damage to his reputation—the man who could not even sell air conditioners to the Arabs! Perhaps he should sell ice cream to children.

If necessary, he planned to cancel a reservation on tomorrow's plane to New York via London and stay an extra day—even though it meant raising money by selling his blood at $40 a pint (in Oman, he heard, you were paid $80). Who would have realized that his American Express card would be as effective as tissue in a gale against ceaseless demands for cash, cash, cash. He knew the Middle East was expensive and had brought twice as much money as he thought he would reasonably spend, but it had all gone.

BLOOD DONATION IS A NATIONAL DUTY said signs along the road, and last night at the bar of the Intercontinental, where credit cards are accepted, he met an Englishman who sold a pint every trip. The American shuddered. It was the sort of thing he read about New York junkies doing. Presumably his blood would now run in the veins of an Arab smashed up in his Cadillac.

In Wisconsin they assumed he was languishing under the stars attended by a dozen nubile slave girls. The size of his bill would confirm their suspicions. In fact, he anticipated such luxury himself when he read the brochure of the *Bon Vivant,* a Chandris Line cruise ship moored in the creek and converted into a "flotel." It had, he was told, "international gourmet cuisine" and a casino for "after-hours excitement" as well as "modern communications," and there were "within a few steps of the wide gangway, air-conditioned chauffeur-driven vehicles."

Hah! It was one of the biggest rip-offs he had encountered. His room was tiny, his bed hard, the bathroom so small that he soaked the toilet when he showered. The food was so bad and expensive ($6 for orange juice) that even the waiters took

Valium because they were ashamed to serve it. At dinner the previous evening their version of *tournedos Rossini* had been tough rump steak topped with a small portion of frozen pâté, and *zabaglione* was crème caramel with a drop of Cointreau. A complaint to the manager had inspired a facetious remark: "Rossini was fired last week." The "casino" consisted of two dozen penny-arcade slot machines. Communications were so "modern" that not only were there no telephone directories in the rooms, but the switchboard operator did not have one either. Telexes waited hours to be sent. No airline timetables were available. The "few steps" to limousines were over fine sand which dirtied his shoes so that he looked as if he had trekked through the desert.

The final insult was that he had to pay a tax that went directly to the PLO of 50 cents on every Telex and $3 for an airline ticket.

"I think you might be lucky today," said Jane as she walked from Mandody's office. The American smiled with gratitude and relief. It had been wise, after all, to sit and wait. Now was his chance.

"Okay," said Jane a few minutes later. "In you go."

The American glided through one of the two sets of swing doors, his satisfaction marred only slightly by the surprise of finding about six other people in the room. Mandody greeted him warmly, asked him to find a seat, and continued a conversation on the telephone.

"I said we would get her the money by tomorrow morning. She will have to wait. What about the other business? Good. I'm not sure how long His Excellency will be here. . . ."

Mandody's jet-black hair was sleek in the manner of a 1950s film idol. He wore a blue suit which nearly shimmered and was a bit too gaudy to be respectable—at least in Wisconsin—a silk shirt that clung to the gentle ripple of his stomach, and a colorful tie. He looked like a cross between a prosperous bookie and Omar Sharif. An ebony cigarette holder languished in his elegantly manicured fingers, and, while still talking on the telephone, he greeted a number of visitors. Some he shook by the hand. Others kissed him, so that sometimes, when he was engaged in a particularly emotional part of the conversation and waved his cigarette hand, it seemed as if such close contact might cause a conflagration. He spoke alternately in Arabic and English, and when he finished on the telephone, he introduced the American to no less a person than local hero Abdulla al Alawi, the newly declared world champion of Petropolis, a version of Monopoly designed to capitalize on money-rush fervor. For a while they discussed the versatility of Swedish girls vis-à-vis a mutually acquainted Norwegian stewardess.

Neville Brook, a senior executive of Costain, came to pay his respects and was welcomed with much familiarity and friendliness. "He's a very good man," said Mandody, and the American began to remind himself for about the hundredth time that optimism, balance sheets, a good product, and hard work are no substitute in this market for the one qualification which ensures success: contacts. He smiled thinly, but anguish showed in his eyes and rivulets of perspiration began to trickle down his face and the nape of his neck. Sweat stains dampened the light brown tropical jacket his wife had bought in an out-of-season sale before waving him an envious good-bye. Christ, if only she knew . . .

"Yes, Mr. . . ." said Mandody. "What do you want with us?"

The World Petropolis Champion looked fascinated, and the telephone rang again.

Surely this was not the time for a serious business meeting, with all these people listening. . . .

"You want to see His Excellency?"

"I thought . . ." began the American.

"You see, it's a difficult time for us at the moment," explained Mandody, managing to sound genuinely disappointed, before the telephone interrupted him once more.

"What I thought . . ." the American started.

"Do you have your card?" asked Mandody. "Can you come back in, say, a month when I know His Excellency will be here and we can try to arrange a meeting?"

"But I have to leave tomorrow. Or," he added hurriedly, "the next day at the latest." The American felt his smile turning into an involuntary grimace. There was nothing he could do to stop the muscles twitching and he felt foolish, like a child unable to stop crying. His last slim hopes were dismembered as Mandody answered another call and then announced, "I'm afraid I have to see His Excellency, who is with the Ruler. If you can come back, I hope we might be able to help. Thank you so much for dropping by."

The American departed for the *Bon Vivant,* disconsolate and aching for the delights of Wisconsin.

I understood how he felt. It was my third visit to Dubai, and I, too, had been promised meetings with the ambassador which somehow never materialized. And I was not trying to sell him anything.

Then Mandody patted my arm. "The ambassador will see you this evening," he whispered. "Can you come round to the house at seven? It's easy to find."

A herd of expensive cars stands idle in the garage, and a retainer insists that you wait at the gate of the £200,000 beach-front home while he checks your appointment. Inside, no servants are in evidence, and the house has an unlived-in, musty air—little to indicate the torrents of money that the ambassador has collected. His wife is not in residence. She has a less grand home, where the paint is peeling, near the customs office. Mandody is here, of course, in a side room, talking sotto voce to a colleague.

His Excellency is a slim man of medium height with crenellated gray hair and skin so smooth there are those who say it is chiseled by a plastic surgeon. He speaks in a slow voice and sits upright, looking you straight in the eye, like the Shah. We spoke about development in the money-rush countries, and he sighed. "I don't think you will find many people agreeing with me, but the changes here have not been good. Money has spoiled the people.

"We are very greedy. Perhaps you have to work hard to earn money, but you have to work even harder to spend it. A rich man should be like an artist. He should collect his money beautifully and spend it beautifully, exactly the way an artist lives. The wealthy man in the Arab world is not an artist. Far from it. He is a greedy pig. Most of our wealthy people can hardly sign their names. How can they control empires?"

"Do you include yourself?"

"No. It has not spoiled me because it is not new as far as I am concerned. I had a very wealthy father, and that makes a difference, because when you make your own wealth, you are more at ease. It is not strange, something you don't know. If you suddenly find you have millions, you lose your balance, and, unfortunately, some of us have done that."

"Does it worry you that people say you take a percentage?" I asked.

"Not a bit. What is written in Britain is for Britishers, and they won't care for a moment if I take five percent or ten percent from the customs. But if it is written for this part of the world, I feel sorry for them because our people know better than that. I am wealthy, yes, but not the only wealthy man in the world."

He paused for a moment, and I was about to ask about specific allegations when he continued in an almost earnest fashion. "Anyone who works hard would be in better shape than the British are now. I don't think they work hard enough. What is really sad is to feel that Britain is losing the will to lead. You will not find many people agreeing with me, and certainly you will not meet another Arab to say in public, 'I love Britain.' But I do. In the past, you exported officers to command armies, to sell arms, or become governors. Today you are contributing more than at any time in history—doctors, teachers, engineers, bankers. And that is a healthy sign.

"There are those who say Britain divided us. Well, they did not have to do that. I would be exaggerating if I said we are now like brothers, but we are trying. The UAE is doing fine. The British achieved many good things. They did not open schools or hospitals—they left that to the Shaikhs on the grounds that they did not want to become involved locally—but they maintained stability, and we enjoyed many happy years of peace. During the war, while you could hardly get an egg once a month in England, we had plenty of everything supplied by the British Fleet.

"I blame the British Government for certain things. After God knows how many years of a relationship, they are the only Western government which knows the Middle East—the Americans don't attempt to understand us. They don't understand that our religion teaches us to like people, not to hate them—yet the British never educated their people to know the Arabs.

"We are to blame too because we have not handled our case as we should. Take U.N. Resolution 242 [see Appendix]. Part of the Arab world is for it, part against, and part neutral. We have never had an Arab policy. But it is a new world today. We have to change.

"In the UAE we had shaikhly rule, and that was marvelous because it gave a tribal, family relationship. The Ruler was like a father to everyone. Fifteen years ago, we did not use police. It is not possible to go back to that system, and we will miss the personal touch. But I am against a compromise—neither ruled in a shaikhly way, nor being a democratic state. At the moment we are lost between the two. We all hope for a democratic way, and we dream of a union. The greatest empire in the world—the British Isles—has crept on its knees to join Europe. What chance do we have in the United Arab Emirates if we live alone with our $8 billion income?

"My dream is that one day all the states of the Gulf will become a union with Saudi Arabia—even South Yemen. People say, 'Oh, no, they're communists.' Good gracious me, is that the only reason I have to give for not feeding a starving child—he's a communist? So what if he's a communist? I have to shoot him? Why not give him a better idea, and start to live with him?

"There is nothing to justify the present situation where $50 or $60 billion comes to part of Arabia while people are starving in the north and south. It is too, too ugly. And I don't think people living here should count on a long honeymoon if we just accept it. It does not look nice, nor does it suit the twentieth century, that my neighbor is starving while I am dying of a quantity of dollars. If we want stability and peace, we must become a union. How can we live otherwise?"

Will Israel be included in this grand union—as many Arabs think, privately, that it could be?

"We hope the Israel problem will be solved. Unfortunately, the Jews have lost the courage to admit the Arabs have a case. Some Jews are as good as any human being can be, and I meet them. I am not against them. I am against the devil whether he is in Jerusalem, Washington, or 10 Downing Street. It just happens that this time the devil is Zionist, so I will boycott everything directly or indirectly to do with Israel. It is not fair to contribute towards arms to kill my brothers in Palestine. We are applying the same method as the rest of the world does to South Africa, Rhodesia, or Chile. It is a human rights case, and the Jews have nothing to do with it.

"But I feel sorry for them. What is the use of the son of a musician, who made millions happy, driving a tank in the Middle East? Or the son of a great archaeologist, who has spent years uncovering tombs in Egypt, flying a Phantom and destroying Damascus? Or the family who were doctors for generations, and whose son fires a machine gun instead of taking over his father's clinic in Harley Street?

"I can understand running away from Russia, but why should a wise Jew leave beautiful England to live in a tiny place like Israel and then try to fight every few years to add a few inches of land? I don't think they can last in that way. Nature is against them. We have 150 million Arabs.

"If I were responsible for Arab policy, I would leave them alone. That is enough to see Israel off the map. It is not Jews who created the state. It is an invention of their enemies, especially the British. When you wanted to get rid of them because you were afraid they would rule Britain, you put the idea in their head of creating a homeland. When the Germans wanted to get rid of them, they gave them enough rope. So when Hitler did that disgrace and killed innocent people, the Germans were not at all upset. Instead they said, 'At last we are free and not ruled by Jews.' The same thing is happening in America now. They are leaving the press to the Jews, the banks to the Jews, and industry to the Jews. Every other American is becoming unhappy and is anti-Jew."

By now he had been talking for almost an hour, with only occasional prompting by me and a number of interruptions from the telephone. The atmosphere in the room, as dusk closed in over the Gulf, was solemn, almost studious, and the problems of the world seemed far more important than unseemly personal allegations. Moreover, I thought, guests were arriving for dinner, so I took advantage of the ambassador's invitation to contact him again later.

I should have known better. I wrote several letters mentioning in vague detail the sort of insinuations being made about him. I took his representatives to lunch and explained why I wanted to see the ambassador, who, unfortunately, never seemed to be in London.

Then, eleven months later, I received a telephone call. "The ambassador will see you tomorrow morning."

I entered the elegant first-floor drawing room of his Rutland Gate home with some misgiving. It is not every day that you ask an ambassador if he accepted £40 million in what some might construe as a bribe. He was affable and courteous, ordered some coffee, and said, "Tons of good rumors go on around me. If people say that Mahdi Tajir's been paid for this or that, it doesn't bother me a bit. I would like you to publish whatever you have heard. If you don't, it will be dishonest. Publish anything, but my one request is this: Be fair."

"All right," I said, "what is your reply to the suggestion that nothing can be done in Dubai without your taking a cut?"

He sighed, and looked sad. "I don't know the BP gentleman who made that remark, and I don't want to waste time on this very cheap and mean comment. I would like to see it published very much, but with another opinion from BP about commission they have been requested to pay in Dubai. BP is a better firm than to have such a sickly opinion.

"I am responsible for giving them"—he paused and corrected himself—"of course, it was Shaikh Rashid who approved it, but I personally was responsible to give them a plot of land at Dubai Airport. I feel sorry for the man who spoke to you. At the end of the day, he might say he paid me for it. Well, that doesn't worry me. If I am to be bothered to collect a few shillings for a lease at Dubai Airport, that will really be the day."

"How about Sir William Luce's comments?"

The ambassador sat back in his chair, relaxed. His three-year-old son scampered into the room to say good-bye before going to the Chessington Zoo, and then ran off shouting the catch-phrase from a television program.

"Stay cool."

"Well," continued the ambassador. "Sir William Luce was a personal friend of mine, and a man with great qualities who will be remembered for many years. Perhaps you will find a lot of

Arabs won't agree with me because they don't understand the man. I do. I worked with him and I know how good he was. In spite of his opinion, I have the highest respect for him, but I am very sorry to say he was not correct. Perhaps he was misled by unfounded press statement."

"Do you represent Costain?" I asked.

"We have no business relationship with them whatsoever. If they are awarded a project, good for them. They are a very good firm, and being accused of taking commission from them will never make me change my mind. I will go on supporting them as long as they are a good firm.

"Let me go further, though. We don't represent any firm working in the UAE, directly or indirectly. We have a business in the UAE, just general import-export, like any other merchant. I am a businessman and very proud of it, and no one denies my organization makes a lot of money. But in Dubai, the decisions are made by His Highness the Ruler, and sometimes I am in a position to influence them. So if I collected any commission, it is a bribe and I feel it is illegal, although there is no law against it."

"Why is it," I asked, "that practically everyone suggests you do take commission?"

"I feel sorry for them. They look at Mahdi Tajir the way they want to look. I'm not going to argue with them. I accept it as the price for being a successful man, but they make one mistake, and it is very simple." He waved his arms around the drawing room. "How could I make all this from Dubai? What is the price of the projects there? A billion. Well, I have more than that—so where do I get the rest? If you gave me all the money the projects cost —not just five percent—I am still richer than that. So they cannot make me rich."

There are other things. Did he take $30 million destined for Kamal Adham to settle the border dispute?

"To start with, I think Adham is worth more than $30 million. As far as I am concerned, he is worth all the money on earth. I'm definitely worth more than $30 million. Apart from that, there is no truth in the story whatsoever."

"Does it worry you that the American Securities and Exchange Commission reportedly suggest that you took $6 million from Boeing?"

"Not a bit. That only gives me an idea of how stupid they are.

Why should I take $6 million from Boeing? I'd rather go and buy them. They're for sale, like everything else in the world. If the President of the United States stands in the Congress and says I have been paid, I don't care."

"It doesn't worry you?"

"Of course not. Why?"

"Because it's a slur."

"So. Who are they trying to say it to? To me? I know better than that. To my government? My government knows better than that. Anyway, what is $6 million? Let us say for argument that Boeing did pay $6 million—that is five percent. Tell me an American firm that would work for less than five percent. Why, when an Arab firm works for five percent is it a bribe, and when an American firm collects ten percent it is legal?

"In the West, you have the hypocrisy of assigning your business when you have public office. I would rather be clear about it. I would rather say, 'I am the ambassador, but I am a businessman.' If anyone is willing to give me a commission, let him come and ask me to do business for him outside the UAE, and I will. There is nothing to be ashamed about. Business is the holiest religion on earth. That is what people miss sometimes."

"Business—the holiest religion on earth?"

"Yes, of course. You go to the church or mosque to meet people, and that is what you do in business. In business you learn how to love, and it teaches you how to promote understanding, how to live together, how to feel towards each other. If it is just for money, then it is stealing."

We paused for more coffee, and discussed his early days in the customs office. "I know people watch me," he said. "I am not going to give them a chance to criticize me. Why have I lasted so long in Dubai? There is no responsible man lasting for twenty-five years in any other Arab state."

But how has he become so wealthy?

"I will go this far. If I ask Shaikh Rashid for anything, I am sure that I will get it—a million, or two, or ten, or anything. I have never had any doubt about that. But to say Shaikh Rashid paid me five percent, or that we work on a percentage basis in Dubai is rubbish. It is a very clean place. There is nowhere like it in the Arab world. Nor in Europe, nor America."

That is not difficult to believe.

"When you hear of a ruling family having a fight, look out for the real estate." U.S. STATE DEPARTMENT OFFICIAL

"You need to adopt the Chinese philosophy—wait long enough and your enemy will float down the river. It saves a lot of wear and tear on the soul if you are forewarned."

FREDERICK J. PITTERA, U.S. BUSINESSMAN

FREDERICK J. PITTERA, an American whose visiting card says he is a K.C., S.O.C., and O.M., resides at the Villa Felice in Switzerland between strenuous bouts of wheeler-dealing in Dubai. He has worked in the Middle East since 1965, when he gave up manufacturing farm tractors in the United States and moved to Saudi Arabia.

"It made sense because they were the ones who always paid cash, and it was straight cash deals which brought me to this area. It's like the Klondike now, but you still have to work harder than anywhere in the West, and don't let anyone kid you. You really sweat, and there is the aggravation of the *insha'allah*, *bukra* bit. 'Tomorrow' goes into weeks, and weeks go into months, but persistence pays off.

"You must be prepared to do business their way. A contract has no real value. If there is good intent on both sides, it will prevail. But they will cancel without compassion or judgment if they want to, and there is nothing that can be done about it.

"It happened to me about two years ago, when I was given

the exclusive license to bring a hotel ship into Abu Dhabi. They wanted it put on the beach in front of the Hilton Hotel, which is like asking for the Sphinx to be brought to New York City. The cost of dredging was not feasible, but after four months of hard work and expense, I reported back to one of the shaikhs. He asked, 'What are you doing here?' I told him. 'But,' he said, 'didn't you get my Telex canceling the deal?' Well, unlike most businessmen forced into that situation, I was not going to grovel for my expenses. I simply said, 'Your Excellency, I'm willing to take a loss. The idea is not practical anyway.' Immediately he turned round and said, 'Well, when are you going to bring the ship?' They play games, you see.

"Any project of note has to go through the ruling families. I don't monkey about with bureaucrats. That way you simply spin your wheels because there is always a middleman who says, 'I have a cousin who can handle this.' They become very impressed with fantasy deals.

"I like to give value, and I am not being a puritan when I say you can make money honestly here. But there is a different tradition. If someone does not get a hunk of the action, the deal does not go through—no matter how much has been spent. They expect you to report and say, 'Here is a piece of the pie,' and if you don't, you are out. You settle in cash, and the normal procedure is through a third party—a bag man—into a numbered account in Switzerland. He is given a bank guarantee based on an attached agreement of work on such-and-such a project. It's as simple as that. The bank guarantee is your protection—so long as you are doing business with the top individual. If you are not, and someone hears about it and has not had his slice, then you will find there is infighting and you might be told for no reason, 'Out you go.' And then what can you do? Who are you going to fight? Who are you going to sue? And where?

"Arabs are not dummies. They have had to fend for themselves for years and can be just as deceptive as some of the people who come here to fool them. You begin with a concept, and the moment it is successful, the squeeze is on. If they ask for 250,000 dirhams, you do not offer 100,000. You offer 50,000, and come up to 90,000 or maybe 100,000. If you don't like it, you can pull up your socks and go home. No one is forcing you to do

anything you don't want. Those puritans in Washington should
be taken out at dawn and shot. They have no idea what goes on.
You will never stop commissions.

"I am ashamed to say that the Americans who come here are
typical of them the world over. They arrive thinking they have
all the clout and say, 'Y'all don't know what you're doing, and
here I am.' The Arabs resent it. They resent the British, too.
They won't forget the old colonial days with Hurricanes flying at
rooftop level to let them know who was in charge. The French,
now, always have the most aggressive ambassador here. He's
doing a hell of a job. He is everywhere. The TV comes on, and
there he is visiting some shaikh or promoting his country's interests. He'll have meetings set up, and he really works hard.

"At present the classic Miami Beach law is creeping in. Two
years ago, no one would have given a $10 bet that the Marbella
Beach Club would have a branch here. It didn't make sense at
all. Yet it is practically oversubscribed before it opens. There
will be a greater demand for deluxe facilities like that, and those
which don't maintain standards will slowly peter out.

"I explored the possibility of tourism two years ago, and there
was a tremendous response from the package-tour operators because there is a mystique about the place. But it's too expensive,
even on reduced fares. The minimum package would be about
$1,500, and you can't really do it for less than $2,000 to $3,000.
For sun worshipers it's a great place. You can see an oasis, *souks*,
and the waters—if they are not polluted.

"The future? Banks themselves have little confidence in the
area. They don't care to touch another pennyworth of hotels, and
I think they are right. Look at the Klondikes in the past. They
became ghost towns after a short while."

Shaikh Rashid does not think he has built a future ghost town.
Years ago, when he sat on the roof of his Palace and counted the
dhows as they called at the customs office next door, he saw
shacks surrounded by desert. Some thought it looked like Venice
or a "maritime San Gimignano" that might have inspired Can-
aletto.[1] To me it looks like a cardboard Shanghai. Tall, solid
buildings cram the waterfront and are squashed together, as in
every civilized city, regardless of acres of empty land behind

them, rising ever higher so that the 39-story $200 million Trade Center, complete with ice-skating rink, towers over others in the Gulf. Progress is so rapid that one Bedou, visiting after an absence of a year, thought he had lost his well-developed sense of direction and wandered bemused back into the desert. Shaikh Rashid sympathizes with such disorientation. He did not understand nor believe that men could have traveled to the moon when he first saw it on television.

Sharjah, down the road, tries hard to be more sophisticated and competes with prestige projects which flatter important foreign countries. There are no taxes, no unions, no foreign exchange controls, and no prohibition on landowning. "We are the ultimate in the free enterprise system," says Bert Paff, an American who was the Ruler's adviser until 1978. "There are lots of opportunities here, but we don't want to become just another tax haven with brass plates and post-office boxes. We want major international corporations that can stand on their own feet and contribute something to the economy." Between 1976 and 1978, the number of hotel rooms increased from 249 to over 3,000 and official brochures boast, "Sharjah isn't too good to be true. It only sounds that way."

It does not to Shaikh Rashid. A few years ago, his son Mohamed tried to clarify a dispute in which Sharjah claimed part of its land was being stolen by Dubai for a road. Mohamed, who is also UAE Defense Minister, flew off in his helicopter but was unfortunately shot down by Sharjah policemen. The helicopter was incapacitated, and he had to take an undignified taxi ride home. Nevertheless, he is philosophical. On a desk in his office is a sign: "It is NICE to be important BUT it is more important to be NICE." Shaikh Sultan of Sharjah, whose degree in agriculture from Cairo University qualifies him as the best-educated Emirate ruler, is apologetic. "It was a mistake," he told me. "These disputes are one of our teething problems." Like the day in 1972, when his older brother Khalid was shot dead in a family squabble and Sultan became Ruler.

Nowadays, most animosity between the families is relieved in a commercial rather than warlike manner, although federal police had to control the overexcitement when Shaikh Rashid discovered Sharjah planned a 44-story building to outclass his own mini-skyscraper. The Dubai Ruler immediately claimed the land, and construction was halted. Billboards near the site now proclaim mockingly: SMILE. YOU ARE IN SHARJAH.

Shaikh Rashid, having exhausted even his urban fantasies with two harbors, two international airports, dry dock, cement factory, aluminum smelter, and wall-to-wall buildings for his 200,000 people, now hopes to attract clean-living world attention by international extravaganzas such as the Dubai International Track and Field Championships. This event was announced in 1977 at a time when they had no athletes, no dates, and no venue, but plenty of money—$2 million in prizes, with $350,000 for the winner of the mile—and American promotional talent in the form of Falconry Sports Enterprises of Chicago. Minor problems seem unimportant, such as the fact that "international" has a limited interpretation if women, Russians, East Europeans, and Israelis are not allowed to compete in Dubai.

Sometimes, to his chagrin, Shaikh Rashid is upstaged. He was not happy when the tiny emirate of Ras al-Khaimah, whose ruler is rumored to be the actual owner of London's Dorchester Hotel, installed one of the world's most advanced earth satellite stations capable of operating 972 Telex channels and able to transmit color television programs live from anywhere in the world. It does seem like overkill, as there are only 12 Telex subscribers and 660 telephones, but Ras al-Khaimah has a precedent for such ambition. Its airport, funded like many other projects by Saudi Arabia, which needs a friend at the mouth of the Gulf but finds Shaikh Rashid too independent and worried when Sharjah had large financial contributions from Iran, has a runway 3,760 meters long to take two jumbo jets at a time. But who wants to go there? Since it was opened in March 1976, its five fire engines, control tower, customs, and immigration have been on twenty-four-hour duty. At first, this was in honor of just one flight a week: from Kuwait.

Shaikh Rashid himself has few personal extravagances. He leads a dull private life, by Middle East standards, and goes hunting in Pakistan rather than in the gamy environs of European brothels. On one of his first visits to London, his ambition was to drive a train in the Underground. Startled officials, accustomed to more sybaritic requests from Oriental gentlemen, let him take the controls between Earl's Court and Acton.

Now in his seventies, with a well-lined face, aquiline nose, and almost perpetual amused glint in his eyes, he has open-house *majlis* most days from 9:00 A.M. until 2:00 P.M. He sits on a settee, kicks off his sandals, puts his feet on the table in front of him, and fills a small brass-lined pipe with tobacco from an old brown aspirin bottle. He rarely uses the numerous ornate boxes he has been given by well-wishers. Sitting around the room are guards with ancient Czech rifles. A procession of Bedouins with camel sticks and Western visitors with contracts and hope wanders in and out. Rashid signs every check, sees every agreement.

"It's amazing how he keeps the figures in his head," whispers his senior aide, Humeid bin Drai. "He is a man of the people, but he does not like publicity—unlike Zayed, who wants to see himself on television every five minutes. That's the difference between the two."

Rashid is the most approachable of money-rush potentates. The Dubai telephone directory lists seventeen numbers for him, including his bedroom, living room, wireless room, yacht, and garden.

It is the same during the summer in London. Anyone can walk in to see him. Almost.

Bodyguards sit both sides of the elevator on the seventeenth floor of the Carlton Tower Hotel in Cadogan Place, Chelsea. As the door opens, they tense and observe the visitor. Another man checks credentials.

Suite 1712, with its uninspiring view of the Battersea power station, has been rearranged to suit its guest. All the bedroom furniture except a television set is removed, and settees and wicker chairs of varying height and shape are placed along three walls. Tables at the back of the room are covered with pink cloths, cups and saucers, and pots of tea. The bar is filled exclusively with Pepsi-Cola.

In front of a mirrored wall at one end sits Shaikh Rashid. His sole concession to London is discarding his sandals in favor of gray socks and black lace-up shoes, which he rests on the table next to an ever-present box of colored paper tissues. Now and again he takes one, and, with disconcerting gusto, coughs phlegm into it.

He is here with twenty retainers, one of whom offers coffee from an Arab pot. His wife and family are staying in a house "somewhere near London airport" says Humeid bin Drai vaguely. From 6:00 in the morning until 10:00, and again from 6:00 in the evening until 8:00, Shaikh Rashid conducts his *majlis*. That morning he greeted—and then chastised—a Saudi who he discovered had tipped the hotel lavatory attendant $20. Conspicuous stupidity is giving the Arabs a bad name. After that he had a long talk with former British Foreign Secretary Reginald Maudling. Coincidentally, it was the day Maudling was to be criticized in the House of Commons for unfortunate business relationships with a convicted criminal, architect John Poulson, so the Arabs thought it politic to deny the meeting. "He definitely did not see us," bin Drai told the London *Evening Standard*. "Perhaps he was visiting someone else. There are a lot of Arabs in the hotel."

A chubby man of infinite charm, bin Drai's flexible attitude toward truth is based on humanitarian instincts. "Mr. Maudling is a good friend of ours. We did not want to add to his problems by admitting that," he told me later as we sat with Shaikh Rashid watching a slide show given by two civic dignitaries from Portland, Oregon. It was accompanied by a stirring "Here is our town, and here is our harbor, and here is our wunnerful mayor" type of commentary which the Ruler listened to, smiling courteously. He does not understand English, so it was probably beneficial that the projector broke down halfway through the show.

Shaikh Rashid's liberal attitude has made Dubai the most acceptable resting place for foreigners on the money-rush circuit; more relaxed than Abu Dhabi, less prissy than Bahrain, not so tumultuous as Tehran.[2] There is no religious authoritarianism—Christmas Day is a public holiday, and the Ruler himself laid a foundation stone for the Anglican church. Although expatriate drunk drivers are deported immediately, alcohol is not banned, and there is a pub, the Rose and Crown, and a country club three miles out of town, which provides a haven of darts playing, drinking and slot machining for expats, as they call themselves, and many of Shaikh Rashid's countrymen who crave excitement.

Such *louche* behavior would not be tolerated further north in Abu Dhabi, where "The Club" treads a genteel course of inoffensive good taste, the only mild excitement being provided by self-styled "sundowners" who drop in casually dressed after work at 5:30 and drink solidly until 8:00, when ties must be worn. "Hey-ho tiddleypush," they say as they leave, grateful that standards are still applied somewhere in the world. The Club's 2,000-strong waiting list is pruned by invitation rather than application, and a cocktail party is sometimes held so the committee can vet potential members.

The Dubai Country Club has more exotic management in the person of Geoffrey Glover-Wright, formerly pop singer Simon Raverne, who arrived in town in 1970 en route to a singing engagement in Vietnam. "That folded, so I did a turn at the Oasis Club here, liked it, and have stayed ever since. I had a record high in the American Top 100 called 'Empty Beaches, Cobbled Streets and City Walls.'"

Some puritanism does exist—an advertising poster for the singing group Martha and the Vandellas was banned because it showed a navel—but the general laissez-faire business morality is reflected in the social life, and has brought eager lower- and middle-management types rushing for $20,000-plus, tax-free salaries. They soon settle into a predictable round of cocktail parties, where, unlike at home, everyone is equal. There are few of the subtle status symbols which identify a family in its own environment so it is possible to invent a past and make the present into a suburban fantasy. Many people do.

It becomes an existence of defensive boredom enlivened by nostalgia—red, white and blue diapers, and bibs with special crests sold rapidly during the Queen's jubilee year. They talk about the disintegration of the "Western way of life," the increasing hold of "Communism," of the poverty of friends back home. Soon, in this brave new world, the money-rush trap is sprung: they are earning more than they could expect anywhere else in the world, children are committed to boarding school because there is no adequate local alternative, and there is a gathering suspicion they have sold out.

Sitting by the swimming pool of the Intercontinental, I met a thirty-three-year-old woman from Brighton whose husband is a senior government official and whose three children were away at school. "I'm pissed off," she said. "My husband is told what to do by eighteen-year-old boys. He is humiliated by people who know nothing and are powerful only because of their money. He dare not say anything because what would he do if he left? Go back to England and become a bus driver if he's lucky. He knows only this part of the world.

"I can't stand it here, but I don't fit in at home anymore. The only thing they seem to say there is 'Oh, really?' If I told them I walked through the desert the other day and was raped by five tribesmen, the only reaction would be 'Oh, really? Did you know Monica's adding an extension to her house?' Property prices and the cost of food. That's all they ever discuss. Well, we have to stay in Dubai now because of the children. We could never afford the [tuition] fees if we lived in England."

It is ironic to consider the thousands of British living abroad because they have convinced themselves it is the only way they and their children will ever be able to afford an eventual good life in England. They assuage their doubts in gin (Dubai must be the only Arab city where Alcoholics Anonymous, under the name of the Dubai Clocktower Group, is allowed to thrive), good works (the annual church bazaar takes in $16,000), and sport. (The Ruler has given them some land on the outskirts for rugby and polo. There is also the Darjeeling Cricket Club, and golf can be played quite well on sand if you don't forget to bring a portable strip of synthetic turf for the tee.)

Life is enlivened by the occasional scandal, such as when Don Revie arrived incognito, disguised in a cloth cap, muffler, and dark glasses, to renege on a five-year contract as English football manager in return for nearly $700,000 over four years as UAE coach. "An offer I cannot refuse, an unbelievable opportunity to secure my family's future," he said, while others were more skeptical of the money rush's real rewards. "Will you really be satisfied studying your bank balance and watching those no-hopers gallop lazily up and down the forlorn strips they call pitches?" asked the *Sun* newspaper. Forlorn strips? The UAE is building a $43 million national stadium twice the size of Wembley.

More serious scandals were not mentioned. The expats are, naturally, managers. They need people to manage, and, as native Dubaians are scarce and rich, workers have to be imported in increasing numbers from India and Pakistan. They are forbidden by law from forming unions and are not allowed to bring their families. As in Saudi Arabia, they are flown home as soon as there is any unrest.

They have little incentive to complain. Many are illegal immigrants lured by the money rush and unaware of the true conditions.[3] They spend their savings on a boat trip to opportunity and are sometimes off-loaded onto a sandbank by unscrupulous *dhow* captains who do not want to take the risk for which they have been paid. On one occasion, in September 1976, 200 people died when two ferryboats, built to carry a maximum of 350 people each, but with a total of 1,150 on board, became stuck in the sand and were then surprised by a police patrol launch. During the journey, which took three times the anticipated four days, the sick had been forced overboard at gunpoint, and others died from hunger or thirst.

Those who escaped arrest from the UAE police managed to find jobs eventually. For their unskilled labor in the broiling sun, helping to develop tomorrow's ghost town and inflate the profits of British construction companies, they are paid between $4 to $6 for a ten-hour day, and housed in primitive tents hidden from sight of the casual visitor. The justification, usually given over a few drinks costing about $40 in a local hotel, is age-old: "You see, old boy, they are better off than at home." In the same way, a kick in the balls is better than decapitation.

Not every Pakistani suffers such humiliation. Twenty-one of them dress in kilts and play bagpipes in the Abu Dhabi Defense Force Band at social events like camel racing. Others make a fortune from reexporting. Hajji Ashraff is one of the richest. He arrived in Dubai in 1966, ". . . because general business was good here." Actually, he means gold smuggling, although he denies it. "You cannot call it smuggling because this is a free country. These days the gold trade is not good because the price is high, so I import rice, cement, and steel." He does not own a car and works from a small, unostentatious office. When he visits London, as he does twice a year, he is an honored and respected guest.

One of his "students," Nasim Khan (a pseudonym), is thirty-seven, languid, striking-looking, and talks with an upper-middle-class British accent developed at London University. "I think I am the only graduate from there who has made a success of smuggling," he claims. He came to Dubai in 1971 after a peripatetic upbringing.

"I've seen three revolutions in my life. At first we lived two hundred miles from Bombay, and after partition in 1947, we were on the wrong side of the border. We had to leave home in the middle of the night because my father was a leading Muslim and we would all have been shot. So we went to Burma. In 1958 the Communists took over our lands there, so we moved to East Pakistan. Then there was a civil war, and, again, we were on the wrong side. I'm what you call a born loser, you see.

"I had started in the silver business in East Pakistan, so I came to Dubai for obvious reasons. I suppose you could say it was smuggling, but it was modest. We took silver from India to Pakistan, then to Dubai and on to our principals in Switzerland or London. There it was refined and sold. I made a lot of money, but, like most traders, lost on speculation.

"Smuggling gold from here to India was very easy, with hardly any question of being caught. I acted as the bank, so to speak, operating a travel agency. We were paid for the gold in Indian and Pakistani currency, and it was my job to transfer it into dollars and have it transmitted here with no questions asked. With an external account you can walk into a bank in London and say you want $40 million, or as much as you like, remitted to Dubai, and it will be done. There are fortunes floating around. One of my friends was arrested in Pakistan, and they found $800,000 cash in his house.

"But gold smuggling stopped almost overnight when Indira Gandhi decided quite rightly that her economy should not be run by bandits like us. She became very strict. A few people were caught, others were scared, and, quite honestly, it is impossible to operate unless everyone is on the take from top to bottom.

"The charlies who worked for me got mislaid—they were either arrested or the boat sank. I lost everything and owed 1.5 million dirhams ($400,000), with nothing coming in. The banks were very helpful. They carried most of us for a while because they knew the problems. I paid them back eventually.

"I decided to start something legitimate, so I imported steel, cement, and orange juice and got up at six o'clock in the morning to flog the stuff. If you are looking for a short-term gain, this is the place to be, but you reach a stage where money doesn't mean much to you. Other things become more important—silly things like the Sunday newspapers. You miss them.

"And you miss someone intelligent to talk to. We start talking in monosyllables like the Arabs and don't realize what is happening in the world. I don't know what is the 'in' thing to wear, a good play to see, or a good book to read. I enjoy those things. Reading the *Financial Times* two days late in Dubai is not the same as reading it on the Underground in London. The whole environment is different, and as we begin to make a success, we wonder, 'What for?' We get very depressed, too, which I think is partly to do with the climate. I am afraid if we live here much longer we will become like them—or our children will. If you want to know about our people, look at their pets and at what animals are indigenous. Here it is hawks and scorpions. That gives you an idea about them.

"My father has practically disowned me. We are a well-known landowning family—there are still monuments to my grandfather —so he is particularly upset that I am a smuggler. He is keen on gardening and has won a gold medal two years running for his vegetables. I try to explain that I find my life frightfully exciting, but he doesn't understand.

"At the moment I am respectable. Tomorrow morning I shall negotiate a loan for $2 million with the manager of one of the most staid, stodgy English banks. If we agree on interest rates, I shall put up a few villas in Sharjah, where the Ruler has given me some land. It is all very humdrum, not at all like the midnight worry of a boat being caught or panic over the price of textiles in Bombay. But it's a living.

"In the evening, as a pastime, I play the commodity market in Chicago. When it's ten A.M. there it's eleven-thirty P.M. here, and we have a direct Telex link with Merrill Lynch. It's just like being there, except we don't have to pay the taxes. I don't make money at it—no speculator ever does. My theory is that all of us who speculate have an inferiority complex. But it's better than going to the bar of the Intercontinental every evening and listening to the $10 million deals being cooked up.

"Dubai is a town full of upstarts, people who have been failures elsewhere and want to make easy money. There is no character. Three of the bank managers are good friends of mine, and they are all leaving. One says he thinks we have seen the best of Dubai. He has all the money he can manage, a good life, and he is going back to Kent and the commuter life with taxes and bad weather because, he claims, he wants his family to grow up in pleasant surroundings. He's a pukka, stiff-upper-lip type and I tell him he is talking like a sentimental Pakistani, but he is right.

"My wife has threatened five or six times to divorce me because she doesn't like living here. It is not the place to bring up a family. We have two daughters and don't need much to live. I have promised we will leave in a year or two and my brother will take over. If there weren't so many Pakistanis in England, I would go there. They have made such a mess of things. It is impossible to prove to the average Englishman that we are not the same, that we don't all want to be porters or bus drivers. Maybe I will go to the Seychelles, spend my summers in England, and play the old colonial way of life with my British friends.

"I am very pro-British. After all, you educated me for $54 a term, payable in installments of $18 a month. Really, what a crazy nation . . . but maybe not, because we all have affection for you. If the British had stayed in this part of the world, the money rush might have worked. It could have operated as in India, where a few families were told, 'Look, you chaps, if you want to rule these beggars we'll show you how to do it, and then let's all have a good time.'

"Instead, it is out of control. It is all very dandy when everything is working in your favor, but the whole place is based on a construction boom which has to end. They can stretch it out with government white elephants, but one fine morning they will wake up and won't know what's hit them. The dry dock will never work. Would you send your multimillion-dollar tanker to one of the most expensive cities in the world, where there is no expertise, and where politically it might be a mistake? The economics are unfavorable, apart from the fact that these people don't have the experience to run a tea shop."

Abdul Ghaffair Hussain, a swarthy man, sat sweating in the disheveled office to which he is entitled as deputy director of Dubai Municipality. His sensuous English secretary perched on the desk and appeared to listen intently to every word of the conversation, punctuated as it was by squawks and whoops from outside. It is a very busy office, like any similar place, but Mr. Hussain is not a normal town hall functionary nor does he radiate traditional municipal penury. He is a 51 percent partner in a £12 million development by the construction firm MacAlpine, and he owns the *Bon Vivant*, apartment buildings, the largest cold storage in the Emirates, and a plastic manufacturing company which has fortuitously won a large local government contract. Black plastic bags sprout throughout Dubai, and old pipes are disinterred to make way for the plastic revolution. Hussain reassured me there was no conflict of interest between his government and business activities. How could there be?

"In fact," he confided, "I am thinking seriously of leaving the government, and so are many of my colleagues. We are not appreciated. We are not being given our rights.

"We are competing and fighting with foreigners," continued the deputy director. "Most of them are here for the money. That is depressing in some ways, but they wouldn't come if they were not encouraged, and we need their expertise. But they should be made to have a local partner—otherwise they take away our money.

"Why give them that chance? When I do something, my money stays here. Why should Sunley or Costain make money here and take it out of the country? What are we getting from them?"

His secretary looked pensive. He smiled at her, and there was clearly nothing personal in his next remark. "Let me tell you I was thankful when the British left here. For a hundred and fifty years they did nothing. On the contrary, they closed the door to civilization and prevented progress. They say they were protecting us, but they were protecting us only from becoming civilized. That is history. Whether you agree or not, it is history."

"It is," said his secretary. "Yes."

"This country is now for us. And our children."

But how can such a small country survive, I wondered, as I set off 150 kilometers across the desert to see President Zayed bin Sultan al-Nahyan, whose deposed brother Shakhbut decided to ignore the money rush in the hope that it would disappear. Shaikh Zayed knows that it will not. Moreover, he has learned quickly that there is one supreme prerequisite for international success today, one qualification without which a ruler is as bereft as his people, one essential by which leaders judge each other. It is something the Gulf Arabs did not understand until blessed with money and earnest Egyptian or Palestinian advisers.

You can have a country. You can have money. You can have tradition. But before you are really respected and join the ranks of the civilized nations, you must have a mammoth bureaucracy to guide your progress. I should have known that civil servants, like the mice who ate through boxes of cash Shakhbut kept under his bed, would begin to plague the money rush sooner or later.

21/FRIENDSHIP FOR SALE

"We have not forgotten our poverty. Now we shall share our wealth." MOTTO OF THE ABU DHABI FUND FOR ARAB DEVELOPMENT

"The Swiss are very dull. They do not enjoy themselves. They go to bed early, and they think only of money. These are the people we should deal with."
SHAIKH ZAYED TO A FRIEND ON A VISIT TO LAUSANNE IN 1971

SHAIKH ZAYED has come to his home town Al Ain, formerly called Buraimi, for an agricultural show. He sits under an awning on a faded orange settee whose style is Western suburbia circa 1930. Behind him are members of his family and local shaikhs who have the ascetic look of desert dwellers rather than the prematurely debauched countenance of the Saudi princes. In front, as always, is a plastic table laden with two unopened boxes of colored tissues.

These gatherings always seem strange to a Westerner because of the lack of female spectators. Shaikh Zayed is never accompanied by any of his wives. He has had about twelve (four at a time), who have provided him with nine sons. His favorite wife, the fecund Shaikha Fatima, who gave birth to six sons and two daughters in nine years, lives in Abu Dhabi. He has two in Al Ain whose dim stirrings of emancipation, characterized by a demand for him to spend a few nights at home, once became so shrill that he was obliged, allegedly, to cancel a meeting with David Rockefeller, chairman of the Chase Manhattan Bank, who has appro-

priately superseded Lord Curzon as the maker of regal progres-
sions around the Gulf.

Today, though, at the back of the viewing stand, is an exquisitely dressed woman with a fresh complexion bred only in the
best British shire families, whom I will meet in unexpected circumstances an hour or so later.

Meanwhile, a group of local musicians plays a traditional Arab
tune adapted to discothèque beat, and schoolgirls carrying plastic flowers attempt a Westernized Arab dance. Shaikh Zayed
looks up occasionally and claps, but is more preoccupied with
his newspaper. His gazes at it intently during a number of short,
fervently patriotic speeches given by several of the show's organ-
izers. Eventually he joins them and other male guests waving
camel sticks in a simple tribal jog. All the while he is photo-
graphed by a spectacularly agile middle-aged man, John Cowan,
one of the leading fashion photographers of the sixties who has
now equipped himself with a Range Rover as a traveling home-
cum-studio and spends much of the year producing glossy and
lucrative reportage of the Arabian peninsula. Competition is
tough because photographers are quick to realize when any area
is crammed with aspirant world leaders who have money to
commission acceptable pictorial records of themselves and their
good works.

Shaikh Zayed ignores Cowan's contortions. He has developed
a film star's insouciance since his country became the Sutter's
Mill of the money rush in October 1973. He is the man who blew
the starting whistle when he—not Saudi Arabia's King Faisal—
operated the first total ban on oil exports, a grave decision with
immediate consequences as the UAE, which few people had
heard of, supplied more oil to the United States than Iran. The
embargo worked more effectively than anyone imagined, and,
even though outsiders still believe it was Saudi Arabia's initia-
tive, Shaikh Zayed's status within the Arab world increased as
rapidly as his income—$5 billion in 1978, ten times the amount of
pre-money-rush days.

He has tried to encourage his people to join the bonanza by
providing them with free housing, medical care, electricity, and
up to $100 a month for sending their children to school. He also
gives out bits of land on which they can build gimcrack apart-

ments and thus join the entrepreneurial elite by renting at exorbitant prices.

As a result, his capital, Abu Dhabi, an island about the size of Manhattan, has a per-capita income of $36,000, a bank branch for every 2,000 people, inflation of 166 percent over three years, and is the most expensive city in the world for visiting businessmen.[1] That is significant to economists, if not to Pakistanis, and means something to American diplomats, whose embassy is crammed into the only reasonable accommodation they could find: four single-room apartments on the top floor of a decaying octagonal building identified only by the words ORIENTAL SUN FLOWER, and costing $60,000 a year rent. The British, whose embassy has 400,000 square feet of overgrown garden in the most expensive area, are building their ambassador a $1 million residence, modest, apparently, as "it falls somewhat short of the normal standards for an ambassador of his rank," explains the Foreign Office.

"It would save everyone a lot of trouble and expense if all the locals went to live in the South of France or Switzerland and left the place to a few technocrats in air-conditioned offices," says one diplomat. "The trouble is, they actually like the place. They are devoted to this basically uninhabitable land."

That being so, the civilized world is quick to bestow all its glittering credentials, and the UAE has been admitted to membership of the UN, WB, IRC, AL, UNESCO, UNICEF, IMF, ILO, ICAO, FAO, OPEC, OAPEC, and so on. Everyone rushes to pay obeisance. John Butter, a Scot who became the ruler's financial adviser in 1970 after twenty years in Kenya (he spoke no Arabic when he arrived) rationed himself to a maximum of four bankers a day, and saw 437 in two years. "It is educative," he says. "I realized then that if I did the opposite to what the experts said, I would probably be right."

But experts provide prestige, and the President now has at least 35,000 of them: bureaucrats who announce numerous enlightened projects oblivious to the inconvenient fact that only one in three is carried out, and have devised a constitution with grand-sounding institutions—Supreme and Consulative councils—regardless of continuing shaikhly rule. Why, he even has a British-style honors system, with six classifications!

The pressures on tradition have been resisted less in the UAE than in Saudi Arabia, partly because the 5-to-1 ratio of expatriates to locals is overwhelming and also because the Gulf Arabs have a less majestic view of their own infallibility. Nevertheless, the tug toward Westernization is sometimes rebuffed with surprising severity. The Saudi-born Chief Judge, opposed with implacable enthusiasm to public enjoyment, had a youth flogged in 1977 for kissing a girl on the beach. There is a mandatory forty lashes for any Muslim caught drinking alcohol, and an attempt is being made to apply *Sharia* law to Westerners and locals alike for seven Koranic sins: murder, theft, highway robbery, adultery, slander, promiscuity, and the use of alcohol.

These Canute-like intentions are supported by a security system which provides the normal vigorous checks on entry into the country. Only those who can prove their prime motive is money-making (bankers, businessmen, lawyers, football managers) are given easy access. Temporary visitors must leave passports with airport immigration to prevent their departing from any of the country's other proliferating airports. The motive is to hamper illegal immigration, the bureaucratic mind being unable to conceive of anyone not living by forms and regulations, but the result is a pile of 16,000 unclaimed passports and frustration for genuine travelers whose only transport within the "united" country is by private plane or taxi. "We shall learn by our mistakes," says Zayed, whose emirate contributes 90 percent of the whole country's budget and who refused to be reelected President in 1976 unless there was more cooperation from the others. "How can we build a union when we cannot agree on a new hospital without first determining if the site is on the soil of Dubai, Sharjah, or any other emirate?"

It is the bloody-minded attitude which worries him. Although he resents subsidizing his old enemy Shaikh Rashid, now seen publicly as his fraternal good friend, the Vice-President, money is not very important. He has plenty left.

His particular vision, apart from unity, is to turn the desert green, and he spends millions on agricultural schemes. Tree planting alone has cost $5 million, equivalent to his total income fifteen years ago, and he hopes that soon the 100-kilometer highway between Abu Dhabi and Al Ain will be a luxuriant leafy boulevard instead of its present vista of decomposing camels and rusting wrecks of cars. A third of his income has been given away to a wide collection of people and causes in thirty-two countries since 1974: the Paris Airports Authority, dams in Jordan, water in Bahrain, electrification in Syria, tourism and railway cars in Tunisia, fertilizer projects in Egypt, water for the Yemen Arab Republic, a Liver Research Unit for King's College Hospital, London, and an odd $1 million to the PLO. Most of the money is transmitted through the Abu Dhabi Fund.

"Are you trying to buy love?" I asked the managing director, Nasser al Noweiss, a man of great charm destined for a leading role in whatever future his country has.

"We hope to gain friendship. We are small and we like to get to know people. A few years ago there was nothing here, so the feeling of poverty is still fresh with us. We understand and know what a hard life is like. Other human beings need our help, and so long as we have money, we are very happy to give it."

But just in case the dream does not last, or people become too greedy, Shaikh Zayed spends a third of his money on defense even though his "brother" shaikhs are still eager to maintain their own private forces. Arms dealers are so sought after that the most successful of them, Sam Cummings, actually refused to help one shaikh waste his money—a heresy that some might find unforgivable. "One of the Emirate shaikhs—I won't tell you which one—wants me to build him a small-arms factory. He says, 'We have the money.' I tell him, 'That's fine. Build another desalinization plant.' I try to convince him that it would be more economical to buy the arms, rather than set up a factory, but he says he wants to be self-sufficient.

"They already have a whole lot of things they don't need. We try to tell them. Unfortunately, it falls largely on deaf ears because arms sales are not based on real needs. The last reason they are bought, in the quantities they are, is for legitimate defense. They are bought for prestige and in some cases for the income it brings to certain individuals. Bribes? One follows the local rules on the basis that the customer is always right. We have paid large commissions in some countries, but in others we pay none at all.

"In my own view, though, these weapons will never be used.

I've seen them rotting to pieces all over the Middle East. Nobody needs all the arms that exist in the world today, but you cannot control this sultan, or that shaikh, or president. A sovereign state is sovereign. They buy materiel they cannot use, often materiel they cannot physically store, which will become obsolete before they get it out of the packing cases."

Cummings shrugged with the air of a man conditioned to the world's absurdities. "The military armaments business worldwide is essentially based on human folly," he said. Such folly provides him with an excellent living. From a luxurious base in Monte Carlo, where he lives with his Swiss wife, he directs operations at his offices throughout the world. Now in his fifties, he started selling guns at twenty-six, when, on a trip to Europe from America, he bought surplus Second World War guns which were rusting on the battlefields. He still earns money from them, as well as more modern weapons. He supplied the former dictator of the Dominican Republic, Rafael Trujillo, with machine guns and Vampire jets which he bought in Sweden. He sold guns to Castro before the revolution, and afterward. He equipped the Sudan cavalry with lances which he picked up in Argentina.

His warehouses are in Virginia, Singapore, and Manchester, which is where I met him. He had celebrated my arrival by hanging a Scottish flag outside the steel door with its double locks, spy hole, entry phones, and television scanner. Unfortunately, I did not notice until I left, and then he gave me a key ring decorated with an imitation silver bullet. Truly, selling arms is a cozy business, and as we began a tour of the seven-story building, he intoned a commentary as if we were viewing some fine historic masterpieces: "We have a total of 200,000 square feet here. The place used to be a *Sunday Times* warehouse. We have an example of everything we have handled, so that provides an immediate reference library of all the standard weapons. We like firearms for their own sake—historically, mechanically, and artistically. We have about one thousand in the company collection going back to the seventeenth century.

"You can get a pretty good idea of men's follies right here. There's the Gatling gun, which was rejected by General Custer

when he went to fight the Indians at Little Big Horn. He said
the gun wasted ammunition. End of General Custer."

There were bits of rusting M15s from Vietnam, cannons, two
Purdeys owned by the late Duke of Windsor, and cases of guns
marked with a champagne glass—the international sign for delicate cargo.

"We have our own rifle range downstairs, so we are able to
test the guns we remodel. Then they are ready for another lifetime of faithful service. I look forward to the day when I can
buy them back. Guns become quickly obsolescent in the folly of
the military arms race, and we can transform them into sporting
rifles. It makes a good profit for us, and no one has been hurt by
that particular gun. That is what is happening in the Middle
East. We are recycling our hard currency into buying oil. They
are recycling their unused weapons back to us through a sieve of
sand."

We drove in his Cadillac to a local pub for lunch. He had a
large glass of water and a well-cooked steak. "I look on myself
as a businessman who might just as well be selling baked beans,"
he said. "I don't believe that any inanimate object is ipso facto
good or bad. We are trading in items which have the capacity to
kill—yes. But it's only the use or misuse which makes it good or
bad."

The same argument could be used by a bartender providing a
drunk driver with another large whisky.

"I would be the last to agree that my business is corrupt,"
Cummings said. "People die driving cars—do you stop car manufacturing? People even go blind reading books, you know. Of
course, governments do ninety-nine percent of the arms business
—both legitimate and clandestine. Let's be brutally realistic.
They are the gunrunners. I am just obsolete, but I don't know it
yet."

I asked if there was anyone to whom he would not sell.

"The question doesn't arise because we don't make a policy
for ourselves or determine any transaction. Governments have to
provide a license. Take your friend General Idi Amin. I don't
know this gentleman at all, but one day I was in Monte Carlo
and my phone rang. A deep voice on the other end said, 'You
don't know me, but I know you.' It was General Amin. He said,

'I'm sending up my private jet. I want you to come down and give us a modernization program for our Army.'

"I said, 'Before I come down, I have to see if we can get licensed approval from the British or the United States for delivery to you.' I did check him out with the British and the Americans. They said, 'No. Forget about General Amin.'

"He sent his plane up anyway, and I said, 'I'll leave you a big envelope of catalogs at Nice Airport, and you can pick it up.' He did. Afterward he sent a small mission to see me, but I knew nothing was possible. In the meantime he has received ample supplies from the Soviet Union largely funded by Colonel Qaddafi.

'I would not sell to any government I thought would use the materiel against our own country—but in the world we live in, that is hard to estimate. We do only what governments allow, and we do it for economic gain. Governments imagine they do it for political long-range gain, or that someone will love them. We have our illusions, but that is not one of them."

He chuckled loudly. It is difficult not to like him and easy to forget that his job in the money rush is to provide guns for people to kill each other. He does not see it that way.

"Will it aggravate war? It is impossible to answer that. I would turn the question round and ask you, 'Has the tremendous effort of the East and West in rearming since World War Two aggravated the chance for world peace, or not?' Logically you would say that the more weapons you buy, the more chance there is to use them. But the history of our civilization, if one can call it that, since the war, indicates the opposite. The easiest way to explain it is to say that it is bound to lead to a holocaust—but it has not. It is paradoxical and defies all logic."

It does not defy logic at all, it just requires time. The arguments of Cummings are those of arms suppliers and some politicians—*before* war happens. Afterward it is different. "It was the arms race between the great powers which made 1914 inevitable," said British Foreign Secretary Lord Grey in retrospect.

A few weeks after I met Cummings, I had a drink in London with Colonel Khalifa Nabooda, the UAE's Deputy Minister of Defense. He was in a pensive mood over the brandy, articulate, and far less military than when I had met him previously in

Dubai. I asked how he was managing with all his brand-new weapons.

"Who are we going to fight?" he said. "Why do we need all these things?"

"Well, why?"

He ordered another drink. "If people knew the answer to that, they wouldn't buy them. It is all a game, and we are caught up in it."

Some game. But it delights the arms suppliers who have sold Shaikh Zayed two early-warning systems—Rapier and Crotale—as well as numerous tanks, rifles, and jet fighters camouflaged in green and brown in anticipation presumably of some mysterious jungle war. He says he would lend them to front-line Arab states in a war against Israel. But there are few skilled pilots, and not much of a coordinated Army has developed from the rag-tag of private troops conscripted by the various shaikhs in self-defense.

"It must be hell," I suggested to General Awad al Khaldi, a genial and efficient Jordanian who was imported as Chief of Staff in 1976. (King Hussein has offered to help the UAE military because he is so worried about the country's future.)

"It has been very difficult to amalgamate the different armies," admitted the general. "They had so many teachers—British and Jordanians—but they have the caliber, and I think they will be able to take over from foreign officers in five years, and have full technical capability in about ten.

"The trouble is that sudden wealth spoils people, especially the military. No one wants to join the Army because they can make more money outside. They are not motivated. I try to give it to them by telling them that to preserve their money they must prepare for war. Although we have very friendly neighbors and feel we live in a peaceful spot, I tell them about Lebanon. There was a country with more money than the UAE, but look what happened when radical elements got in. It will be the same here if there is not a strong force to preserve the wealth. It could be another Beirut if we don't deal very sharply with radical elements which come from outside."

The start of the headlong rush into the twentieth century was more stable than most people predicted. "Everyone is so busy making money that they don't have time to think of revolution,"

says Dr. Adnan Pachachi, former Iraqi Foreign Minister, who is
Shaikh Zayed's personal representative. "But we can't be choosy
about adjusting to a different style of life. We have to take the
good with the bad.

"There is nothing fundamentally contradictory about the
Arabs practicing democracy. It is not just for Western countries,
and we will probably learn in a shorter time than it took the
West. At the moment we are under pressure from local fanatics—
not from Saudi Arabia—but it is clear you cannot really run a
modern state on shaikhly lines."

Shaikh Zayed knows that. He realizes that when he and his
contemporaries have gone, the social changes could be as vast as
the economic ones have been, but less comfortable. He just
hopes that nothing happens before that. He read in the newspaper, for instance, about the Shah's "help" to Oman. He prayed
that such "help" would not be needed here, that he could keep his
country free for the pure, unpolitical gathering of money.

Like other Arabs, he suspected the Shah's intentions despite
protestations of brotherly love. The UAE had already been
flicked like a pinball when it became a hindrance to British domestic policy or Iranian military aggression. When the Shah went
on "holiday," who would take over Britain's nanny role? A
diamond necklace of a country, shaped like a *khanja* (curved
dagger) along the West bank of the "Arabian" Gulf, the UAE
was a tactical prize for both East and West.

What, wondered Zayed, did the Shah really think?

"A patch of sand," said His Imperial Majesty, the Shahanshah,
etc., casually in a way that would have given His Highness
Shaikh Zayed palpitations. "In twenty years' time the oil will be
finished—and then what? They must see it that way, and some of
them do."

We were discussing his attitude to the Arabs, and I mentioned
I had been told that his lips actually curled into a sneer when
they are mentioned. Was he contemptuous of the Arabs? "That
is a misinterpretation. But I have to say that we always helped
them and never received anything in return. We helped mor-
ally on the international scene, in the United Nations, in our declarations, and in everything behind the scenes. The only thing

we received was that they declared the Persian Gulf is the Arabian Gulf and many other unfairnesses."

So they have no need to be frightened? "Of course not. It's ridiculous. I had the occasion of taking back Bahrain, which we claimed for one hundred fifty years, but what would I want with that patch of sand?"

They—the UAE, and all other Arab money-rush countries—are convinced they are more than patches of sand. They are being told so by the West and are building new societies, developing industries. Just like Iran.

"How can they? They have not the climate nor the population. History will be the proof—in twenty-five years' time."

In that case, it seems strange that His Imperial Majesty was willing to risk international condemnation, with particularly strong ripples from Tripoli and Dallas, by grabbing a small "patch of sand" from Britain on the eve of the UAE's birth. But some of the ironies of today's money rush cannot be appreciated fully without a brief understanding of why the British were there in the first place, keeping everyone else out, their chaste knee-length khaki shorts flapping in the breeze, their gung-ho enthusiasm and pink-cheeked integrity bringing a touch of godliness and authority to barren parts.

22/PROTECTING THE ARABS

"Blessedly without robes or wig (or any scrap of legal training), we would pronounce. After a morning remanding a dozen men in custody and deporting twenty others; authorising a shaikh to buy sub-machine guns; issuing visas for a lord or foreign ambassador; and allowing the police chief to import a crate of beer, we had undoubtedly earned the sentry's springing to attention and present arms as we drove our old Ford Zephyrs home from work."

FORMER ASSISTANT POLITICAL AGENT IN ABU DHABI, MICHAEL TOMKINSON, THE UNITED ARAB EMIRATES

As WITH OMAN, the British arrived in the Gulf in the early nineteenth century to protect imperial ambitions and the trade to India. At the time, ships were being hampered unsportingly by the Qawasim tribe of Ras al-Khaimah which not only claimed to be descended from the Prophet but had a small armada of 876 vessels and 19,000 men with which, they announced, they wanted to protect their coastline.

This, retorted the British, was an excuse for blatant piracy. So, in 1809, after the Qawasim tried to extract tribute from foreign ships and then captured the *Minerva*, killing the crew and ransoming an officer's widow, the British attacked with 2,000 Indian troops and a detachment of the Bombay Artillery. They burned sixty boats and numerous houses, but could find no Qawasim chief to acknowledge a surrender. They tried again in 1816 with equal humiliation. A representative from Bombay arrived, threatening "the displeasure of the British Government" if captured property was not returned. Unfortunately, the weather was bad, and the representative had to leave before his ultimatum expired. When he returned two days later, he was attacked. He left hurriedly in a gunboat, firing shots which fell short because the powder was damp. No empire is without its small defeats.

Finally a British soldier who could speak Arabic, Captain Thomas Perronet Thompson, was sent out as political agent, and, with his wife's calligraphic assistance, drafted the General Treaty for the Cessation of Plunder and Piracy in 1820. Captain Thompson, then aged thirty-seven, was the son of a Methodist lay preacher and he considered his one mission in life was to encourage "the moral regeneration of the Arabs" whom he hoped to convert to Christianity by providing copies of the Bible in Arabic. "If I were called upon to place the different competitors for my father's favour," his son wrote, "I should say that a Negro, a Wahhabi, and a chimpanzee run a dead heat for his affections with a Radical tailor a bad fourth." He was unsuccessful in his attempted Reformation, but inspired an evangelical lilt to the treaty, which begins, "In the name of God, the Merciful, the Compassionate. Praise be to God who hath ordained peace to be a blessing to his creatures."

The Perpetual Maritime Truce (see Appendix), after which the coast was named the Trucial States, followed in 1853 and was supplemented forty years later, when the Russians and French tried to weaken Britain's hold, with an Exclusive Agreement in which individual rulers pledged "on behalf of myself, my heirs, and successors . . . that I will on no account enter into any agreement or correspondence with any power other than the British Government . . ." and "without the assent of the British Government I will not consent to the residence within my territory of the agent of any other Government." Now and again the agreements were reinforced by stern warnings, as in 1914, when a Greek merchant looked as if it was becoming too successful. The political resident wrote ominously to the shaikhs, saying, "it would be altogether disadvantageous if any of you were to grant concessions to foreigners (*sic*) in connexion for pearls or sponges."

"Protecting" the Arabs from outside influence and attack was easy compared to stifling the vicious feuds which took place among tribes and within families. Shaikh Rashid was so relentless in his raids on Abu Dhabi that travel facilities had to be stopped for Dubaians and mail steamers prevented from calling at Dubai until he agreed to be less provocative. "Don't be under any illusion of what the Gulf was like," says John Wilton, now British ambassador in Saudi Arabia who has spent many years as a diplomat in the area. "When I was a political fellow there in 1950 I remember an occasion when a bullet was put through the windscreen of my car. Luckily, I used to go around with twenty or thirty chaps—three or four jeeploads. We got into position behind some rocks, and after a while, a man with a huge white flag came out of a fort and said it had all been a big mistake. That was the Ruler of Rams, a small fishing village. He wanted independence. It is all very well nowadays to say we should have drilled for water or started schools, but first we had to establish peace. Even the oil companies could not explore without risk to life."

Nor could those born into a family of ambitious brothers. Passions remained unrestrained, perhaps in anticipation of subsequent psychological thought, with alarming results. Thirteen of Shaikh Zayed's predecessors have been murdered by male relatives. A former political resident, Sir Lionel Haworth, recalls:

Some few years ago the Shaikh of Abu Dhabi died and left several sons. The eldest inherited. After some years, a brother asked him to dinner; as the Shaikh left after dinner, his brother followed him downstairs, and, having incontinently shot him in the back, reigned in his stead. This brother was the Shaikh when I took over the appointment as Resident, and I have never seen a man with fear so written on his face. I gave him a year at most to live; he proved me wrong. He lived eighteen months. He was also asked to dinner by a brother, who, however, did not shoot him in the back; the Shaikh came upon an ambush on his way home and was shot in the front. The last brother was a wise man and put his nephew on the throne, and now the sons of the last murdered man are already maturing their plans to murder the new Shaikh.[1]

The new Shaikh was Shakhbut, one of four brothers by the same mother, Shaikha Salama, a powerful woman who kept a palm-frond mat hanging on the wall to remind them that it was once their total worldly possessions. After her husband was assassinated in 1926, she made the sons[2] promise never to fight against each other. Islamic punishment for breaking such an oath is to forfeit the right to paradise, and, for this reason above others, the Saudis were unsuccessful in attempting to bribe Zayed with $60 million to sell out to them on the Buraimi dispute, and it took longer than anticipated to depose his brother—forty years.

At first, there was little problem. Life continued in the same meager way as it had for centuries. Abu Dhabi, with a population of 15,000, most of whom lived in *barastis* (palm-frond huts), had a small income from the sale of postage stamps. The British raised an army, the Trucial Oman Scouts; mostly rejects from Aden who murdered their first commanding officer and sold their weapons to tribesmen. A desultory five-year development plan was started in 1956 with $800,000 provided by Britain.

Then, in 1962, oil was discovered.

Shakhbut, soon overwhelmed with money, refused to spend any. He crammed it in boxes under his iron bed. When finally persuaded to deposit the money in a bank, he demanded to count the notes after a week and was flabbergasted to discover he was paid interest. He thought it was some form of prank. On vacation in London, he ran out of cash and sent his secretary back to Abu Dhabi for another sack of rupees. "Why didn't he write a check?" asked the bank manager. "He did," replied the secretary. "I've brought it with me." In Paris in 1960, he was astounded to be told by his hotel that they would not accept rupees in settlement of the bill.

Sir Hugh Boustead was sent from Oman to encourage a more positive attitude to development—without much success. Only one scheme was accomplished during his three and a half years: piping water from the interior. Shakhbut refused to commission an initial survey because of the expense—he knew where the water was, he said. And he was correct—so a respected American firm which had completed similar work in Kuwait was asked to tender for the $2 million contract. Unhappily, the company was not warned of Shakhbut's aversion to signing his name to any-thing that resembled a contract. When one of their directors brought a legitimate letter of intent for signature, Shakhbut tore it up, handed back the pieces, and declared, "You are trying to trick me."

A British firm, Paulings, was then suggested. "Having heard of the company, the Ruler said he would not deal with a common person as general manager, but that he must have a lord," recalls Sir Hugh. The request, relayed tactfully to Paulings, was for a "gentleman of eminence and integrity not connected with the firm."

Alas, they could think of no one until a director remembered that his father, who was chairman of the South African Automobile Association, had spoken highly of a man with the same job in Britain. What was his name? Ah, Lord Brentford. He became chairman pro tem and went to Abu Dhabi. "Shakhbut and I got on well," he recalls. "He said, 'I am a Bedou. All my people are Bedou. We are accustomed to living with a camel, on a goat, in the desert. If we spend this money, it is going to ruin my people, and they are not going to like it.' He has been proved right. The character of the people has changed, and I think for the worse."

Nevertheless, Shakhbut had to go. It was no use having a miser as ruler of a fabulously wealthy country. His income was approaching $100 million a year, and by 1966 he had spent only $4 million. He was even niggardly about paying for his own private army, the Abu Dhabi Defense Force, formed by an imported British officer, Colonel E. B. "Tug" Wilson.

"Every day I had to struggle with him for money," says Colonel Wilson. "He would send a man to count the soldiers to check I wasn't exaggerating the numbers and stealing their pay. I had a lot of useless equipment bought in some sort of swindle—World War One greatcoats, steel helmets, and arctic boots. Not much use in the desert. But I come from Yorkshire, and once I decide something, I'm determined to succeed. I did in the end. When I left, the Force was 6,000 strong with thirty-six airplanes, ten patrol boats, an armored car regiment, and two infantry regiments."

Encouraged by the British, Zayed decided finally that there was no alternative to a peaceful overthrow of his brother. Colonel Wilson helped in the planning. "I would not allow the soldiers to have anything physically to do with removing the Ruler because that would set a precedent. We just seized the telephone exchange. Later, I broke into Shakhbut's room. On every pillar there was a mirror, and in the middle of the floor was a Louis Quinze chair. He obviously sat looking at himself around the room. And there were tins and tins of money, some of it nested in by mice and rats."

Zayed spoke to his brother on the telephone for an hour, apologized for the inconvenience and said he had no real alternative. Four hours later, an RAF Pembroke was taking Shakhbut on the exile route to Bahrain and then London where he lived in a Kensington mews house for a few months before returning quietly to Al Ain where he now lives contentedly, some say smugly, watching the money rush and its problems pass by. For weeks after the coup, Zayed did not dare tell his mother what had happened. When at last he was courageous enough to do so, she thought he was joking and refused to be convinced he was telling the truth. The subject was never raised again.

The coup coincided with British withdrawal from Aden and the establishment of a new military headquarters in Bahrain. Forces there and in Sharjah were doubled to 6,000, but soldiers were told to be discreet and forbidden to wear uniforms off duty lest they encouraged antiimperialist thoughts. There were worried murmurings among Gulf shaikhs, now conveniently obliterated by the money rush, that the fashion for Arab nationalism and Britain's declining status might combine to leave them stranded without "protection," vulnerable innocents in a world full of muggers.

Do not worry, said their ex officio nursemaid, Britain's Defense Minister Denis Healey, who understood "the real risk in the Gulf is that much of the oil is produced in tiny countries which cannot protect themselves and which, if we left, might be the subject of an attack by three at least of their neighboring large countries going in together."

It would also, he added, result in millions of unemployed in Britain, although such a parochial consideration would not influence him. "If we could be certain of the stability of the government with which we made a commercial agreement on the basis of common interests—fine. But the risk at the moment is that a disorderly British departure before there is an alternative basis for stability in the area could lead to a prolonged conflict. I agree that if our presence there becomes an irritant rather than a stabilizing factor, that would be one of the signals for us to reduce our presence. But that is not the case at present."

As reassurance, he sent his junior minister, Goronwy Roberts, fluttering around the Gulf in November 1967 to pledge unfailing support. There was, after all, a "perpetual" treaty.

Perpetuity lasted another couple of months until money (imported by the Treasury) beat obligation (as advertised by the Foreign Office) and Britain announced it would, after all, withdraw from the Gulf within two years. A hapless Roberts was shunted back to soothe outraged shaikhs and to explain that what seemed at first glance like a betrayal was in fact a . . . realistic assessment of the situation? a wonderful opportunity for self-determination? the natural course of history? The Conservatives thought it an outrage and resolved to "reconsider" if returned to power. When they were, in 1970, indignation had decomposed into a realistic assessment that nothing could be done except persuade Sir William Luce to travel tirelessly round the Gulf arranging the least embarrassing retreat from an undistinguished imperial role.

The main problem was the Shah, even though he had not yet been accorded notoriety as international demon. "His horizon in those days was limited to the Straits of Hormuz and Russia," said Sir William. "In later years he developed a messianic sense of mission. When I met him again, in 1973, he was talking about the furtherest reaches of the Indian Ocean and how he must get the Russian and American fleets out of the way. When I asked how he would achieve that, he was not quite sure."

Sir William's task was to try to form a union between the seven shaikhdoms, plus Bahrain and Qatar. The Shah, however, said he wanted Bahrain on the basis of Persian occupation in the seventeenth century. "It was nonsense to us," said Sir William, "a bit like Britain claiming the United States. But he was serious. All Iranian students had been brought up to believe Bahrain was part of Iran. He never allowed by one jot or tittle that his claim was not one hundred percent valid."

It was, however, bluff. The Shah's real motive was to gain control of three islands: Abu Musa, administered by Sharjah; and the Greater and Lesser Tumbs, supposedly owned by Ras al-Khaimah—in the Straits of Hormuz which effectively controlled entry to the Gulf.

"When I was negotiating," said Sir William Luce, "he told me, 'You and your people have no idea what it cost to give up my claim to Bahrain.' He laid it on as hard as he could. I accepted that it was a considerable sacrifice and was a factor in his attitude to the islands but he did not know the detailed history as well as I did. I had studied it with the Indian Government and had no doubt that Abu Musa belonged to Sharjah. Nevertheless we arranged a Falkland Islands type of agreement by which each side continued to claim sovereignty without prejudice, and there was a fifty-fifty working arrangement. Iran was allowed to occupy a designated area and much to my surprise, has made no infringement whatsoever. I quite frankly expected that within a year Sharjah would be quietly pushed off.

"The Tumbs was a more arguable case. I reckoned it was sixty percent in favor of Ras al-Khaimah, and we tried everything to reach the same sort of agreement as with Sharjah. Unfortunately, early in 1970, a tanker carrying oil to Eilat was attacked with a bazooka by a launch which had called at the Tumbs. That made a deep impression on the Shah, and he mentioned it on a number of occasions. He said he would never allow any risk of the Tumbs being used by ill-disposed people to attack tankers passing through. The Tumbs are nearer to Iran than Arabia, he said, so he should have control. We couldn't accept that argument, or we would have to hand over the Channel Islands.

"I suppose it had some force to it, if you don't mind discarding the historical claims of the Ruler of Ras al-Khaimah. We did mind because we had protected him for years. Every so often, as a sort of ritual, the Iranians put a buoy by the islands. In due course we sent it back to the shore with a note saying, 'Your buoy is lying off the coast of Sharjah and you are welcome to come and get it any time.' We had quite a number which they could not collect because that would be admitting they were wrong.

"However, the day before Britain formerly withdrew from the

Gulf, on November 30, 1971, Iran attacked the Tumbs. One Arab policeman and three Iranian soldiers were killed—a modest victory for the Ruler, in a way," commented Sir William. But Iran stayed on the islands and thus controlled the Straits. "I knew the Shah was going to attack twenty-four hours in advance," said Sir William. "What is more, I told the Ruler of Ras al-Khaimah and suggested he remove his police force from the island because no one wanted a loss of life. He said he could not do that because it was against his pride and self-esteem. Perfectly understandable. The whole thing was very difficult, but you have to remember what the issues were at the time: our relationship with the Shah, and his with the Arabs if he did not take control of the islands. He attacked when he did because he did not wish to start his relationship with a new country by seizing part of their territory."

So the UAE was born to the accompaniment of that ubiquitous diplomatic trio: *realpolitik*, fury, and bluster. The British Foreign Office remarked disingenuously that it could not be expected to uphold a treaty obligation the day before it was revoked. A furious Muammar Qaddafi offered Ras al-Khaimah immediate military aid. The Ruler declined politely and sent the Libyan President a signed photograph of himself as a present, after which Qaddafi's fury took eight days to coalesce into action. Then he nationalized British Petroleum, which had a half share in the Saris oil field with Nelson Bunker Hunt, the Texas multimillionaire. He justified his action by saying the company was 50 percent government owned and therefore culpable by proxy. BP retaliated by threatening worldwide litigation, as if they were once more dealing with Mossadeq in Iran:

> The Libyan Government's wrongful acts are under international law incapable of depriving the company of its rights under the agreement. Accordingly, the attention of all those who may be concerned with these developments, whether as purchasers of oil or otherwise, is drawn to the continuance of the company's rights. It is the intention of the company to assert those rights wherever and whenever necessary against those who infringe them.

But the world had moved forward two decades. The money rush was about to begin, and an entirely different set of rules now operated. BP's rhetoric was as effective as a faded lawyer burbling in the bath about his bygone triumphs, and Qaddafi was emboldened to give the United States "a good hard slap on its cool and insolent face" by nationalizing Hunt's oil interests as well. Hunt was sitting in his Dallas office when he heard. "One has to expect a few disappointments in life, and I was disappointed," he told me in uncharacteristic Texan understatement. "There wasn't a whole lot the American Government could do, short of military intervention, and we never anticipated they would do that. But in our view the other oil companies did not live up to their obligations to us.[3] I don't think nationalization was inevitable. Nothing is except death and taxes."

Hunt was paid $48 million. "It was peanuts, but I had to take that or nothing. Our investment in Libya was $150 million before the field went into operation. One thing these countries overlook is that there was no oil until foreign firms came along with their technical ability to find it and their financial ability to develop it. In all fairness, perhaps the producing countries were not getting quite so much as they should have, but to me it's a great tragedy they do not stick to their deals. When you get to the stage where a written agreement does not mean anything, it's pure and simple law of the jungle.

"I never did meet Qaddafi. One of the clauses in our contract was that we should not engage in internal political affairs. On three occasions the CIA asked me to put agents in there. They said they would furnish a geologist or engineer. I refused because I didn't feel it would serve any purpose and could see it might be construed as meddling. We had a comparatively small organization—maybe five Americans and twenty-five Libyans. It would have been pretty obvious. Interestingly enough, I heard later that they had put a man in, an engineer I hired for eighteen months but who didn't perform well so I did not renew his contract.

"When I first went to Libya in 1956, Tripoli was a nice little city, small, clean, and with few vehicles. You had pleasant horse-drawn taxis which could move along at a nice whip because there was not much else on the street. Then, several years later, I was amazed to encounter traffic jams. It's a worldwide phenomenon: how are you going to keep them out of the desert when they've seen the city?"

23/THE SHAIKH, THE LADY, AND THE COLONEL

"If you support the Arabs you get it in the neck."
FORMER BRITISH LABOUR MEMBER OF PARLIAMENT, MRS. MAR-
GARET MCKAY

*"There can be few deeper satisfactions than to have played a
part in helping a country or a people forward to a life of peace,
under an honest government."*
COLONEL SIR HUGH BOUSTEAD, FORMER POLITICAL AGENT IN THE
GULF, THE WIND OF MORNING

MOST OF SHAIKH ZAYED's family are too restless to take part in
rustic folk-dancing now that they are leaders of a country which
has grown to such international importance in so short a time. He
himself still has the bedou mentality, wandering from place to
place, but instead of a camel he uses a VC10; instead of a casual
majlis, he is surrounded by Palestinian advisers, as befits a world
statesman; and instead of simple delights like hunting with an old
musket, he takes an unsporting machine gun to the pheasants,
according to neighbors at his former British home, Buxted Park.

His eighteen-year-old son, Mohammed, had inherited a romantic nature, it seemed, when he bought $600 of equipment and set
out to camp on Dartmoor. But it began to rain, and he returned
hastily to the comforts of a $3,000-a-week hotel, temporary lodg-
ings while he neglected to attend the language course for which
he had been sent to England.

Shaikha Fatima has formed a much-publicized women's movement, but has never been seen by a man other than her husband

since puberty. "For me to be without the *burqa* would be the same as a Western woman to walk the streets naked," she says. When she made an official visit to Egypt, sidewalks were cleared along her route so that no man would see her.

"You can imagine how difficult it was," says her secretary and companion, Abla Nuweis, a beautiful twenty-nine-year-old Egyptian who has lived in the UAE for nine years. "But Shaikha Fatima promised Shaikh Zayed that she would never let a man see her. It is not jealousy. These people do not want to alter their ways. But change is coming. Seven years ago, she did not leave her house at all. Now she goes all over the place."

For all she sees and hears, she might well remain at home. "When we go to London," continues Abla Nuweis, "we take about thirty other women. The plane is met by a Rolls Royce, and we go straight to Shaikha Fatima's house in the Boltons. We never see a man. The chauffeur is a woman. Shaikha Fatima does not go shopping. Harrods send clothes for her to try. If you asked me to live like that, I could not. But it is her custom and she is happy. It's a strange life."

The rush to respond to feminist pressure has its peculiarities. Aisha Ali Sayyar, director of Social Services in Abu Dhabi, keeps her veil in the bottom drawer of her desk as a precaution. She feels that some men expect her to wear it, she told me.

But what about the trickle of UAE students who have been educated abroad and are beginning to return home with strange ideas? Shaikh Zayed's respected Foreign Minister, Ahmed Khalifa al-Suweidi, was nonplussed when confronted by a group who had been invited to ask him questions. Instead of the innocuous remarks he anticipated, they said, "Why can't we vote?" and "Why should the Ruler dispose of oil money in any way he likes?" Visibly shaken, he muttered to a British friend, "I suppose that is what you call democracy. It is not something we are used to."

Zayed thinks the British are partly to blame. "The tragedy remains that they did not prepare the area or its people for independence of any sort. We were suddenly left on our own. It was a hasty decision. What worried me most was the failure of Britain to fulfill its responsibilities."

Adnan Pachachi adds, "It was not deliberately malicious. No

one asked them to make it a flourishing paradise, but after the Second World War, many Arab states were prepared to do something for themselves and were not allowed to. We would have been ten years further ahead if we had been given more freedom."

The British legacy is viewed less charitably by most, including the UAE Minister of Information, Shaikh Ahmed bin Hamed. Sitting in his office surrounded by indignation, he made his opinion perfectly clear, "The British did nothing. I insist they did nothing. In Aden, where they had self-interest, they made a heaven with television, roads, and an airport. Here we did not benefit at all. They did nothing for the good of the country."

There are, however, individual British with an enthusiasm for Arabia not based primarily on money. "Tug" Wilson left Abu Dhabi in 1969 to become a staff instructor at Camberley, re-signed to breed trout unsuccessfully, and returned at Zayed's invitation in 1975 to look after horses "and other jobs." Edward Henderson, a former British ambassador in Qatar, is working on historical records. And former Labour M.P., Mrs. Margaret McKay, a seventy-one-year-old widow who claims she was thrown out of Parliament by "a mysterious group of Trotskyites and Zionists" because of her pro-Arab views, lives rent-free in a three-bedroom apartment in Abu Dhabi. The wallpaper was peeling when I met her—"It's going to be redone next week," she explained—and the view across the sea had recently been obstructed by yet another apartment building erected a few yards away without any apparent planning consideration. "Shaikh Zayed invited me to come here in 1970, and then they didn't know what to do with me, so I wrote a book. I get a salary, but I was one of the first people here, and it remains the same as when I arrived. Shaikh Zayed does not know, and I will not remind him because I can live on it. I don't need a lot. I have no car."

It is a curious place to find a woman who started work at thirteen years of age for $1 a week as a weaver in the village of Oswaldtwistle, joined the Communist party when she was in her twenties, became chief woman officer of the Trades Union Congress, and then Labour M.P. for Clapham. She is perky and lively in spite of several cancer operations, and gets up at 4:00 every morning to work on a 7,000-year history of the Arabs.

She became interested in their cause in the mid-sixties when it was unfashionable, and brought political disaster upon herself by accepting $200,000 from Shaikh Zayed to open an Abu Dhabi campaign center in Piccadilly and buy the seventeen-year lease of two houses in Pont Street, Chelsea, which she hoped to turn into a cultural center. "We put the kibosh on it, though," said her landlords, Cadogan Estates, who pointed out the residential nature of the lease. Her local party said it no longer wanted her as an M.P. "Maybe I should have presented my case in a different way," she admitted as we sipped tea in the comfortably furnished drawing room and gazed across the concrete landscape. "I was a little overactive. But I never dreamed how pro-Zionist Harold Wilson was.

"I was accused of all kinds of unimaginable things—a plot to kidnap Charles Clore, diamond smuggling, trying to blow up an Israeli plane. I had death threats and everything. They slandered me, they maligned me, and they lied about me. I remember going to Douglas Houghton, then chairman of the party, and saying to him, 'You've done everything else—for God's sake, why don't you X-ray me?'

"Honestly and truly, I don't miss much about England. Some of the colleagues I desperately wanted to see are dead, and the era I represented has gone. I have friends still in the House of Commons who do little things for me like photocopying and sending me books. As a political person, I feel a bit out of touch here although I listen to the BBC news at six o'clock. I'd probably be bored to death if I returned to England, apart from the fact it would be too expensive and I don't think I could stand the climate. We are in another world here.

"I had six years in Parliament, which was a pretty fair run, but I don't bless those who threw me out. And why did they do it? For putting the Arab case and bringing delegations here. Looking back, I see I was a bit previous. Now we have Jim Callaghan and others turning up following in my footsteps. In fact, they are doing more than me. They are coming to beg. I never did that."

Colonel Sir Hugh Boustead, K.B.E., C.M.G., D.S.O., M.C., Vladimir with cross swords, St. George's Military Medal with one Palm, a member of the Athenaeum, doyen of the expats, was born in 1895 on a tea estate in Ceylon where his father was a planter. His earliest ambition was to join the Navy, a desire not hindered by the fact that his uncle Algie was Admiral of the Fleet Sir Algernon Lyons. He entered Dartmouth Naval College, became a midshipman and went to South Africa with H.M.S. *Hyacinth* in 1915 before deciding that seasickness seven times in an hour, claustrophobia, and a love of horses were not compatible with his chosen career.

So he deserted.

He left his uniform in a public lavatory at Cape Town, changed into civilian clothes, took the name of McLaren (which he often forgot, to his embarrassment), and joined the South African Scottish Regiment which was off to fight the Germans in France. He won several decorations, received a royal pardon for his desertion, and, after the war, returned to England, where he decided it would be fun to go to Oxford for a year while he awaited an Army commission. "I had been brought up in anything but an academic atmosphere. I had to sit an exam of sorts and was then accepted as an undergraduate. I decided to read Russian." There were one or two beastly inconveniences caused by the fact that he was a jolly good boxer, shortly to become Army lightweight champion. One evening, when he promised to attend the Trinity Commencement Ball with some enchanting Danish girls, "as luck would have it, I was called to fight that same night in the lightweight competition against a French services team. My fight was put on early, about eight o'clock, as I had told the President I had to get back to Oxford. My Frenchman was a good deal heavier, but rather fat, and I was able to knock him out in the third round to an enthusiastic response. I hared off to Paddington to catch the nine o'clock and changed in the train into white tie and tailcoat."

A year later, in 1920, he captained the British pentathlon team at the Antwerp Olympics. "We were beaten in all the events by the Swedes. This was disappointing, but we had a magnificent view from special seats of the stadium events." After that he raised and subsequently commanded the Sudan Camel Corps before joining a 1933 Mount Everest expedition, "enormously interesting" but "hellish" nevertheless. When forced to retire because of frostbite, he returned to base camp, had a shave, bought a sheep, and rode a pony across Tibet—"the journey was one of the most memorable and enchanting I can remember."

Boustead then became a British political representative in many parts of Arabia before being invited by Shaikh Zayed to live out his retirement training horses at Mazyad, a village near Al Ain. Today, because Shaikh Zayed has come to the agricultural show, Sir Hugh thinks it is possible he might make a detour to see the stables. He has not been there for such a long time.

Coincidentally and less dramatically, I also planned to visit the colonel. He is difficult to contact as he does not have a telephone, spends some of the year traveling, and a few months at his home on the New Mountain in Tangier. But two weeks earlier, in Muscat, we had made a tentative luncheon engagement through a third party he was visiting. He had said, "Just ask. Anyone will know where to find me."

As my rickety taxi bumped along the road from Al Ain, I held little prospect of locating him, and even less of lunch. Mazyad is a single narrow street with one general store, and no one seemed to have heard of Colonel Sir Hugh. There were vague pointings to the right, and we drove a few kilometers off the road, past some *barastis* and brick buildings with corrugated iron roofs until, convinced of our mistake, we turned back toward the Hilton in Al Ain and a mutton dip to which I had been invited. The thought of succulent baby lamb, crinkling over a barbecue, made me lick my lips. I tasted bitter dry dust from the desert which blew through the taxi's open window and hovered in specks before clinging loosely like prickly chiffon to the skin.

Just then, I noticed a cluster of green trees to the left; a mirage no doubt, to which we drove in the certainty it would disappear before we arrived. But it stayed, an ersatz Hampshire garden in this desolate piece of sand. There was a gate into a small drive, and, behind that, a bungalow weighed down with unexpected greenery. An Indian appeared carrying a wooden spoon, which I assumed was a cooking implement rather than an offensive weapon.

"Colonel Sir Hugh?" I inquired dismally.

"Hello, old boy. Glad you could make it. Come on in."

An elderly man, stocky, slightly stooped but with fine sparkling eyes and weather-beaten freckled face almost hidden by a wide brimmed floppy brown hat, had materialized from the corner of the garden. "Beer?" he asked, before introducing himself, and then "Boustead."

I felt I should have managed a sharp salute, handed over a cleft-sticked message from the Queen, and retired with a posse of cavalry into the distance. Instead, I was disheveled, overweight, a Londoner concerned about missing lunch and about to do feisty battle with an Arab taxi driver who clearly expected a gargantuan fee for having brought two outlandish Britishers together.

"The others back?" Sir Hugh asked his cook.

"Not yet, sir."

The taxi driver and I played the traditional game of mutual incomprehension, swore at each other for respective greed, and Sir Hugh took me through his small kitchen into a drawing room furnished with bachelor comfort rather than style. He has never married.

A portrait of Shaikh Zayed dominated one wall. Against another was a glass-covered cabinet full of strange medicaments. A desk cluttered with bits of paper was in front of a window framed by a tangle of orange bougainvillea, white oleanders, and Japanese hibiscus which stirred faintly in a breeze from the mountains stretching toward Oman in the distance. This was the heart of the Rub al Khali—the empty quarter—scene of so many diplomatic quarrels and oil-company duplicity.

"Would you like a dip before lunch?" Sir Hugh asked. "We have plenty of water here."

The setting seemed too ascetic for a swimming pool. Perhaps he was suggesting a bath.

"I have a tank outside," continued Sir Hugh. "Did you bring a costume?"

It had not occurred to me.

"I'll see if I can find you one."

His room was cluttered, clothes were on the floor and chairs and double bed. Memorabilia of his soldiering days were tucked into odd corners and there seemed to be everything but a spare suit.

"Pity," said Sir Hugh. "Better not go in starkers. Do you mind if I have a dip?"

The "tank" was a concrete structure erected above ground to a height of about seven feet. There were steps to the brim which Sir Hugh climbed with agility and plunged in. The water looked dank and was covered with leaves. He swam four lengths in a gentle breaststroke, carrying on conversation most of the time, clambered out, put on his hat, walked down the steps and went to change. "Glorious day," he said.

Inside the house a whiff of perfume mingled with the smell of curry, and lingered like sweet lilies—altogether too dainty for such a resolutely bachelor establishment. It must be imagination.

"Do you know Lady Pamela?"

I turned. Sir Hugh had entered the drawing room with the woman I had noticed earlier at the agricultural show.

"Lady Pamela Egremont,"[1] said Sir Hugh, and then to her, "Did you manage to get your hair done?"

"Yes," she said. "But I only just got away before this mass of cars and soldiers came up to the entrance."

"Lady Pamela went to have her hair done at the Hilton after the show," explained Sir Hugh.

"Quite," I replied.

"She's here on holiday."

We sat down to an excellent curry lunch, talked about London literary life (her son Max had just written a book), and Shaikh Shakhbut. "Of course he was extremely entertaining, with quite a sense of humor, and he used to listen to all the news," said Sir Hugh. "He insisted it was much safer to listen to Israeli radio because they are more truthful than the Arabs. He hated Egyptians.

"But he was mean [stingy]. He even kept his tea locked up. If he had a guest, a servant would come in, Shakhbut would go to a cupboard, unlock some tea, and then it would be brought back again afterwards. And he always forgot to pay people. One day the chief of police came and said, 'Look here, you had better pay. You haven't for four months.' So Shakhbut got a box of rupees from under his bed and it was full of silverfish. They had eaten the whole lot. That shook him. It was after that he agreed to put it in the bank.

"Another time he was persuaded to put up some loos by the beach at Abu Dhabi. You see, the problem was that everyone used the beach as a loo, and that didn't seem a very good idea in a seaside resort. So he got some contractors. But the Arabs didn't like the toilets. They thought they were insanitary and didn't use them. Shakhbut thought he had been swindled and put the contractor in prison."

Sir Hugh spends much of the day as a doctor, treating Bedou who come from all around. "I see about twenty a day. They are jolly good chaps." In the evening, he rides for one and a half hours on one of the fifty horses stabled nearby. Every day he awaits a visit from Shaikh Zayed, who since he became a world leader seems to have lost interest, but he enjoys living in such an out-of-the-way spot. "I think it is largely the background one has grown up with, the people one has been working for, and been interested in over the years."

I left and returned in the amnesial afternoon to Al Ain. Traffic was stopped at a traffic circle for Shaikh Zayed's Cadillac to pass. A couple of police cars were in front and a jeep behind, manned with two machine guns. He waved from the window but was deep in conversation with an unidentified man in a Savile Row suit. Being a world statesman is tough.

From across the sand, the chant of the *muezzin* quivered for a while in the languorous air and vanished into the disappearing day. The *ulemas* often tape-record their message now, and mosques are fitted with stereo equipment. The money rush makes real people redundant.

Across the sands Sir Hugh cantered, waiting for a visit that never came.

Part Six

Bahrain, Qatar, Kuwait, Iraq

"Your neighbor is your enemy, and your neighbor's neighbor is your friend." ARAB SAYING

"The deterioration in manners is the fault of the Europeans. Many of them have strange ideas as to how to behave to people of a different race. The following remark, made by Lord Morley, could well apply to Americans and Europeans in Bahrain, 'While bad manners are a fault anywhere, they are a crime in a native territory.'" CHARLES BELGRAVE, PERSONAL COLUMN

MONEY-RUSH CONTESTANTS sweep into Bahrain at the rate of about one million a year, using the island as a bolthole to sanity, refreshing themselves in its comforting atmosphere of energetic philistinism. No one expects much style, a commodity generally developed by the poor for emulation by the rich; but after the deprivations of Saudi Arabia even limited attractions are like brackish water to a man dying of thirst.

Comparison with other Arab countries, combined with the normal sycophancy of the money rush, allows Bahrain to be judged lightly. Its twittering provincial pretensions become embarrassing rather than offensive, the ridiculous self-importance of ministers like Tariq al Muayyid (Information) and Shaikh Abdul Aziz bin Mohammed al Khalifa (Education) is comic rather than harmful, the Ruler is endearingly batty rather than dangerous, the indigenous Brits are complacent rather than arrogant and are allowed to retain the squeamish values with which their predecessors met an earlier invasion. "Soon American wives began to arrive; they added a good deal of colour to the social scene and some of them startled the staider inhabitants of Manama by their expressions. We saw a lot of them and they came to At Homes which we used to have every Wednesday. Once a lady who we did not know well surprised the company by saying, during a pause in the conversation, 'Well, folks, I don't think I'll play tennis. I'm pregnant.' My mother-in-law, who was staying with us, never forgot the remark," wrote Sir Charles Belgrave, who became Adviser to the then Ruler in 1926 after seeing the job advertised in the personal column of *The Times*. He had to contend with other newfangled ideas, such as the cinema which opened in 1937 and "caused a deterioration in manners and morals. I have always attributed to some incident in a film the terrible habit of suicide among women by pouring petrol over their clothes and setting themselves alight, which has become prevalent in recent years."[1]

In fact, Bahrain is maiden aunt to the money rush, prissy, and vaguely contemptuous of nouveau riche neighbors who have neither such an archaeologically reputable history stretching back to the Paleolithic era, nor education, nor an efficient workforce wrought by sixty years of "Westernization," but who nevertheless provide acceptable bribes (a $40 million sports city, a military base, and cash inducements of hundreds of millions) to keep auntie's *virgo intacto* and ensure she remains unviolated by beastly radicals who scent easy submission, and uncompromised by imperialist Americans who offered $4 million a year rent (up from $600,000) in a vain attempt to keep a naval base at the port of Jufair after the lease ran out in July 1977.

The Ruler, Shaikh Isa bin Sulman al-Khalifa, K.C.M.G., takes his orders tacitly from the Saudis as he once did from the British; and his relaxed and relatively hedonistic society is tolerated in much the same way as trinket sellers are allowed in St. Peter's: it is a bit gaudy, but prevents the peasants being ripped off elsewhere. A twenty-five kilometer causeway is being constructed between the island and mainland, its $800 million cost paid by the Saudis, so it will soon be even easier for them to slip into town for a boozy weekend. Shaikh Isa jokes to friends that he will build a drying-out hotel on the border, but knows he has to be careful. While the money rush lasts Saudi Arabia rules. An excess of pleasure is considered as dangerous as an excess of democracy—and will be curtailed just as quickly.

There has already been one near-escape. In 1973 a constitution was published in Bahrain guaranteeing freedom of speech, conscience, and religion. A Parliament was elected for the first time, by 85 percent of the adult males eligible. It was assumed that the right-wing merchants who supported the status quo would have a large majority. Instead, the deadly "black-red" alliance of reactionary religious leaders and left-wingers which characterizes so many money-rush hurdles, particularly in Iran, gained most seats and began to pursue their incompatible aims. One day they would try to exclude women from public life; the next they suggested a takeover of the oil company. Finally they combined in August 1975 in a refusal to sanction detention without trial, whereupon the Ruler suspended them protesting that they "tried to take advantage of the democratic system . . . to achieve their own goals." He now rules by decree with members of his family in key positions and everyone, including his brother the Prime Minister, can continue to make money unhindered by the inconvenience of having to justify their actions.

They are protected by the most elaborate security in the Gulf, devised by a former superintendent of police in Kenya during the Mau Mau era, Ian Henderson. Some estimates suggest that one in three telephones is tapped. Undesirables are prohibited from entering the country, and potential troublemakers are whisked off without trial to Jidda, a rocky island prison to the West. Bahrain is the sort of place where police detainees are likely to jump out of prison windows, suffering bruising and broken legs, in order to "expiate for their crimes."

Trades unions are banned, and censorship is as ludicrous as elsewhere in the Middle East. A special Bahrain issue of the *Investor's Chronicle* in November 1976 was prohibited because an editorial map omitted the Hawar Islands off the coast of Qatar which have been subject to rival claims from the two countries for years. An English language newspaper, the *Gulf Mirror*, is self-censored by its predominantly British journalists whose livelihood depends upon maintaining the myth that Bahrain is not far short of the Garden of Eden which legend suggests it could be. If they need help, it is provided by the ever-watchful James Belgrave, son of Sir Charles, who runs a sensible public relations firm, drives a Cadillac, has the ear of the Ruler and ministers, and smothers the *Gulf Mirror*'s editor like a mother hen lest an embarrassing fact should appear. He intervened when the Minister of Education threw an injudicious tantrum and accused the elite St. Christopher's preparatory school, with its 500 British and 60 Bahraini pupils, of representing "imperialist arrogance in its ugliest form" and being run by people "of narrow-minded, arrogant imperialist mentality. They treat the Bahraini pupils and the children of the Asian community in a humiliating manner. In fact the presence of this school, with the mentality with which it behaves, collides with the country's freedom and independence."

The information that the minister's daughter attends the school, and that his outburst could have been connected with a sharp letter reminding him he had not paid her fees, was a perspective which, through his influence, Mr. Belgrave was able to deny readers of the newspaper.

Minister of Information Tariq al Muayyid, is equally adept at trying to lobotomize news which might reflect badly on Bahrain. He was infuriated by an accurate Reuters account of a fire at the two-story Chase Manhattan building in the center of the banking district. He berated the journalist concerned, saying it should never have been reported—particularly as the local fire brigade was inept. National security, otherwise known as money, was at stake.

But the tense political situation still obliges commitment, as it does in all Arab countries. You are either "for" the Israelis, or "for" the Arabs—which means an uncritical acceptance of one side or the other and leads to a distrust which seems absurd. "I see a Zionist behind every person who walks through that door," said Yousif Shirawi, Bahrain's Minister of Development, when I met him at his office. "The West does not want to hear our point of view, does not want to understand us." He is reputed to be the island's most intelligent government official.

Bahrain's oil will run out in the 1980s, so it is trying to become a service center, a Singapore or Cayman Islands to the money rush without pejorative overtones of a tax-swindling haven. Its pretensions suffer a setback now and again, particularly when prestigious new buildings appear to be collapsing as frequently as they do in less sophisticated Gulf countries where ambition is more pervasive than expertise. Government House, designed and managed by George Wimpey & Co., and the Gulf Hotel, designed and contracted by the same company, both became precarious as a result of improper sand and cement mix, a problem caused by the Good Lord, according to Wimpey's managing director, D. G. Fitzgerald. "You are not going to get facts, or chapter and verse from us," he told me with the defensiveness which infects people familiar with the Middle East. "There were impurities in the mix. We were not aware of certain chemical reactions, and neither were many people. It was the state of scientific knowledge at the time."

The country's self-importance and feeling of cosmopolitan significance was given a boost when the British Concorde used London-Bahrain as its inaugural route on January 21, 1976. Such prestige. Such world recognition. A preening of ministers took part in the lavish ceremonies.

What would they have said if they knew the truth: that the British Government had tried desperately to persuade British Airways to go anywhere but Bahrain, a place which even the chairman of the airline considered a "nonevent." But where else? The Americans would not let Concorde land in New York or Washington, and British Airways had to travel somewhere in January because the French refused to delay their first flights between Paris and Rio de Janeiro. In all the world, Bahrain was the only suitable place even though it was commercially disastrous, sometimes involving travel with no passengers at all. "Valuable experience for the crew," said British Airways. "We never expected the service to be overcrowded."

Bahrain is not a fortuitous location. When the first Imperial Airways plane landed there in 1932, amidst similar pomp for the inaugural trip to India, it sank into a disused water tunnel on takeoff and had to be hauled out with ropes.[2]

Any money-rush country desperate for prestige is a perfect target for con men, and they came to Bahrain from all over the world to sell junk to shaikhs and junk jewelry to their wives. It was a paradise for those with imagination. The great manure swindle is remembered fondly, and, even though it was not successful, several prestigious newspapers seemed to believe in the project.

It began in 1974 when a small American company, RJB Sales Export Inc., of Sequim, Washington, announced with much publicity that it had a three-year contract to provide Bahrain and Dubai with at least 50,000 tons of liquefied cow manure a month —enough to cover every square mile of the Garden of Eden with 3,600 tons, eventually. The cost was $1.2 billion, and a broker for the deal, Mitch Randazzo of World Wide Brokers in Galliano, Louisiana, said the Arabs agreed to deposit $50.2 million a month with Chase Manhattan Bank in New York.

Farmers were to be paid five cents a gallon for a substance that had been previously a worthless, smelly nuisance. "This will save our lives," Virgil Baker, a farmer from Orting, Washington, told *Time* magazine in December. "We've been operating $2,000 a month in the red, but now we could make up to $4,000 a month on manure. It seems like a fairy tale."

A man calling himself Prince Khalid signed a contract on behalf of the Bahrain Government—or so it was thought—and arrangements were made to deodorize the manure with a chemical invented by Richard J. Briggs (hence RJB Sales Export Inc.) to prevent a dangerous buildup of methane gas on the journey to the Gulf in an oil tanker. Once there, the manure would be mixed with pulverized wood chips, spread on the sand, and planted with grass.

The *Financial Times* wrote a full account in February 1975 about the "export potential of the humble cow pat," discovering in its story such hitherto-unknown geological formations as "the Dubai to Kuwait desert valley" through which, it claimed, there was already a pipeline capable of taking the manure. It would then be pumped onto the desert through 48-inch pipes.

Alas it *was* a fairy story. "Prince Khalid" was former airline clerk Mohammed Khalid Ebrahim. The Dubai to Kuwait desert valley does not exist. There are no pipelines like those mentioned. And the scheme would have taken one-third of Bahrain's national budget.

Banking is a more plausible and safe activity than mythical agricultural breakthroughs for a relatively poor and tiny country surrounded by other people's excess cash, so in 1975 Alan Moore, formerly with merchant bankers Williams and Glyn, was recruited to set up an offshore banking facility. It was so successful that at one time it attracted $1 billion of new capital a month. Chase Manhattan, Citibank, Grindlays, American Express, Algemene Bank, Lloyds, Midland, The National Westminster, and the Swiss Bank Corporation were among thirty-two of the world's leading banks with assets of $15.7 billion in Bahrain's offshore banking by the end of 1977. "If you tried to find the ideal location for international banking, you would come up with Bahrain," says Mr. Moore. "The time zone is in its favor, and it has good communications."

But Ivy League–style bankers from Wall Street make more stringent demands than their British counterparts, and are more selective than Texas roughnecks and assorted wheeler-dealers who comprised the American community until then. As the number of American firms doubled in Bahrain during 1976, facilities became inadequate. "The deterioriation of the quality of life and services available accelerates," said an American Embassy report. "Telephones and Telex, about which Bahrain used to boast, have deteriorated over the past year, and the telephone system is both expensive and unpredictable.

"All the things that Bahrain used to manage so well, such as its port, its road system, its power plants, are in the throes of deterioration because of radically increased and obviously unanticipated demand. All these problems are shared in the region, but the case of Bahrain seems to be particularly full of pathos because it once was so good.

"Westerners and 'decadence'-seeking Saudis have always viewed and used Bahrain as their watering hole. This role has increased over the past year, and prospects for the future are practically unlimited unless the puritanical Wahhabi hand extracts some social restrictions from the relatively liberal-minded and -acting Bahrainis."

As everywhere else in the money rush, success creates tensions which prosperity can subdue only temporarily. Even bankers and their wives, sunning themselves by the Gulf Hotel pool, can see through the wire fencing to where Pakistanis, Baluchis, Indians, and less fortunate Arabs live in cardboard boxes on the beach. Even blinkered ministers and advisers have not forgotten the shock results of the 1973 elections. Even the ever-smiling face of jovial Shaikh Isa hides worries that the money rush has deprived him of British protection and thrust him into a tumultuous world of international intrigue, greed, and skulduggery. Once, when his private plane was delayed by fog and had to circle the airport several times, he was convinced there had been an attempted coup. He gave the pilot permission to land only after his son went to the control tower to assure him personally that there was no danger.

Shaikh Isa came to power in 1961 when he was thirty-three, the eighth member of the family to rule since his ancestors came from Kuwait in 1738 to capture Bahrain from Persia. The al-Khalifas are comparatively docile with a reputation for gentle eccentricity rather than violence. In the early thirties, when his grandfather Hamad built a palace "rather like an Indian railway station," according to Sir Charles Belgrave, he shopped in London for furnishings and became so impressed with the latest bathtub that he bought enough to have two in each bathroom, even though there was no running water. When a rival shaikh expressed surprise at such concern for cleanliness, and asked why two bathtubs were needed in each room, Hamad replied with disdain, "One for hot and one for cold, of course."

Shaikh Isa is content to leave the actual running of the country to others, and he has only one real rival in the family: his envious younger brother Muhammad. Most afternoons, as guards make sure drivers obey the instructions on their licenses ("the holder must comply with the rules of the traffic, and stop the vehicle on the right side during the passing of His Highness the Amir of Bahrain"), he travels 30 kilometers along the dual highway to his private beach.

There he sits in portly splendor chatting to a selection of the six hundred Gulf Air hostesses, 60 percent of whom are British, who live on the island and have done much to stimulate its exaggerated image of debauchery among other Arab states. True, some girls have left the island with cases of money, and His Highness was warned by the British to curb his allegedly gargantuan sexual appetite. But he appears to be an extraordinarily happy man, and his generosity is not restricted to girls. When a

British battleship paid a courtesy visit prior to Bahrain's independence in 1971, he was invited on board for lunch and took with him 278 watches: gold for the officers, silver for the men. Sir William Luce had to ask him, tactfully, to restrict his gifts in future.

Shaikh Isa is joined on the beach by Margaret, a dark-haired girlfriend who flies out from England several times a year. Shaikha Hasa, his wife, first cousin, and mother of his nine children, is an understanding lady who busies herself with lucrative property deals.

In front of his green-tiled bungalow, the clear blue water laps gently against white sand in an almost idyllic setting. The Ruler allows Europeans, but not fellow Arabs, to cavort with him here. Three armed soldiers patrol the road to check that the regulation is obeyed. Some English wives picnic with their children, sitting at plastic tables on the beach. The Ruler's table is there, too, identical to the others, except his chairs are tied together with string to stop visitors from taking them away. Behind his bungalow, a stall is opened to dispense free soft drinks and biscuits as it does every day. Shaikh Isa smiles at the children and urges them to have a good time.

He motions to a couple of stewardesses to take tea with him and Margaret. They giggle and wonder if they will be invited to a party. They have heard stories.

"This is a nice place," says one of the girls.

"Yes," says Shaikh Isa.

"A bit boring after a while, though," suggests the girl.

The Ruler does not answer. He smiles and shrugs.

"With all your money you could live anywhere," continues the girl. "Why do you live in this dump?"

Her friend looks embarrassed, but the Ruler continues to smile.

"There is one reason for that," he says, patting her on the knee.

"What? Go on!" teases the girl anticipating a lascivious innuendo.

"Because," says the Ruler, "it is my home."

And was long before the money rush began to loosen the feudal system, churn up family loyalties, and create fear for the future. Out here, at the beach, everything is placid. The snakes in the Garden of Eden have been safely caged, and there is time for another party.

How soon will it end? Twenty years, predicts the Shah. Maybe sooner, if Mr. Henderson's security police lose their tight hold. The problem for Shaikh Isa is that he lacks an essential commodity of the money rush: cascades of cash to buy off the opposition. Maybe his cousins in Kuwait and Qatar have had the right idea.

25/QATAR CRUMBLE AND KUWAIT FLU

"When I see all these industrial and constructive projects, I feel the happiest man in the world."
SHAIKH KHALIFA BIN HAMAD AL-THANI, EMIR OF QATAR

"There are three superpowers: Russia, America, and Kuwait."
KING FAISAL OF SAUDI ARABIA, MAKING A JIBE AGAINST THE ARROGANCE OF KUWAITIS

QATAR (pronounced "Gat-a") has less need to worry about its image than most, if only because it is hardly noticeable. It is not so dangerous as Iran, so influential as Saudi Arabia, so vulnerable as Oman, so vulgar as Kuwait, so tense as the UAE, so cosmopolitan as Bahrain. Nevertheless, the Emir does not lack all the money-rush attributes. He and his mammoth family are constructing the conventional white elephants on their acres of sand inhabited by 100,000 people: a $400 million iron and steel complex which will depend upon imports of ore from Brazil, flour mills, fertilizer plants, petrochemical installations, and the most modern hospitals in the world (but not so many doctors). In 1977 Qataris managed the remarkable achievement of spending $1 billion more than their $2 billion income. It does not matter. They have one of the best credit ratings in the world which allows them to borrow the odd half-billion from Chase Manhattan, and their spending power ensures that sordid embarrassments are hushed up abroad. In the summer of 1977, a member of the royal family was arrested in an Oxford Street store for allegedly stealing a handbag. The store detective was telephoned that evening at home by a man he took to be a senior Foreign Office official and warned that if the charge was not dropped, he would be out of a job. The charge was dropped.

Qatar is a sliver of sand jutting from the east coast of Saudi Arabia like a thumb 100 miles long and 50 miles wide. Growth in the capital, Doha, has been leisurely and well planned, and the society has a tolerable balance between the spivvery of Dubai, ascetism of Saudi Arabia, and internecine rivalry of the UAE although it is not without family squabbles. The previous ruler, who was deposed in 1972, imported two electric chairs—playthings for his son—which were kept in the palace basement. No one is really sure whether or not they were used.

The Saudi influence is resisted as much as possible, even though Qataris come from the same Wahhabi sect. There are cinemas in Doha, a national theater is planned, and foreigners can drink at the local speakeasy—Room 501 of the Gulf Hotel—or apply for a liquor license from the British embassy. A licensed restaurant-cum-nightclub was closed, however, after Saudi complaints.

Some expats may need more than one drink to calm their nerves as they hit the ubiquitous, yet still unexpected, problem of the money rush: rush is often more evident than money. A British firm, Turriff Construction Corporation, discovered this when a panic-stricken member of the royal family asked it to rebuild the country's magnificent new football stadium which another member of the family (there are 202 different shaikhs of the al-Thani family in the Qatar telephone directory, and 12 shaikhas) had bungled. It had to be completed within four months, by March 21, 1976, for the Gulf football championships which were to be opened by King Khalid who was paying his first visit to the country. Imagine the disgrace if it fell down, as it threatened to at any moment. Turriffs worked, regardless of cost as it had been told, and the stadium opened on time. The company presented certified accounts for $20 million. It was paid $17.5 million, and haggling continued years later.

Meanwhile, the championship was such a success that Qatar took a third of a six-page advertisement in *Time* magazine in June 1976 to tell the world of their achievement. So effective was their bland Ministry of Information prose that parts of it were reprinted verbatim six months later in a special editorial report in the *Guardian* about Qatar. These "supplements" which also are published by the *Financial Times* and *The Times* bring lucrative advertising to newspapers and some assumed prestige to the countries concerned who are not encouraged to understand the difference between them and legitimate editorial coverage.

They give, too, a spurious respectability to what is so often pure greed. The pretense that most money-rush contestants are actually helping to build a country, rather than their own bank balances, sometimes causes emotional strain. Here, at least, it has been identified as the Qatar crumble. Dr. Sayed Tajeldin, Director of Preventive Health, who has been in the country for ten years, told me, "People think they will make money, but there are a lot of psychological problems for foreigners. They don't know if they will stay for one, two, or three years. Their children are usually in the homeland, so they can't live as a family. Also the high humidity and temperatures effect blood fluidity. Combined with perspiration, which works on the central nervous system, it makes one depressed and can also form blood clots. Heart disease has increased enormously.

"So, in the summer, more than five thousand patients will be sent to Europe for treatment. Seventy percent will just be going for recreation—paid for by the government. It is far too many, but it is common now for Qatari women to need psychiatric help, or to go abroad for two or three months because their situation is changing so rapidly. The old pressures still apply, yet they have much more freedom, and an educated woman will no longer agree to marry an ignorant husband."

Gone are the days when an innocent girl, fearful of an accidentally ruptured hymen, pushed a sheep's bladder full of blood into her vagina on her wedding night to "prove" virginity. Or the days when a bride was wrapped in a carpet and rolled into the room where her bridegroom waited to see her for the first time.

In a shop in Doha I watched a young Indian man wearing tight satin trousers walk into a crowded radio shop followed by four black bundles, who, seconds later, came out cackling with high-pitched girlish laughter. The Indian stared after them dumbfounded. "Do you know what they did?" he said to no one in particular. "They goosed me!"

Such frivolity would be unthinkable a few hundred miles north, in Kuwait, where the money rush has lasted for longer than anywhere else and has produced the world's most advanced social security system, and a semicomatose population of a million people who have little to fight for, nothing to complain about, and whose only excitement is the anticipation of leaving.

I timed my first visit badly—a few days before a religious holiday, when everyone was preparing for a week in Europe or Bahrain to recuperate from the puritanical restraints of home. It takes indulgence quite beyond my capabilities to remain unmoved by the sight of hundreds of unshaven, unglamorous Kuwaitis in dirty clothes, with inelegant olfactory habits, clamoring to withdraw thousands of dinars from a sweaty, overcrowded bank—particularly as my own $100 travelers checks were treated with scorn.

For years, Kuwaitis have been among the world's richest and most cosseted citizens[1] with an income now of $25 million a day. Everything is free: education, medical care, clothing for children, and there is low-cost housing. Naturally there are no taxes.

The real wealth began in 1952, when annual revenues trebled to $56 million as Kuwait sold more oil to make up for the embargo of Iran. During the fifties and sixties, individual Kuwaitis had a unique opportunity to make money when the government decided to spread wealth by buying land from its citizens at inflated prices. Thousands made enough to live in comfort for the rest of their lives. Others are now paid high salaries and given civil-service sinecures if they cannot find a job.

I had a typical meeting with one of them, Hatim Abdul Ghani at the Ministry of Information. He spent most of the time chatting to a friend on the telephone, gave me no information whatsoever, and when I left for an appointment at another ministry, he directed me to a building that had been vacated a year earlier.

The residents of a slothful, snobbish, and wealthy nation can afford not to give a damn what anyone else thinks because money buys them all eventually: Iraqis who invaded when the British left in 1961, Palestinians who make up a quarter of the population and run essential services, the PLO, front-line Arab states, major industrial nations—including Russia—eager to supply ever more weapons so that the inconsequential Kuwaiti armed forces can pretend to defend themselves, and expats earning vast salaries.

In the Bristol Hotel, where a tatty room with cheap furniture and no bath (the communal bathroom was filthy with no soap, no plug, and a dirty toilet with a broken seat) cost about $80 a night, I met a British truck driver from Hull who was taking it easy after earning $10,000 for six weeks' work.

"It's simple," he claimed. "I go from London to Saudi Arabia with a truckload of goods. It takes about twelve days, and I'm paid $2,000. I stay in Saudi for a few weeks, driving between the main cities. From Jidda to Riyadh, which takes three days with a twenty-ton truck, you are paid $1,000. A forty-ton truck pays double. From Jidda to Dammam, which is five days, pays $2,000. Then there's whisky. You buy it for $50 in Jidda, sell it for $80 or so in Riyadh, or bring it here. They are probably even more corrupt here than in Saudi."

But it is not politic to say so, even in jest. Why should anyone upset a country which has 10 percent of the world's known oil reserves, $50 billion in foreign assets, huge cash deposits in several major banks, and whose true financial involvement in foreign companies is treated with the utmost circumspection. The holdings of Kuwait, as well as Saudi Arabia, are impossible to quantify because there is no clearly defined line between the royal families and the State. As in Britain several centuries ago, the royal family "owns" everything. All royal families are specifically excluded by law from disclosing any assets in Britain, so many Kuwaiti and Saudi investments are obscured by the words "Bank of England Nominees."

Even so, known shareholdings make Kuwait the largest investor in Britain of any Middle East country. Kuwaitis have spent at least $1.2 billion in shares of insurance, banking and newspaper companies,[2] $400 million in property, and $4 billion in long-term securities in Britain since the money rush began. Spare currency is gambled in casinos or the Kuwait Stock Exchange which, with only thirty-three listed companies, had a turnover of £1.8 billion in 1976—slightly less than the Paris Bourse. Only Kuwaitis are allowed to play the game, and when massive speculation is followed by an inevitable crash, as it was early in 1978, the government is there to invest heavily and stabilize prices. On that occasion it cost $6 million.

But if arriving in Kuwait is like falling into a giant cash register, there are many who find the till slammed uncomfortably on their fingers. Two German firms, Thyssen and Mannesman, which won a $26 million contract in 1969 for part of a computer-controlled water-distribution project, claim that delays by the government cost them $40 million and were followed by prevarication over arbitration. At one stage the Minister for Electricity, Yousef al-Ghanim, insisted that 30,000 relevant documents, covering 6,000,000 words, should be translated into Arabic. Suddenly, international lawyers who had been speaking English to their opposite numbers for years, found them feigning a lack of understanding. "It is regrettable and alarming that the minister has decided to render arbitration procedures inoperative," said one, Terence Lane, after the government refused to extend a three-month deadline for the arbitration tribunal to make an award.

"This is a hardheaded mercantile community, and disastrous disappointment lies for anyone who counts his chickens too soon," warns British ambassador Archie Lamb.

There are occasional hiccups to spoil the atmosphere of manufactured calm and progress. In August 1976, on Saudi advice, the royal family suspended democracy in the form of a National Assembly which had existed since 1963. Members were becoming too critical, or as a Kuwaiti diplomat told me, "We have flu at the moment. If we don't treat it, it will become bronchitis. We are a bit ashamed, though, that we have not developed faster."

And, along the northern border soldiers fidget, wondering if and when Iraq will again back its claim with military intervention. Relations between the countries are less strained than a few years ago. Some Kuwaitis drive to Basra for the weekend, instead of jetting to Bahrain, to indulge those pastimes proscribed at home. There is even a street in the heart of town named after them. But they suspect, as do others on the money rush, that Iraq is incubating the very forces that could one day spoil the whole game.

"The oil companies represent imperialist logic, the logic of plunder and impoverishment of the masses."

AHMED HASSAN AL-BAKR, PRESIDENT OF IRAQ

"They [the Russians] won't be satisfied until the whole world becomes Communist. By allowing ourselves to be drawn into spheres of influence, we Arabs are ensuring that we will become an East-West battlefield."

SADDAM HUSSEIN, VICE-PRESIDENT OF IRAQ'S REVOLUTIONARY COMMAND COUNCIL, NEWSWEEK, JULY 17, 1978

THERE ARE THOSE for whom Baghdad, the capital of Iraq, evokes childhood memories of stories about the thousand and one nights, Sinbad the sailor, Ali Baba, magic carpets, and exotic oriental unreality. To others, the exotic oriental unreality masks one of the most dangerous and vicious regimes in the world, a haven for political terrorists and sinister Russian-backed saboteurs. For some, Iraq is the only money-rush country making a genuine attempt at independence—even though "independence" is sometimes advertised in a barbaric fashion.

In the summer of 1978, twenty-one Communist Army officers who had been in prison for three years accused of treason were shot, despite pleas for mercy from Russia and East European countries. This was a deliberate warning by Iraq's leaders that they would not tolerate the sort of infiltration taking place in South Yemen, the Horn of Africa, and Afghanistan. A few days later, there was a less dramatic, although personally painful and humiliating, warning to the British, which was to culminate in uniquely insulting diplomatic tit for tat—and deaths in a Paris street.

One evening in Baghdad, Richard Drew, a communications officer at the British embassy, was dragged from his car and beaten up in front of his pregnant wife by Iraqi secret police. It was assumed to be retaliation for an incident the previous April in London during which an Iraqi diplomat claimed he was similarly ill-treated by the British police. Apparently, the diplomat left a West London restaurant at midnight, and, according to the British version, drove off at 80 miles an hour on the wrong side of the road. An unmarked police car began to follow. The diplomat panicked, assuming the occupants to be an assassination squad. He sped even faster to Acton police station, where he crashed the car against a wall, and dashed inside to demand protection from the startled duty sergeant. He was pursued by the equally bemused Q-car men. When he proved he was a diplomat, he was handed over to an embassy official, unharmed except for any damage he might have caused to himself.

"Well now," observed one of those involved in the subsequent diplomatic fracas. "The combination of bad behavior, ignorance, and money does tend to annoy people. When those qualities appear in a drunk diplomat at one o'clock in the morning, I can see it might cause problems."

Meanwhile, though, many Iraqi diplomats were under Special Branch surveillance because it was thought they were involved with two assassinations and at least one attempted murder in London. In January 1978, Said Hammani, the moderate PLO representative, was shot in his Mayfair office. Seven months later, a former Prime Minister of Iraq, General Abdul Razzak al-Naif, was gunned down outside the Intercontinental Hotel. And there was the gruesome story of Dr. Ayad Allawi, who had left Iraq when he became disenchanted with the government. He awoke one night at his home in Epsom to find an Arab about to cut off his head with an ax. He moved quickly, was badly injured, but lived.

Following this activity, eleven Iraqis were expelled from London "on security grounds," and the Iraqis retaliated by expelling ten diplomats from the British embassy in Baghdad. A few days later, the Iraqi ambassador in London was about to enter his car when he was summoned back to his office to take a telephone call. Seconds later, a hand grenade exploded under his car, injuring two passersby. A nineteen-year-old girl was arrested running from the scene.

Four days later, an Arab gunman walked into the Iraqi embassy in Paris, took eighteen hostages, and demanded the release of the girl held in London. After a siege lasting most of the day, he surrendered to French police but as he was leaving, was shot at by Iraqi security guards. In the ensuing battle, one of the guards and a French policeman were killed.

At last, said some, the country which masterminds and finances so much terrorist outrage is the subject of attacks itself. A bomb had gone off outside the Iraqi embassy in Brussels a few days before the London attack.

Unfortunately, though, the streets of Europe were being used for the shootouts instead of the more bloodstained gutters of Baghdad. Three days after the Iraqi embassy siege in Paris, that city's moderate PLO representative, Essedine Kalak, was assassinated in his office by two gunmen who fired sixteen bullets into his body. Arab feuds and the complex internecine hatreds, now financed amply by the money rush, are based on one fundamental dispute: whether or not Israel should be recognized.

Because of Iraq's refusal to acknowledge what it calls the Zionist entity, or Occupied Palestine, and the conviction of the country's leaders that war is inevitable (an easy enough principle to hold as they are not a front-line state), Baghdad has become headquarters for the most militant Palestinian organizations. These include Dr. George Habash's Popular Front for the Liberation of Palestine, and "Black June," set up by Abu Nidhal (born Sabri Khalil Banna in Jaffa about forty-two years ago) who founded the Fateh branch of the PLO with Yasser Arafat in the early sixties but broke with him in 1974.

The windows of Abu Nidhal's secret headquarters a few miles outside Baghdad are boarded and covered with bulletproof panels. Very occasionally he travels to Europe, but remains mostly incommunicado as one of the world's most wanted men—hunted by the secret services of Israel, the United States, conser-

vative Arab countries, and under sentence of death from the
PLO, which has called Saddam Hussein, Iraq's de facto leader,
"a professional killer and specialist in the slaughter of innocents"
for harboring so many extremists, and claims that the assassination of their Kuwait representative, Ali Nasser Yassin, also in
1978, was carried out by "cowards who are protected, sheltered,
and guided by the intelligence services of Baghdad."

In addition, Iranian religious leaders like the Ayatollah
Khomeini, who was expelled from his country after riots in 1963,
have been guests of the Iraqi government. Khomeini lived in the
holy city of Najaf, and his speeches, smuggled into Iran, were an
inspiration to those who felt the Shah's restrictive regime should
be replaced by Allah's restrictive regime. Eventually, in the fall
of 1978, Khomeini was expelled quietly, and took up residence in
Paris. It was said he was becoming an embarrassment to the government. . . .

But before you can unravel the intricate skein of Iraqi politics,
another knot is twisted and the whole bundle is lost in confusion.

Baghdad seethes with suspicion and fear "like Russia in the
Stalin era" says one ambassador, and there is a jittery feeling
that it is a testing ground for some of the world's most advanced
spy technology. One embassy found fifty different "darts" carrying microscopic transmitters fired into the walls leaving marks
undetectable by the human eye.

Diplomats are not allowed to travel outside city limits without
written permission and find it almost impossible to mix with
Iraqis. Local staff are automatically considered to be spies, and
many "disappear" overnight. Ambassadors whisper what they
consider to be the truth only when the air conditioning is turned
to maximum power, and consequent noise, and the visitor stands
close.

Even allowing for melodrama endemic to the money rush, and
a real fear of violence which exists in Baghdad, paranoia is at a
more advanced state than in other countries. One day I horrified
the Baghdad representative of one of the world's largest firms by
telephoning his office to make an appointment. When we met
later, he motioned me to silence before I had a chance to say
anything, and indicated that I should follow him into the garden.
There he told me, "You have already broken the first rule here

by telephoning me. Your phone is bound to be tapped, and you are sure to be followed."

He led me into the street. "We must talk here, so that everyone can see our relationship is open and there is nothing to hide."

"Are you sure this is necessary?" I asked. My skepticism annoyed him.

"Didn't you see that car just go by?" he replied. "The red one, with four men in it. They are watching every move you make. You shouldn't have come here."

"That's crazy," I said.

"They're bonkers, of course. But what can you do? Give my regards to —— [name deleted] when you get back to London. Now go. Quickly."

I drove disconsolately around town, past signs providing reminders that autocracy is the least articulate form of government. In Arabic and English I was exhorted to remember that "The experience of autonomy shows the humanitarianism and democracy of the revolution. Let us safeguard it"; or "Let us work together for consolidating the foundations of national unity as set up by the revolution to secure a strong and advanced Iraq"; or "Let woman play her role in the revolutionary process."

Such messages may not be wholly effective in a country with 60 percent illiteracy, but maybe they are less harmful than cigarette advertisements in the West which are, I suppose, their equivalent. And they compensate for the lack of consumer goods which are curiously lacking in a country with a $10 billion a year income and potential wealth indicated by the second largest oil reserves in the Middle East next to Saudi Arabia.

"This is a complete contrast to the laissez-faire mentality of Kuwait," said a businessman. "And many of the contrasts are favorable—there is less corruption, and they are trying genuinely to spread the wealth by making sure the state owns nearly everything. But the economic determinism is also applied to human beings. The first priority of the leaders is survival. They pursue it uncompromisingly, and anyone who stands in the way gets very short shrift indeed."

The brutality of the leadership may horrify visitors, but to some Iraqis it is unremarkable. "It is a problem we have had for two thousand years," says Dr. Awni Shakir, director general of planning for the Iraqi oil company. "You learn to keep silent here. If everyone is allowed to speak, the government would change every two days.

"But we have no feeling for the community. Businessmen are used to such quick changes in government that they want to invest in the morning and take their profit in the evening. They cannot afford to plan ahead because no one knows what the future will bring. Democracy will come with time . . . a very long time."

In this almost bored tolerance of harshness, Iraq is more like Iran than any of its Arab neighbors. There are other, less alarming, similarities. Western dress is almost universal, alcohol is available, and morality is not determined by religious dogma. Women are unveiled and participate in the revolution, a freedom which at times seems more like an obligation.

"Last year we trained 18,000 women to do anything from driving a tractor to typing," says Dr. Souad Barnouti, secretary of research for the 200,000-strong General Federation of Iraqi Women. "We jump in to fulfill any need."

Dr. Barnouti, middle-aged, slightly prim but attractive, has a Ph.D. in social science from the University of California at Los Angeles, where she spent seven years. "In America, everyone is discriminated against unless they are strong. That means people have to fight for justice. Here, we diagnose a problem and try to deal with it sensibly. In Iran a woman thinks her role is to become a socialite, buy dresses in Paris, show up in ballrooms, and be written about in society pages. When she feels guilty, she sets up a charitable organization—making sure, of course, that the poor remain poor and investing in her good works by having her picture in the papers.

"Here we don't accept the personal freedoms of the West, the way governments leave things to the individuals so they can behave without regard to social limitations, the complete disrespect when you walk down the street . . ."

"What do you mean?" I asked.

"You know what I mean."

"No, I don't."

"People will do anything in the streets in the West—the way

they dress, walk with their girlfriends, you know what I mean. It is indicative of personal freedom without regard to social behavior."

"You sound very Victorian."

"It is not Victorian. We want to strike a balance. We are individuals, but we are also social creatures. If you want a healthy society, you need healthy social relations. We don't find the solutions in the West."

In Iraq the two men seeking these and other solutions can be seen everywhere, their black-and-white portraits brooding over streets, shops, and offices: President Ahmed Hassan al-Bakr, and forty-two-year-old Saddam Hussein, Vice-Chairman of the Revolutionary Command Council. They are more decorous than the Shah and Empress Farah. In fact, they look like a couple of undertakers. There is little to indicate that Saddam buys his clothes from Cardin in Paris, and favors jazzy, almost spivlike, ties. He is a former lawyer, and it shows both in his discreetly smug face and the unintelligible gobbledygook of his speeches. "Everyone should bear in mind," he says, "that the practice of democracy does not flow through one channel. It has to flow through two channels: the 'lower' channel in its relationship to the 'higher' and vice versa. That is to say, the 'higher' should adhere to democracy and stick to democratic practices in its relationship with the 'lower.' And the same goes for the latter. This should be viewed as one of the basic laws of the Revolution and the Party."

Quite so, I thought, as I went to see the head of foreign press relations, Amir Helou. His name means "Sweet Prince" in English, and he is, indeed, a handsome man. He took slow and infrequent puffs at a Havana cigar as he stared at me over his desk.

"Welcome," he said. Then he asked whom I would like to see in Iraq, shuffled some papers while I told him, and replied, "Welcome. You are welcome."

"Will I be able to see any of these people? I'm not really keen on seeing farms and factories." They are the normal itinerary in such countries.

"We will arrange. It is very hot."

"Yes."

There was silence while he puffed deeply at his cigar, flicked away the ash, and sat back in his chair as if about to make a profound statement. He stared at me again, then at his cigar, but said nothing.

"I'm glad to be in Baghdad," I remarked.

"You are welcome."

"Thank you."

"Welcome."

I nodded.

"Why," I asked eventually, "are there so many signs in English?"

He thought for a while, looked at me, and weighed his words carefully before replying. "A lot of people speak English, I think."

"I see."

"Welcome."

"I would like," I said, "to see as many people as possible, as soon as possible. I have a deadline."

"It is hot," he said.

"Yes."

Another long silence. Finally he stood up and said, "We have arranged for you to see the museum. It is time to go."

It is a melancholy fact that most of Iraq's greatest treasures are not in Baghdad, but in London at the British Museum. "We vandalized the place," admits a British archaeologist.

"Why not?" shrugged an Iranian politician. "Iraq is only a figment of Winston Churchill's imagination."

The country which is now Iraq was formerly Mesopotamia ("the land between the rivers"—Tigris and Euphrates) and was established by the Sumerians as one of the earliest centers of civilization in 3000 B.C. But its modern history is less flattering and, although it has many similarities with other money-rush countries—bureaucratic incompetence, intolerance of intellectual freedom, a background of Western domination which has been replaced by autocratic leadership—it goes further than any in rejecting both Israel and the embrace of Western capitalism. "They [the West] are making wealth a means of corrupting the Arabs," says Saddam Hussein, whose strident criticism of "imperialism" is based on comparatively recent experience.

After the First World War, Iraq became one of five new countries—together with Syria, Lebanon, Transjordan and Palestine—created from what remained of the Ottoman Empire. Under Article 22 of the Covenant of the League of Nations, they became Mandatories: territories which were to be administered by "advanced nations." France took Lebanon and Syria. Israel was created in Palestine. And Winston Churchill decided over dinner at the Ship Restaurant in Whitehall, according to his special adviser, T. E. Lawrence, that Iraq and Transjordan should be hereditary monarchies like Britain. As a sop to Hussein, Sherif of Mecca, who thought he had been promised an independent Arab state in return for help against the Turks, his sons became kings. It did not make much difference because British advisers still ran the country. There was even an Anglo-Indian government suggestion that Iraq should become part of the empire and be used as a settlement for Indian peasants.

The first king of Iraq, Feisal, ruled until 1933 and was succeeded by his flamboyant son, Ghazi, who killed himself six years later in a sports car crash. He was followed by his brother-in-law, Abdulillah, who acted as regent for the infant Crown Prince Feisal.

The family and their Arab retainers, such as Prime Minister Nuri-es-Said, became "Arab parodies of Windsors or Hanoverians."[1] They had Scottish nannies, English tutors, sent their sons to Harrow, and drove in ornate state landaus tended by white-gloved English grooms. They copied the life-style of British country gentry and conspired in the sham of "independence" which was declared in 1932. When the inevitable revolution occurred, on July 14, 1958, feelings of pent-up nationalism were released with ferocious obscenity. Abdulillah, the Crown Prince, Nuri-es-Said and others, including three American "colonialists," were shot and dragged around Baghdad tied to the back of a truck so the mob could hack them to pieces.

"The crash came, and in one day the old links with Iraq were severed, never to be restored," wrote Sir Humphrey Trevelyan (later Lord Trevelyan) who became British ambassador that year. One of the few reminders of the British presence are red double-decker buses which even now give a touch of London to the streets of Baghdad.

The military government under General Abdul Karim Kassem, which succeeded the monarchy, lasted for five years. Then it, too, was overthrown and Kassem shot. The new leaders were Army officers and members of the Ba'ath party which had been founded in 1941 in Syria and was dedicated to Arab unity and socialism. There was vicious anti-Communist purge and a series of coups, countercoups, and assassinations until July 17, 1968, when General Ahmed Hassan al-Bakr became President, dismissed the whole Cabinet, chose loyal friends to surround him, and began a regime that was to last longer than any other.

Many of the new Revolutionary Command Council came from Tikrit, al-Bakr's home town 175 kilometers from Baghdad, and were connected by marriage. The son-in-law of the President was brother of the Vice-Chairman's wife, and so on. It was unfortunate that a country attempting to discard all traces of imperialist colonialist mentality should resort to nepotism, the most ridiculed of all such traits, and embarrassing that it was obvious because Iraqis add their birthplace to the end of their given names. The growing numbers who could read (education is now compulsory and free) and think about such things began to wonder why so many of the leaders were Tikriti.

There was a simple solution: abolish the system. So in 1977 the traditional designation was made illegal. The leadership no longer appeared so Tikriti-based, but thousands of Iraqis became confused about their own identity and that of their friends. "No one knows who they are anymore," said a diplomat.

I asked one of the Iraqi ministers involved why the change took place. "We thought the designation was backward, connected with tribal divisions. The revolution wants to create a common feeling of equality amongst the citizens," he explained.

Later one of his aides took me aside and added, "I should explain to you about the Tikritis. Naturally when you have a revolution you want to be surrounded by friends you can trust. Such people would normally come from your home town. You should not be too upset about it. It's not that serious. I know at least three Tikritis who have been shot."

"Why?"

He smiled. "Perhaps they did not do as they were told."

The next day, I accepted a Ministry of Information invitation to visit a collective farm, spent several hours looking at sugar beet and listening to an energetic defense of the regime from the manager. After that, I was given a conducted tour of an electronics factory.

Back in Baghdad, I asked Amir Helou if I would see the people I requested.

"Welcome," he said.

I asked the Minister of Information, Sa'ad Kassem Hamoudi, the same thing. "Welcome," he beamed, and produced a massive tape recorder on which to immortalize our talk. As additional reassurance, a man whom I was told was one of the highest-ranking journalists in Iraq sat down with a huge pad and took verbatim shorthand notes.

The conversation did not really warrant such attention. It was full of pedantic praise for the revolution, and the minister has an inpenetrable facade of deception.

"Why is there no real freedom here?" I asked.

"Freedom is guaranteed by law for Iraqis."

"Why is there censorship?"

"We have no censorship."

"Has Iraq been misinterpreted then?"

"Yes. Iraq is a revolutionary socialist progressive country which opposes imperialism and Zionism, and it is natural that people will take a stand against us and distort our image."

"Why was a British diplomat beaten up?"

"An accident."

"Why do diplomats need passes to leave Baghdad?"

"Every country has restrictions. Even those which appear most open are secretly following people. Why should we hide it?"

"What is your hope for the future?"

"We believe the Arabs have a common interest and must have a single political system. We cannot coexist with different regimes, but we don't believe in change by force. It is the people themselves who hold the reins."

"Surely Iraq could not coexist with Saudi Arabia?"

"It all depends on the outcome of the struggle in Saudi Arabia at the moment."

"It does not seem a very effective struggle."

"That is because there is a blackout on news."

"By whom?"

"By the regime and its allied organizations. But change is continuous and people will always be in possession of their own destiny."

"Is change inevitable in Saudi Arabia?"

"Sooner or later."

In Iraq, too, it is inevitable. Since 1968 there has been ruthless repression of opposition which comes from several different sources. There is a mutual and unneighborly hatred of Syria and its rival Ba'athist interpretation. There is internal religious aggravation because the leadership is *Sunni* while the majority of the population is *Shia*. And there are the Kurds, who were promised an independent state at the end of the First World War but are now divided between Turkey, Iran, and northern Iraq. Non-Arabs, they are a determined, though helpless, pawn in the international power politics for which Iraq is a central arena.

For years, their cause was backed by American money, the Israeli secret service, and Iranian finance and weapons. Then, on March 6, 1975, the Shah and Saddam Hussein agreed to a quid pro quo in which they settled a long-standing dispute over the Shatt-al-Arab waterway which marks the southern borders of the two countries in return for Iranian neutrality on the Kurdish question. The revolt collapsed immediately, and Kurdish leader Mustapha Barzani fled to Washington, where he lived under the protection of the American Government until his death in March 1979.

Ever since, there have been sporadic reports of a new uprising, many of which are propaganda. Lord Kilbracken, an Irish peer who belongs to the British Kurdish Society, visited Kurdistan in 1978 and was surprised by what he saw. "I am very confused," he told me, "because I was getting bulletins saying there was activity throughout the area. It is crawling with military, but they are all unarmed and relaxed, and there was no sign of tension. It is different to my expectations, but it is difficult to come to any definite conclusion."

The Iraqis have given a certain amount of autonomy to the Kurds who have their own television channel, newspapers, and are allowed to wear national dress. But it is a situation which could be ignited at any moment either by the Syrians, the Iranians, or Americans whose CIA assistance began to wane in 1975.

It is no doubt a coincidence that the following year America started to import oil from Iraq for the first time, and its trade with Iraq increased to $382 million—from $60 million in 1973.

The American embassy in Baghdad was closed as a reprisal for supporting Israel in the 1967 war, but they are represented by a seven-man "American interests section" of the Belgian embassy. "Things were coming up roses until the boycott law was passed in the United States," says a trade official. But even though Iraq is a determined supporter of the boycott, and contracts for any firm doing business there have clauses which Americans cannot accept without risking criminal prosecution, conditions are waived when the need is great. The money rush does not have to be halted for Presidents seeking votes or autocrats in search of idealism. Both sides are confident that a good business relationship will continue and be enhanced in the years to come. Nothing will change, they believe. Or, as a senior State Department official said, "The Ba'ath party think they are molding the new Arab man and stamping out the traditional Arab personality. I wish them luck." Such sorcery, he implied, could never work.

Can it? Should it? Will it?

It is easy to condemn, criticize, or mock. But Iraqis have moved from poverty and repression under the British to comparative wealth and a sort of freedom through education and increased living standards under their own repressive government. Why should they build a society based on Western or Russian examples?

"Which would you prefer, though? This or Saudi Arabia," an American news magazine correspondent asked as we sat expiating our boredom over half a bottle of whisky which cost $40 in Baghdad's cavernous Moulin Rouge nightclub.

Neither, really.

All around, the tables were packed with expatriate workers and "hostesses" who had, through some unforeseen misadventure, alighted here from everywhere, including Chile and Ireland, to watch the cabaret—a mediocre dance troupe from Southern California.

They cheered, they clapped, they drank, they looked morose. It was a bleak enough reward for another day of frustration, boredom, hard work, and the fruitless task of trying to transform yet one more country into a version of the Western ideal.

It was also one day nearer the end of the money rush.

EPILOGUE

"Here is the crux of the matter summed up in a sentence: beneath the veneer of civilisation our spirit remained primitive."

LEBANESE POET NIZAR QABBANI, FOOTNOTES IN THE BOOK OF
DEFEAT

"It used to be the yellow peril: chasing the Chinese and cutting off their pigtails is part of our history. Now we have the Arabs on whom to vent our mistrust and suspicion."

AMERICAN DIPLOMAT IN JIDDA

SO MANY FORECASTS with which the money rush began have turned out to be exaggerated that only the foolhardy would attempt to predict the future. Who can tell what will happen when Russia needs to import oil in a few years? Who knows what maneuvers will change the geopolitical balance in an area of complex and fragile alliances?

The only certainty is that the money rush will continue. Its excesses may diminish and its aspirations become less tawdry, but the scars of the first few years will remain forever, a monument to greed and unplanned development.

"Mankind could be better occupied than transporting vast amounts of merchandise to rot and rust in the deserts of Arabia," said a British ambassador, himself heavily involved in arms sales. "But," he shrugged, "what about our balance of payments?"

Fundamental disruption is inevitable. Industrialization which took one hundred fifty years in Europe, one hundred in America, and thirty in Japan, cannot be squeezed into ten years without problems. "And there is another important point," says an American State Department official. "These are the first countries in the history of the world to dispense money without first collecting it in taxes. That scrambles every concept and does not conform to anything we understand. Moreover, all Western political concepts have failed to take root in the area. The mourning for the National Assemblies which have been dissolved takes place largely in the embassies of Britain and America."

Nevertheless, the money rush has given potential for freedoms of another kind. It has provided schools, hospitals, and houses—as well as tanks, Lamborghinis, jet fighters, and enough bribes to finance a medium-sized country for a decade.

It has provided an opportunity for the rebirth of a culture squashed by centuries of apathy—yet it has encouraged even more apathy for everything except the acquisition of money. It has provided buildings—yet few are of any architectural merit. It has attracted con men, hucksters, interior designers, and men who paint pictures by the yard for undiscerning shaikhs—whereas in the past, money was used to encourage artists, writers, and poets. It has transformed bigots into statesmen, allowed the meretricious to be called magnificent, given hostage to corruption, and made prejudice almost respectable.

It is too early for an epitaph; but now that the first dash is over, there is no reason why the direction should not be changed. It is time, as it always has been, for less avarice and more understanding. It will be irony indeed if the money rush, which began with blackouts in the West, ends with ghost towns rotting in the sand of the Middle East amidst the broken dreams of what could have been and the shattered limbs of those who thought nightmares could be exorcised with cash.

APPENDIX

CALENDARS

The Iranian calendar introduced on March 21, 1976, and revoked two years later, was based on the coronation of Cyrus the Great.

The Muslim calendar is based on the lunar year, approximately eleven days shorter than the solar year, and begins from the year of the Prophet's flight from Mecca to Medina in A.D. 622, known as the *hijra*. The months are:

Muharram	Shaaban
Safar	Ramadan (the month of fasting)
Rabia I	Shawwal
Rabia II	Dhu'l Qa'da
Jumada I	Dhu'l-Hijja—the month of the
Jumada II	*Hajj*, pilgrimage to Mecca.
Rajab	

The corresponding years are:

Gregorian	Iranian	Islamic
1978/79	2537	1399
1979/80	2538	1400
1980/81	2539	1401

THE PAHLAVI DYNASTY

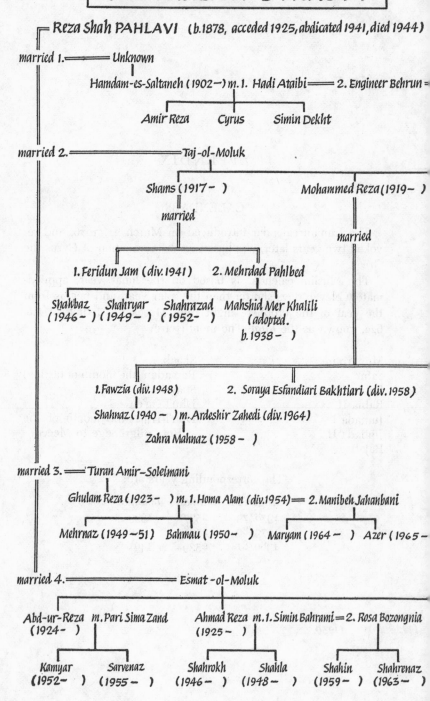

Reza Shah PAHLAVI (b.1878, acceded 1925, abdicated 1941, died 1944)

married 1.======= Unknown

Hamdam-es-Saltaneh (1902–) m.1. Hadi Ataibi ===== 2. Engineer Behrun =

Amir Reza   Cyrus   Simin Dekht

married 2.================= Taj-ol-Moluk

Shams (1917–)   Mohammed Reza (1919–)

married   married

1. Feridun Jam (div.1941)   2. Mehrdad Pahlbed

Shahbaz   Shahryar   Shahrazad   Mahshid Mer Khalili
(1946–)   (1949–)   (1952–)   (adopted.
                                     b.1938–)

1. Fawzia (div.1948)   2. Soraya Esfandiari Bakhtiari (div.1958)

Shahnaz (1940–) m. Ardeshir Zahedi (div.1964)

Zahra Mahnaz (1958–)

married 3.====Turan Amir-Soleimani

Ghulam Reza (1923–) m.1.Homa Alam (div.1954)=== 2.Manibeh Jahanbani

Mehrnaz (1949~51)   Bahmau (1950–)   Maryam (1964–)   Azer (1965–

married 4.================= Esmat-ol-Moluk

Abd-ur-Reza   m.Pari Sima Zand   Ahmad Reza   m.1.Simin Bahrami=2. Rosa Bozongnia
(1924–)   (1925–)

Kamyar   Sarvenaz   Shahrokh   Shahla   Shahin   Shahrenaz
(1952–)   (1955–)   (1946–)   (1948–)   (1959~)   (1963~)

═══ 3. *Amir Aslani*

Ashraf (1919 –)   *Ali Reza* (1922 – 54) m. *Christine Cholewsky* (div. 1948)

                Ali Patrick (1947 –)   *Christian* (adopted. b. 1940 –) m. *Yahna Afsher*

married

                                      Xavier

1. *Ali Qavam* (div. 1941)   2. *Ahmad Shafiq* (div. 1959)   3. *Mehdi Busheri*

  Shahram (1939 –)   *Shahryar*   *Azadeh*

3. *Farah Diba*

Reza (1960 –)   *Farahnaz* (1966 –)   *Ali Reza* (1966 –)   *Leila* (1970 –)

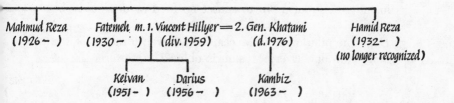

Mahmud Reza   *Fatemeh* m. 1. *Vincent Hillyer* ═ 2. *Gen. Khatami*   *Hamid Reza*
(1926 –)   (1930 –)   (div. 1959)   (d. 1976)   (1932 –)
                                                                 (no longer recognized)

            Keivan   *Darius*   *Kambiz*
            (1951 –)   (1956 –)   (1963 –)

NINETEEN POINTS OF THE SHAH-PEOPLE REVOLUTION:

1. Land reform.
2. Nationalization of forests and pastures.
3. Sale of government factory shares to support land reform.
4. Introduction of profit-sharing system in factories and workshops.
5. Reform of electoral law.
6. Formation of literacy corps.
7. Formation of health corps.
8. Formation of development corps.
9. Formation of equity courts.
10. Nationalization of natural water resources.
11. Reconstruction of the country.
12. Administrative and educational revolution.
13. Expansion of ownership base of industrial and manufacturing units.
14. Price stabilization and campaign against profiteering.
15. Free education.
16. Provision of free nutrition and care for all children from birth up to the age of two years.
17. Provision of health insurance to general public.
18. Rise in land prices will not exceed inflation.
19. Assets of all civil servants must be openly declared.

THE FIVE PILLARS OF ISLAMIC FAITH:

1. *Shahadah.* The creed: There is no God but Allah, and Muhammad is his Prophet.
2. *Salat.* Prayers five times a day.
3. *Zakat.* Almsgiving. This was fixed by the law books at one-fiftieth of all income, but today the amount is left to individual conscience.
4. *Ramadan.* The month-long fast in the ninth month of the lunar year. From dawn to sunset no food or drink may be taken.
5. *Hajj.* The pilgrimage to Mecca, in the twelfth month of the lunar calendar. Every Muslim is obliged to perform this at

least once in his lifetime, and thereafter he can assume the
title *Hajji*. Such a prefix is invaluable for obtaining scarce
seats on Saudia or Kuwait Airlines airplanes, as the devout
are given first option.

THE SONS OF H.M. KING IBN SAUD

1.	Turki	1900–1919	
2.	Saud	1902–1969	former King
3.	Khalid	1903–1903	
4.	Faisal	1904–1975	former King
5.	Fahd	1905–1919	
6.	Mohammed	1910–	
7.	Khalid	1912–	present King
8.	Sa'ad	1914–1919	
9.	Nasir	1920–	
10.	Sa'ad	1920–	
11.	*Fahd	1921–	Crown Prince
12.	Mansur	1922–1951	
13.	Abdullah	1923–	Commander, National Guard
14.	Bandar	1923–	
15.	Musa'id	1923–	
16.	Abdulmuhsin	1925–	Governor of Medina
17.	Misha'al	1926–	
18.	*Sultan	1926–	Minister of Defense
19.	*Abdulrahman	1927–	
20.	Mit'ab	1928–	Minister of Housing
21.	Talal	1930–1931	
22.	Badr	1931–1931	
23.	Talal	1931–	
24.	Mishari	1932–	
25.	Badr	1933–	Deputy Commander, National Guard
26.	*Turki	1933–	Deputy Minister of Defense
27.	*Naif	1934–	Minister of Interior
28.	Nawwaf	1934–	
29.	Fawwaz	1934–	Governor of Mecca
30.	Majid	1934–1940	
31.	Abdulilah	1935–	

32.	*Salman	1936–	Governor of Riyadh
33.	Majid	1937–	Minister of Municipalities
34.	Thamir	1937–	
35.	*Ahmad	1940–	Deputy Minister of Interior
36.	Mamduh	1940–	
37.	Abdulmajid	1940–	
38.	Abdulsalam	1941–	
39.	Hidhlul	1941–	
40.	Sattam	1941–	Deputy Governor of Riyadh
41.	Mashhur	1942–	
42.	Miqrin	1943–	
43.	Hamud	1947–	

* Sons of Hassa bint Ahmad al-Sudairi.

THE AL BU SA'ID DYNASTY

1.	1749–1783	Ahmed bin Said
2.	1783–1784	Said bin Ahmed
3.	1784–1792	Hamad bin Said
4.	1792–1804	Sultan bin Ahmed
5.	1804–1806	Badar bin Seif
6.	1806–1856	Said bin Sultan
7.	1856–1866	Thwaini bin Saud
8.	1866–1868	Salim bin Thwaini
9.	1868–1871	Azzan bin Qais
10.	1871–1888	Turki bin Said
11.	1888–1913	Feisal bin Turki
12.	1913–1932	Taimur bin Feisal*
13.	1932–1970	Sa'id bin Taimur
14.	1970–	Qaboos bin Said

* *From Taimur:*

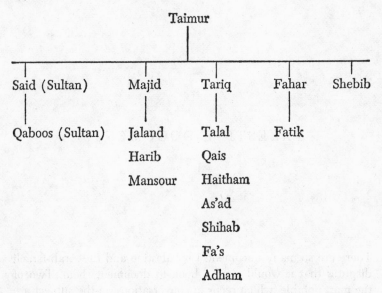

Taimur

Said (Sultan)	Majid	Tariq	Fahar	Shebib
Qaboos (Sultan)	Jaland	Talal	Fatik	
	Harib	Qais		
	Mansour	Haitham		
		As'ad		
		Shihab		
		Fa's		
		Adham		

PALESTINE DOCUMENTS

There are so many documents on Palestine and the Arab-Israeli disputes that it would need a book to document them. Two of the most notable, which recur in conversations on the subject are the Balfour Declaration and U.N. Resolution 242.

The Balfour Declaration was a letter from the British Foreign Secretary, Arthur James Balfour, to Lord Rothschild on November 2, 1917. It reads:

Dear Lord Rothschild,

I have much pleasure in conveying to you on behalf of His Majesty's Government the following declaration of sympathy with Jewish Zionist aspirations, which has been submitted to and approved by the Cabinet.

His Majesty's Government view with favour the establishment in Palestine of a national home for the Jewish people, and will use their best endeavours to facilitate the achievement of this object, it being clearly understood that nothing shall be done which may prejudice the civil and religious rights of existing non-Jewish communities in Palestine, or the rights and political status enjoyed by Jews in any other country.

I should be grateful if you would bring this declaration to the knowledge of the Zionist Federation.

Yours sincerely,
Arthur James Balfour.

U.N. Resolution 242, proposed by the United Kingdom after the Six Day War and adopted unanimously by the Security Council on November 22, 1967, says:

The Security Council,

Expressing its continuing concern with the grave situation in the Middle East,

Emphasizing the inadmissibility of the acquisition of territory by war and the need to work for a just and lasting peace in which every State in the area can live in security,

Emphasizing further that all Member States in their acceptance of the Charter of the United Nations have undertaken a commitment to act in accordance with Article 2 of the Charter,

1. Affirms that the fulfillment of Charter principles requires the establishment of a just and lasting peace in the Middle East which should include the application of both the following principles:

(i) Withdrawal of Israel armed forces from territories occupied in the recent conflict;

(ii) Termination of all claims or states of belligerency and respect for and acknowledgement of the sovereignty, territorial integrity and political independence of every State in the area and their right to live in peace within secure and recognized boundaries free from threats or acts of force;

2. Affirms further the necessity

(a) For guaranteeing freedom of navigation through international waterways in the area;

(b) For achieving a just settlement of the refugee problem;

(c) For guaranteeing the territorial inviolability and political independence of every State in the area, through measures including the establishment of demilitarized zones;

3. Requests the Secretary-General to designate a special representative to proceed to the Middle East to establish and maintain contacts with the States concerned in order to promote agreement and assist efforts to achieve a peaceful and accepted settlement in accordance with the provisions and principles in this resolution;

4. Requests the Secretary-General to report to the Security Council on the progress of the efforts of the special representative as soon as possible.

TREATY OF SIB

In the name of God, the Compassionate, the Merciful.

This is the peace agreed upon between the Government of the Sultan, Taimur bin Feisal, and Sheikh Isa ibn Salih ibn Ali on behalf of the people of Oman whose names are signed hereto, through the mediation of Mr. Wingate, I.C.S., political agent and consul for Great Britain in Muscat, who is empowered by his Government in this respect and to be an intermediary between them. Of the conditions set forth below, four pertain to the Government of the Sultan and four pertain to the people of Oman.

Those pertaining to the people of Oman are:

1. Not more than 5 per cent shall be taken from anyone, no matter what his race, coming from Oman to Muscat or Muttrah or Sur or the rest of the towns of the coast.
2. All the people of Oman shall enjoy security and freedom in all the towns of the coast.
3. All restrictions upon everyone entering and leaving Muscat and Muttrah and all the towns shall be removed.
4. The Government of the Sultan shall not grant asylum to any criminal fleeing from the justice of the people of Oman. It shall not interfere in their internal affairs.

The four conditions pertaining to the Government of the Sultan are:

1. All the tribes and sheikhs shall be at peace with the Sultan. They shall not attack the towns of the coast and shall not interfere in his Government.
2. All those going to Oman on lawful business and for commercial affairs shall be free. There shall be no restrictions on commerce, and they shall enjoy security.
3. They shall expel and grant no asylum to any wrongdoer or criminal fleeing to them.
4. The claims of merchants and others against the people of Oman shall be heard and decided on the basis of justice according to the law of Islam.

Written on 11 Muharram, corresponding to 25 September 1920.

PART OF LORD CURZON'S SPEECH IN 1902
AT THE SHARJAH DURBAR

Chiefs of the Arab Coast who are in Treaty relations with the British Government,—I have come here as the representative in the great Empire of India of the British authority which you and your fathers and forefathers have known and dealt with for more than a hundred years; and my object is to show you, that though you live at some distance from the shores of India, you are not forgotten by the Government, but that they adhere to the policy of guardianship and protection which has given you peace and guaranteed your rights for the best part of the century; and that the first Viceroy of India who has ever visited these waters does not quit them without seeking the opportunity of meeting you in person and of renewing the assurances and engagements by which we have been so long united.

Chiefs, your fathers and grandfathers before you have doubtless told you of the history of the past. You know that a hundred years ago there were constant trouble and fighting in the Gulf; almost every man was a marauder or a pirate; kidnapping and slave-trading flourished; fighting and bloodshed went on without stint or respite; no ship could put to sea without fear of attack; the pearl fishery was a scene of annual conflict; and security of trade or peace there was none. Then it was that the British Government intervened and said that, in the interests of its own subjects and traders, and of its legitimate influence in the seas that wash the Indian coasts, this state of affairs must not continue. British flotillas appeared in these waters. British forces occupied the ports and towns on the coast that we see from this desk. The struggle was severe while it lasted but it was not long sustained. In 1839 the Maritime Truce was concluded, and was succeeded by the 1853 Treaty of Perpetual Peace that has lasted ever since.

Chiefs, that Treaty has not, of course, prevented occasional trouble and conflict; it has sometimes been neglected or infringed; but on the whole it has well deserved its name; and under it has grown up a condition of affairs so peaceful and secure that the oldest among you can only remember as a dim story the events of the past, while the younger have never seen warfare or bloodshed on the seas. It is now eleven years since the last disturbance of the peace occurred.

Chiefs, out of the relations that were thus created, and which by your own consent constituted the British Government the guardian of intertribal peace, there grew up political ties between the Government of India and yourselves, whereby the British Government became your overlords and protectors, and you have relations with no other Power. Every one of the States known as the Trucial States had bound itself, as you know, not to enter into any agreement or correspondence with any other Power, not to admit the agent of any other Government, and not to part with any portion of its territories. These engagements are binding on every one of you, and you have faithfully adhered to them. They are also binding in the reciprocal effect upon the British Government, and as long as they are faithfully observed by the Chiefs there is no fear that anyone else will be allowed to tamper with your liberties.

Sometimes I think that the record of the past is in danger of being forgotten, and there are persons who ask—Why should Great Britain continue to exercise these powers? The history of your States and of your families, and the present condition of the Gulf, are the answer. We were here before any other Power, in modern times, had shown its face in these waters. We found strife and we have created order. It was our commerce as well as your security that was threatened and called for protection. At every port along these coasts the subjects of the King of England still reside and trade. The great Empire of India, which it is our duty to defend, lies almost at your gates. We saved you from extinction at the hands of your neighbours. We opened these seas to the ships of all nations, and enabled their flags to fly in peace. We have not seized or held your territory. We have not destroyed your independence, but have preserved it. We are not now going to throw away this century of costly and triumphant enterprise; we shall not wipe out the most unselfish page in history. The peace of these waters must still be maintained; your independence will continue to be upheld; and the influence of the British Government must remain supreme.

The Sovereign of the British Empire lives so far away that none of you has ever seen or will ever see his face; but his orders are carried out everywhere throughout his vast dominions by the officers of his Government, and it is as his representative in India, who is responsible to him for your welfare, that I am here today to exchange greetings with you, to renew old assurances, and to wish you prosperity in the future.

PERPETUAL MARITIME TRUCE MAY 4, 1853

We, whose seals are hereunto affixed, Sheikh Sultan bin Suggur, Chief of Rass-ool-Kheimah, Sheikh Saeed bin Tahnoon, Chief of Aboo Dhebbee, Sheikh Saeed bin Butye, Chief of Debay, Sheikh Hamid bin Rashed, Chief of Ajman, Sheikh Abdoola bin Rashed, Chief of Umm-ool-Keiweyn, having experienced for a series of years the benefits and advantages resulting from a maritime truce contracted amongst ourselves under the mediation of the Resident in the Persian Gulf and renewed from time to time up to the present period, and being fully impressed, therefore, with a sense of the evil consequence formerly arising, from the prosecution of our feuds at sea, whereby our subjects and dependants were prevented from carrying on the pearl fishery in security, and were exposed to interruption and molestation when passing on their lawful occasions, accordingly, we, as aforesaid have determined, for ourselves, our heirs and successors, to conclude together a lasting and inviolable peace from this time forth in perpetuity and do hereby agree to bind ourselves down to observe the following conditions:

ARTICLE 1

That from this date, viz., 25th Rujjub 1269, 4th May 1853, and hereafter, there shall be a complete cessation of hostilities at sea between our respective subjects and dependants, and a perfect maritime truce shall endure between ourselves and between our successors, respectively, for evermore.

ARTICLE 2

That in the event (which God forbid) of any of our subjects or dependants committing an act of aggression at sea upon the lives or property of those of any of the parties to this agreement, we will immediately punish the assailants and proceed to afford full redress upon the same being brought to our notice.

ARTICLE 3

That in the event of an act of aggression being committed at sea by any of those who are subscribers with us to this engagement upon any of our subjects or dependants, we will not proceed immediately to retaliate, but will inform the British Resident or the Commodore at Bassidore, who will forthwith take the necessary steps for obtaining reparation for the injury inflicted, provided that its occurrence can be satisfactorily proved.

We further agree that the maintenance of the peace now concluded amongst us shall be watched over by the British Government, who will take steps to ensure at all times the due observance of the above Articles, and God of this is the best witness and guarantee.

NOTES

ONE

1. In an Opinion Research Centre poll carried out for *Middle East International,* September 1977, 53 percent of those questioned thought that Iran was an Arab country. There was evidence for this belief. Praising the signing of a £400 million missile swap with the Shah, the *Daily Express* wrote on November 19, 1976: "The deal comes as 11 United States Senators are touring Iran looking into the Arab State's need for military equipment which in recent years has been supplied by the U.S." *Time* magazine included Iran in a half-page map of "imports from the Arab world" on October 22, 1973. The *Investor's Chronicle* (February 4, 1977) illustrated an article about Iran's attempts at oil barter with a picture of a heavily robed Arab. The New York *Village Voice* (January 19, 1976) called Marion Javits, wife of the senior senator from New York, Jacob Javits, "the chic of Araby," and provided a picture of her wearing Arab headdress when it was discovered she was earning $57,500 a year for public relations advice to Iran Air. The London *Sun* headlined a story about Tehran nightclubs: "The teenagers who flew straight into an Arab vice den." (September 29, 1976.)

TWO

1. November 8, 1977.
2. *Arabian Time Machine* by Helga Graham (London: Heinemann, 1978) was printed with a Middle East map that failed to include Israel and showed pre-1967 borders. There was a

large prepublication order from Qatar's Ministry of Information.

FOUR

1. *Washington Post,* May 8, 1977.
2. Reza Baraheni, *The Crowned Cannibals* (New York: Vintage Books, 1977), p. 9.

FIVE

In addition to interviews in Tehran, London, and Washington (where the Shah's former son-in-law Ambassador Ardeshir Zahedi was most helpful), two books in particular provided source material for this chapter: the Shah's own autobiography, *Mission for My Country* (London: Hutchinson, 1961), and by R. J. Karanjia, *The Mind of a Monarch* (London: Allen & Unwin, 1977).

1. Hassan Arfa, *Under Five Shahs* (London: John Murray, 1964), p. 90.
2. Princess Soraya, *My Autobiography* (London: Arthur Barker, 1963), p. 68.
3. Margaret Laing, *The Shah* (London: Sidgwick & Jackson, 1977), p. 51.
4. Gerard de Villiers, *The Imperial Shah* (London: Weidenfeld & Nicolson, 1976), p. 93.
5. Leonard Mosley, *Power Play* (London: Weidenfeld & Nicolson, 1973), p. 14.
6. Henry Longhurst, *Adventure in Oil: The Story of British Petroleum* (London, 1959), p. 144.
7. "I do not deny that payments could in some cases conceivably have been made. I frankly have no firm evidence either way," wrote the Shah, in his autobiography. More recently he has suggested the figure of $70,000. The $19 million estimate comes from *Iran: The Shah's Empire of Repression,* the Committee Against Repression in Iran, p. 9.
8. *Newsweek,* April 23, 1962.

SIX

1. Oriana Fallaci, *New Republic*, December 1973.
2. *The Times*, June 7, 1976.

TEN

1. There are about 5,000,000. A report, given limited internal circulation in 1976, put the total population at 7,102,642. At least 2,000,000 of these are assumed to be foreigners, including other Arabs, Pakistanis, and Koreans. There is no knowing how many people were counted twice or more.

ELEVEN

1. Saudi investments abroad increased from $785 million in 1969 to $62 billion in 1977. According to a survey by the First National Bank of Chicago, published in September 1977, Saudi investments could be earning $10 billion a year by 1981. But this is highly speculative, and banks disagree. Chase Manhattan estimate that the current account surplus of OPEC nations will fall from $38 billion in 1976 to $24 billion in 1980. Morgan Guaranty say it will fall to $10 billion. Economic forecasting is a branch of witchcraft.
2. *Der Spiegel*, December 29, 1976.
3. North Yemen's program is $220 million. Jidda airport is costing $4.5 billion.

TWELVE

1. Since 1973 there has been a twelve-fold increase, to 2,500,000, in live sheep making the 18-day voyage from Australia. Stockmen spend the return voyage cleaning the ship. Few make more than one trip.
2. In December 1977, Ghaith Pharaon, son of one of King Khalid's closest advisers, offered $20 each for Lance's shares in the National Bank of Georgia. This is $3 more than Lance paid in 1975, and more than double their value of $8.50 at the end of 1977. The profit no doubt helped Mr. Lance repay

part of his $5.3 million liabilities, and gave Mr. Pharaon some sort of access to President Carter.

3. In October 1976, the American tax law was changed, reducing allowances and exemption for Americans working abroad from about $25,000 a year to $20,000. This would produce a meager revenue of $48 million a year, but the American Society of Civil Engineers claimed it so discouraged expatriate Americans that it would "place in jeopardy $22 billion in overseas construction work and 400,000 jobs." The Stanford Research Institute said that an American in Saudi Arabia earning $61,000 a year would have to pay an extra $6,720 in tax.

FOURTEEN

1. *Daily Express,* October 12, 1977. What would happen if they wrote about a "greedy Jew" or a "lascivious black"?
2. Anthony Sampson, *The Arms Bazaar* (London: Hodder & Stoughton, 1977), p. 198.

FIFTEEN

There are relatively few sources for historical background to Saudi Arabia. In attempting an overall picture, I have relied on a number of books mentioned in the bibliography. Three have been particularly helpful: H. St. J. Philby, *Arabian Jubilee,* Ameen Rihani, *Ibn Sa'oud of Arabia,* and Gabriel Kolko's *The Politics of War.* Further information was gathered in Saudi Arabia, and I am grateful for the help given by King Khalid's senior adviser, Dr. Rashid Pharaon.

1. Although the founder of Saudi Arabia was known in his own country as Abdul Aziz, I have tried to avoid confusion by calling him Ibn Saud, the name by which he was known in the West.
2. Ali Bey, *Voyages* (Paris: 1814).
3. The stallions were the Darley Arabian, the Godolphin Arabian, and the Byerley Turk.
4. Ameen Rihani, *Ibn Sa'oud of Arabia* (London: Constable, 1928), p. 53.

5. Senate Inquiry: *Petroleum Arrangements with Saudi Arabia,* 80th Congress, 1948.
6. Loans to Saudi Arabia:

   From

Year	SoCal	British Government
1940	$2,980,988	$403,000
1941	$2,433,222	$5,285,500
1942	$2,307,023	$12,090,000
1943	$79,651	$16,618,280

7. Leonard Mosley, *Power Play* (London: Weidenfeld & Nicolson, 1973), p. 123.
8. Winston Churchill, *The Second World War* Vol. VI—*Triumph & Tragedy* (London: Cassell, 1954), p. 348.
9. *Time,* March 4, 1974.
10. Figures from the Organization for Economic Cooperation and Development (OECD). In 1977 Saudi Arabia gave aid to countries which included Egypt, $2.5 billion; Jordan, $500 million; Syria, $1 billion; Pakistan, $500 million; Sudan, $250 million; Somalia, $220 million.

SIXTEEN

1. At the beginning of 1976 more than 80 percent of all skilled workers in Oman were foreign, according to figures in the *Economist,* December 10, 1977.
2. "In June last year Qaboos paid a private visit to London. There he met senior members of the CIA, who put the proposition that the CIA should finance his regime. The Americans insisted the deal should be implemented through the Saudi Arabian Government. A sum of money was suggested (alleged to be $150 million)." *Economist Foreign Report,* February 3, 1972.
3. Every visitor needs an NOC (No Objection Certificate), authorized by a reputable sponsor and collected at Muscat Airport on arrival, in addition to the normal visa. Lest this be insufficient for the bureaucrats, there is a sixteen-question disembarkation form which is to be completed on internal as well as international air travel.

4. "The Sultan of Muscat and Oman has dealt adroitly with the problem of jealousy among his 18 wives in the design of his new £1,500,000 marble palace by the seaside at Muscat. He has made sure that the doors of their 18 bedrooms are hidden from each other. So, when he visits one wife, none of the other 17 will know." *Sunday Express*, March 24, 1974.

5. David Smiley, *Arabian Assignment* (London: Leo Cooper, 1975), p. 40.

6. Hugh Boustead, *The Wind of Morning* (London: Chatto & Windus, 1971), p. 222.

7. John Townsend, *Oman: The Making of a Modern State* (London: Croom Helm, 1977), p. 59. Townsend was economic adviser to the Oman Government from 1972 to 1975, and his book is an invaluable guide to the events of those days.

SEVENTEEN

1. James Morris, *Sultan in Oman* (London: Faber, 1957), p. 132.

2. Harold Macmillan, *Tides of Fortune* (London: Macmillan, 1969), p. 641.

3. Harold Macmillan, *Riding the Storm* (London: Macmillan, 1971), pp. 270–77.

4. Smiley, *Arabian Assignment*, pp. 5, 17. Amery, however, maintains the myth that "the Sultan of Muscat asked Col. David Smiley to reorganise and command his forces"—*Daily Telegraph*, May 22, 1975.

5. For a detailed description, see by Wendell Phillips, *Unknown Oman* (London: Longman, 1966).

6. *The Times*, August 3, 1970.

NINETEEN

1. In a report submitted to the United States Securities and Exchange Commission in June 1977, BP said it paid commissions of up to 40 percent in the Middle East to secure contracts. They were booked as commissions, except two payments totaling £2,600 described as "repairs" and "car hire." A BP subsidiary, unrelated to the oil business, paid

£283,000 in commission to an unnamed agent in a Middle East country, but these payments were stopped when the agent appeared to render no service. Details are in pp. 45–47 of BP Preliminary Prospectus to the SEC, June 16, 1977.

2. Quoted by David Holden, *Farewell to Arabia* (London: Faber & Faber, 1966), p. 186.

3. For further information, see *Gold*, published by Consolidated Gold Fields in 1977. The Middle East takes nearly a third of all gold supplies and has revitalized the Italian jewelry industry with total purchases estimated at £640 million in 1978. In 1975 Saudi Arabia imported £12 million of gold from Italy; by the following year, it was £51 million.

4. The report, dated January 30, 1973, was mentioned in the London *Evening Standard* on October 26, 1977. But they had no further evidence and did not disclose the country, the firms or the people involved. An unnamed spokesman from "the firm" denied the story and said, "The whole thing is incredible."

TWENTY

1. Donald Hawley, *The Trucial States* (London: Allen & Unwin, 1970), p. 19.

2. The managerial—as opposed to entrepreneurial—money rush began in 1976. In January of that year, the UAE embassy in London issued 400 visas. By December the figure had risen to 3,000. Another illustration is the increase in the amount of mail: 41 million items in 1975, 85 million the following year.

3. There are no reliable statistics, but it is estimated there are 150,000 Pakistanis in the UAE without proper authorization, out of a total of 250,000. By 1977, according to the Ministry for Overseas Pakistanis in Islamabad, the migration to the Middle East had dramatically reduced the numbers going to Britain.

TWENTY-ONE

1. In January 1978, the *Financial Times* surveyed 59 cities. Using London as a base for the index (100), Abu Dhabi was 232, Bahrain 219, Oman 185, and Tehran 156. Saudi Arabian

cities were excluded because the alcohol ban distorts the figures. If apartments had been included, Bahrain would have been top—a furnished apartment there is $580 a week, compared with an average of $150 a week in New York.

TWENTY-TWO

1. *Persia and The Persian Gulf,* Journal of the Central Asian Society, 1929, vol. 15, pt. 4, p. 501.
2. Shakhbut (born 1903), Hazza (1905), Khalid (1906), Zayed (1918).
3. Hunt maintains that the major oil companies acted in collusion and did not support him when his firm was nationalized, as they had agreed. He filed a $13 billion suit against Mobil Oil in New York, but dropped his case in January 1975.

TWENTY-THREE

1. Widow of the sixth Baron Leconfield, John Wyndham, who became the first Baron Egremont in 1963, and was private secretary to Harold Macmillan.

TWENTY-FOUR

1. Charles Belgrave, *Personal Column* (London: Hutchinson, 1960), pp. 82, 92.
2. In spite of Concorde's unpromising trips, British Airways has doubled the number of passengers to the Middle East since the beginning of the money rush. Gulf Air, its rival on the routes, took 120,000 passengers in 1973—and 1.2 million in 1977.

TWENTY-FIVE

1. According to the World Bank, Kuwait's per capita Gross National Product was the highest in the world in 1976: $15,480. America is $7,890—sixth behind the UAE, Qatar, Switzerland, and Sweden. Britain is twenty-fourth. No one asks if GNP actually means anything.
2. The Kuwait Investment office in London controls 5.83 percent of Trafalgar House Investments, owners of the Express

Group of newspapers. The Kuwait shareholding is three times as large as Trafalgar's chairman, Nigel Broackes, anticipated.

TWENTY-SIX

1. James Morris, *Farewell the Trumpets* (London: Faber, 1978), p. 261.

GLOSSARY

abbaya (abaya)	thin black cloak covering a woman's dress
abra	water taxi
Alhamdulillah	thanks be to God
ANM	Arab Nationalist Movement
aqal	black band which keeps the ghotra in place
Aramco	Arabian American Oil Company
Ayatollah	Muslim religious leader, equivalent to Bishop or Cardinal
bait	a subtribe
barasti	hut made from palm fronds and cord
BATT	British Army Training Team (in Oman)
batula	beak-shaped mask for women
Bedou	desert nomad
bukra	tomorrow
burqa	black mask for women
chador	black cloak worn by Iranian women
dhow	boat
dishdasha	white gown worn by Arab men
diwan	meeting room
djebellah	woman's cloak
DLF	Dhofar Liberation Front
Eid	a religious festival
falaj	underground waterway
firqat	irregular soldiers
ghotra	Arabian headdress
Hadith	traditions dating from the Prophet
haj (hajj)	pilgrimage
haji (hajji)	one who has been on pilgrimage to Mecca
harem	women
hijra	migration of the Prophet from Mecca to Medina
ikhwan	"brotherhood," a religious movement started by Ibn Saud

insha'allah (inshallah)	if God wills it
jebel	mountain
jihad	holy war
kaffia (kaffiyeh)	headdress
kayf ha lek?	how are you?
khanja	curved dagger
khor	creek
majlis	Parliament, or conference room
mullah	Iranian religious leader
NOC	No Objection Certificate (for entry to Oman)
OAPEC	Organization of Arab Petroleum Exporting Countries
OPEC	Organization of Petroleum Exporting Countries
PDFLP	Popular Democratic Front for the Liberation of Palestine
PDRY	People's Democratic Republic of Yemen
PFLO	Popular Front for the Liberation of Oman
PFLOAG	Popular Front for the Liberation of the Occupied Arabian Gulf
PFLP	Popular Front for the Liberation of Palestine
PLO	Palestine Liberation Organization
qadi	judge
Ramadan	month of fasting
Rub al Khali	Empty Quarter
SAF	Sultan's Armed Forces (Oman)
salaam alaykum	peace be upon you
SAMA	Saudi Arabian Monetary Agency
sayyid	a descendant of the Prophet
SAVAK	Sazman-i-Amniyat va Kishvar (State Security and Intelligence Organization)
sediki	illicit alcohol ("my friend")
Shaikh	literally "old man," a term of respect
shakrun	thank you (Arabic)
Shariah	Islamic law based on the Koran
souk (suq)	market
thaub (thobe)	white gown worn by Arab men
ulema	Muslim scholars, equivalent to priests
wali	governor
yashmak	woman's veil

BIBLIOGRAPHY

Adams, Michael, and Mayhew, Christopher. *Publish It Not . . . The Middle East Cover Up*. London: Longman, 1975.

Ali Bey. *Voyages*. Paris, 1814.

Amirsadeghi, Hossein, ed. *20th Century Iran*. London: Holmes & Meier, 1977.

Avery, Peter. *Modern Iran*. London: Ernest Benn, 1975.

Baraheni, Reza. *The Crowned Cannibals*. New York: Vintage Books, 1977.

Belgrave, Sir Charles. *Personal Column*. London: Hutchinson, 1960.

Bentwich, Norman. *Mandate Memories*. London: Hogarth Press, 1965.

Bermant, Chaim. *The Jews*. London: Weidenfeld & Nicolson, 1972.

Bibby, Geoffrey. *Looking for Dilmun*. New York: Knopf, 1970.

Blair, John M. *The Control of Oil*. New York: Pantheon, 1976.

Blandford, Linda. *Super Wealth*. New York: Morrow, 1977.

Boustead, Sir Hugh. *The Wind of Morning*. London: Chatto & Windus, 1971.

Brent, Peter. *Far Arabia*. London: Weidenfeld & Nicolson, 1977.

Bulloch, John. *The Making of a War*. London: Longman, 1974.

Bustani, Emile. *March Arabesque*. London: Robert Hale, 1961.

Chisholm, A. H. T. *The First Kuwait Oil Concession*. London: Cass, 1975.

Curzon, Lord George N. *Persia and the Persian Question*. London: Cass, 1892.

Darlow, Michael. *The Last Corner of Arabia*. London: Quartet, 1976.

Deakin, Michael. *Ras Al Khaymah, Flame in the Desert*. London: Quartet, 1977.

Eden, Sir Anthony. *Full Circle*. London: Cassell, 1960.

Engler, Robert. *The Politics of Oil*. Chicago: University of Chicago Press, 1967.

Field, Michael. *$100,000,000 A Day*. New York: Praeger, 1976.

Fisher, W. B. *The Middle East*. London: Methuen, 1950.

Freedman, Lawrence. *Arms Production in the United Kingdom: Problems and Prospects*. Royal Institute of International Affairs, 1978.

Goitein, S. D. *Jews and Arabs*. New York: Schocken Books, 1955.

Halliday, Fred. *Arabia Without Sultans*. New York: Random House, 1975.

Hawley, Donald. *The Trucial States*. Boston: Twayne, 1970.

Holden, David. *Farewell to Arabia*. London: Faber & Faber, 1966.

Howarth, David. *The Desert King*. London: Collins, 1964.

Insight (*Sunday Times*). *Yom Kippur War*. Garden City: Doubleday, 1974.

Karanjia, R. J. *The Mind of a Monarch*. London: Allen & Unwin, 1977.

Kedourie, Elie. *Arabic Political Memoirs*. London: Cass, 1974.

——. *In the Anglo-Arab Labyrinth*. Cambridge: Cambridge University Press, 1966.

Kelly, J. B. *Eastern Arabian Frontiers*. London: Faber & Faber, 1964.

Kiernan, Thomas. *The Arabs*. Boston: Little, Brown, 1975.

Kolko, Gabriel. *The Politics of War*. London: Weidenfeld & Nicolson, 1969.

Laing, Margaret. *The Shah*. London: Sidgwick & Jackson, 1977.

Landen, Robert Geran. *Oman Since 1856*. Princeton: Princeton University Press, 1967.

Longrigg, Stephen Hemsley. *The Middle East*. London: Duckworth, 1963.

——. *Oil in the Middle East*. Oxford: Oxford University Press, 1954.

Mansfield, Peter. *The Arabs*. London: Allen Lane, 1976.

Marlowe, John. *Arab Nationalism and British Imperialism*. London: Cresset Press, 1961.

Miles, S. B. *Countries and Tribes of the Persian Gulf*. London: Harrison & Sons, 1919.

Monroe, Elizabeth. *Philby of Arabia*. London: Faber & Faber, 1973.

Morris, Claud. *The Desert Falcon*. London: Outline, 1976.

Morris, James. *Farewell the Trumpets*. London: Faber & Faber, 1978.

——. *Sultan in Oman*. London: Faber & Faber, 1957.

Mosley, Leonard. *Power Play*. New York: Random House, 1973.

Nirumand, Bahman. *Iran: The New Imperialism in Action*. New York: Monthly Review Press, 1969.

Osborne, Christine. *Gulf States and Oman*. London: Croom Helm, 1977.

Pahlavi, Mohammed Reza Shah. *Mission for My Country*. London: Hutchinson, 1961.

Park, Yoon. *Oil Money and the World Economy*. Farnborough: Wilton House Pub., 1977.

Philby, H. St. J. *Arabian Jubilee*. London: Robert Hale, 1952.

Phillips, Wendell. *Oman: A History*. London: Longman, 1967.

———. *Unknown Oman*. Mystic, Conn.: Verry, 1972.

Prittie, Terrance, and Nelson, Walter Henry. *The Economic War Against the Jews*. London: Secker & Warburg, 1978.

Ramahi, Seif El-Wady. *Economics and Political Evolution in the Arabian Gulf States*. Carlton Press, 1973.

Rihani, Ameen. *Ibn Sa'oud of Arabia*. London, 1928.

Sampson, Anthony. *The Arms Bazaar*. New York: Viking, 1977.

———. *The Seven Sisters*. New York: Viking, 1975.

Skeet, Ian. *Muscat and Oman*. London: Faber & Faber, 1974.

Smiley, David. *Arabian Assignment*. London: Leo Cooper, 1975.

Thesiger, Wilfrid. *Arabian Sands*. London: Longman, 1959.

Tomkinson, Michael. *The United Arab Emirates*. London, 1975.

Townsend, John. *Oman, The Making of a Modern State*. London: Croom Helm, 1977.

Trevelyan, Humphrey. *The Middle East in Revolution*. Boston: Gambit, 1971.

Vicker, Ray. *The Kingdom of Oil*. New York: Scribner, 1974.

Villiers, Gerard de. *The Imperial Shah*. Boston: Little, Brown, 1976.

Warin, Olivier. *Le Lion et le Soleil*. Paris: Stock, 1976.

Wilber, Donald N. *Riza Shah Pahlavi*. Hicksville, N.Y.: Exposition Press, 1975.

Williams, Kenneth. *Ibn Sa'ud*. London: Jonathan Cape, 1933.

Winstone, H. V. F. *Captain Shakespear*. London: Jonathan Cape, 1976.

Wright, Denis. *The English Amongst the Persians*. London: Heinemann, 1977.

Zonis, Marvin. *The Political Elite of Iran*. Princeton: Princeton University Press, 1971.

INDEX